Rethinking Soviet Communism

Rethinking World Politics

Series Editor: Professor Michael Cox

In an age of increased academic specialization where more and more books about smaller and smaller topics are becoming the norm, this major new series is designed to provide a forum and stimulus for leading scholars to address big issues in world politics in an accessible but original manner. A key aim is to transcend the intellectual and disciplinary boundaries which have so often served to limit rather than enhance our understanding of the modern world. In the best tradition of engaged scholarship, it aims to provide clear new perspectives to help make sense of a world in flux.

Each book addresses a major issue or event that has had a formative influence on the twentieth-century or the twenty-first-century world which is now emerging. Each makes its own distinctive contribution as well as providing an original but accessible guide to competing lines of interpretation.

Taken as a whole, the series will rethink contemporary international politics in ways that are lively, informed and – above all – provocative.

Rethinking Soviet Communism

Peter Shearman

First published 2015 by
PALGRAVE

Palgrave in the UK is an imprint of Macmillan Publishers Limited,
registered in England, company number 785998, of 4 Crinan Street,
London N1 9XW

Palgrave Macmillan in the US is a division of St Martin's Press LLC,
175 Fifth Avenue, New York, NY 10010.

Palgrave is the global imprint of the above companies and
is represented throughout the world.

Palgrave® and Macmillan® are registered trademarks in the United States,
the United Kingdom, Europe and other countries.

ISBN 978–0–230–50786–9   hardback
ISBN 978–0–230–50787–6   paperback

This book is printed on paper suitable for recycling and made from fully
managed and sustained forest sources. Logging, pulping and manufacturing
processes are expected to conform to the environmental regulations of the
country of origin.

A catalogue record for this book is available from the British Library.

A catalog record for this book is available from the Library of Congress.

Typeset by MPS Limited, Chennai, India.

Printed in China.

For my sons, Peter and Michael

Contents

List of Tables

Foreword

Students of international affairs coming to intellectual maturity over the last few years have experienced a world so profoundly different from that in which the author of this book and the writer of this Foreword grew up, that it sometimes feels as if they (and we) have lived almost totally different lives on almost completely different planets. For 'us' of course the existence of the Soviet Union and an ongoing Cold War between two superpowers locked in an apparently permanent struggle that stretched from the heart of Europe to the paddy fields of South East Asia seemed entirely normal. This reality in turn determined the way we understood the world, the political choices we were then forced to make in that world, and more directly what we were actually taught about the world in our universities. Indeed, one of the most important academic fields back then was 'Sovietology' a branch of nearly everything else whose primary function at the end of the day was to understand the USSR ('know the enemy') and try and explain what it was up to. As I wrote many years ago, the conflict between what some liked to term 'actually existing socialism', and others the 'free world', had so insinuated itself into the DNA of the West that we could almost think of the Cold War as being the most important relationship in all our lives.

But not only that. A very large part of what passed for International Relations after the Second World War was very directly influenced by the reality of the Cold War. Indeed, as Peter Shearman so tellingly reveals in his panoramic study, one of the more obvious reasons why the discipline of IR failed to see the end of the Cold War coming was precisely because many of its key practitioners had forged a set of ideas which appeared to provide an intellectual rationale for it. Few may like to be reminded of the fact now, but it is worth reminding ourselves that the most influential writer on IR—the very great Ken Waltz—made part of his reputation in the 1960s by suggesting a direct link between global stability and bipolarity. Twenty years on and one of the most distinguished international historians of the time—John Lewis Gaddis—was making the equally strong case that instead of thinking of the Cold War in terms of the dangers it posed, we should, he felt, be focusing on it as having created what he termed a 'long peace'; and though he did not make the point explicitly, there was every reason to think, possibly hope, that this peace order would go on for a very long time to come.

But the wider debate about the Cold War was premised on something else: namely the continued existence of a very special kind of state opposed to the world capitalist order and driven, according to conventional western wisdom, by an urge to expand. Now whether the sources of Soviet expansion flowed from its ideology, its history, its geography, or an insecurity caused by the competition with a more powerful American rival mattered very little. What mattered was that the USSR would continue to remain an outsider power in a divided world. That said, the impact it was to have on the world throughout the seventy-five years of its existence was absolutely immense. From the rise of fascism in the inter-war years, through the way the Second World War began in 1939 and ended in 1945, and on to the global competition that so shaped the post-war world, the USSR was in many ways the axis around which the world pivoted. Indeed, it is one of the many strengths of Peter Shearman's study that he is able to show in vivid detail the impact that the Soviet communist experiment was to have on the twentieth century; an era 'in which world politics' according to Shearman 'were in large part determined by events that took place in the former Soviet Union after 1917 when the Bolsheviks set about creating an alternative system to capitalism'. Moreover, even after it had passed from the stage of history as it finally did in 1991, it left a very powerful legacy behind it, not only in Russia itself but across the globe from China—still ruled by a Communist Party formed in the early Soviet years—through to Afghanistan where a disastrous Soviet decision to intervene in that country in December 1979 not only caused such grief to the country itself, but set off a series of catastrophic events that led, over time, to a terrorist attack in 2001, one that changed the United States and the international order for ever.

There is every need therefore for students today to return to the past and with Peter Shearman's help, to rethink the Soviet experiment—not just because it is an interesting story in its own right, or because they need to reclaim the history of the twentieth century. But rather because so much of their own lives—whether they think about it or not—has been shaped by the fall-out of what finally and unexpectedly happened to the Soviet system of power between 1989 and 1991.

Professor Michael Cox
General Editor
LSE IDEAS
August 2014

Acknowledgements

This book has been a long time in the making, and I appreciate the patience from the team at Palgrave Macmillan. Many people over the years have had an influence on my thinking on the former USSR and the Russian Federation. Colleagues and friends at Essex University, in what was a very vibrant and stimulating environment for Soviet Studies in the 1980s, were more important to my development than they will possibly appreciate (even as some will take issue with the things I write). I would particularly mention here Mike Bowker, Shaun Bowler, Peter Clarke, Catherine Danks, the late Peter Frank, Alastair McAuley, Mary McAuley, Steve Owen, Neil Robinson, Cameron Ross, and Richard Sakwa. Melbourne University, my academic home for 15 years, was a dynamic and exciting place to be during the changes then taking place in the former Soviet Union. Here I would like to acknowledge my former colleagues and friends Remy Davison, Bobo Lo, Leslie Holmes, Robert Horvath, Tony Philips, Andrei Suchkov, Matt Sussex, Vladimir Tikhomirov, Yuri Tsyganov, and Stephen Wheatcroft. I wish to give a special thanks to Mick Cox for his support and encouragement and friendship over the years. Thanks to Margot Light for reading a draft of the book and for her useful comments and suggestions. Finally, I am very grateful to Steven Kennedy at Palgrave Macmillan for keeping faith with me, and for his very insightful and helpful comments on a draft of the book.

List of Acronyms

ANC	African National Congress
ASEAN	Association of Southeast Asian Nations
CCP	Chinese Communist Party
Cheka	Soviet Emergency Committee for Internal Security, forerunner of the KGB
CFM	Committee of Foreign Ministers
CIA	Central Intelligence Agency
CMEA	Council for Mutual Economic Assistance
Cominform	Communist Information Bureau
Comintern	Communist International
CPA	Communist Party of Australia
CPGB	Communist Party of Great Britain
CPRF	Communist Party of the Russian Federation
CPSA	Communist Party of South Africa
CPSU	Communist Party of the Soviet Union
CPUSA	Communist Party of the United States
FNLA	National Front for the Liberation of Angola
FRG	Federal Republic of Germany
GDR	German Democratic Republic
ILP	Independent Labour Party
IR	International Relations (the academic discipline of)
KAPD	Communist Workers Party of Germany
KGB	Committee of State Security
KOMSOMOL	The All-Union Leninist Young Communist League
LAI	League against Imperialism
LDPR	Liberal Democratic Party of Russia
MPLA	Popular Movement for the Liberation of Angola
NAM	Non-Aligned Movement
NATO	North Atlantic Treaty Organization
NEP	New Economic Policy

NGO	Nongovernmental Organization
NIC	Newly Industrialised Countries
NJM	New Jewel Movement
NSC	National Security Council
PRC	People's Republic of China
PRUC	Party of Russian Unity and Accord
RSDLP	Russian Social Democratic Labour Party
RSFSR	Russian Soviet Federative Socialist Republic
SPD	German Social Democratic Party
TFC	Treaty of Friendship and Cooperation
UNITA	National Union for the Total Liberation of Angola
UNSC	United Nations Security Council
UR	United Russia
USSR	Union of Soviet Socialist Republics
WTO	Warsaw Treaty Organization

Introduction

This book reassesses the impact that the Soviet communist experiment had during its lifetime and its continuing influence today. World politics in the twentieth century were in large part determined by events that took place in the former Soviet Union after 1917 when the Bolsheviks set about creating an alternative system to capitalism. The ensuing long era of contestation between the Soviet Union and the West finally came to an end with the demise of communism as a powerful alternative ideology in the 1980s, and the ensuing unravelling of the Union of Soviet Socialist Republics (USSR) in 1991. The influence of the October Revolution in 1917 was pervasive, and although its immediate impact on the subjects of the former Russian Empire was dramatic, the revolution also had profound consequences in wider global politics. Communism was to become the most influential cross-border idea in modern history to challenge both liberal democracy and the organization of world politics.

The consequences of the Russian Revolution and the Soviet experience are still with us today. It is not possible to fully understand, for example, the current issues in Southwest Asia without an appreciation of the Soviet impact in that region, including the war in Afghanistan. The same holds true for the international politics of Central Europe and the former Soviet territories in the Caucasus, including the short war between Russia and Georgia in August 2008, and in 2014 the conflict over the future of Ukraine.

The starting point for this book is the end point of the Cold War. It will be argued that the failure of scholars, both in Soviet Studies and International Relations (IR), to predict the disintegration of the Soviet Union and the accompanying end of the Cold War reflects a failure in their analyses to pay sufficient attention to the twin forces of communism and nationalism. The twentieth century was an ideological age, when religion gave way to secular ideational belief systems that would provide meaning in people's lives and political legitimacy to governments. It is truly remarkable that scholars in IR tended to ignore the power of Marxist-Leninist ideology in the conduct of world politics, while specialists on the Soviet Union, and indeed theorists on nationalism too, largely discounted the role of ethnicity and nationalism as a mobilizing force in the communist bloc. At the same time politicians in the West misunderstood or exaggerated the influence that ideology played in the foreign and security policies of the USSR. This book's objective is to rethink the role of Soviet Communism in the international politics of the last century by giving detailed attention to the twin and often contending forces of communism and nationalism. While communist ideology privileges class as the basis of collective solidarity at the international level, nationalism stressed place-based solidarities linked to distinct historical narratives, cultures, and languages.

This book is not simply another narrative interpretive history of the Cold War. In the last decades of the twentieth century, scholars in the discipline of IR saw the end of the Cold War as evidence that the previously dominant theory of Realism was now moribund. A new, younger generation of scholars, many self-consciously working within the general parameters—dare one say "paradigm"—of Constructivism, now focused on the 'politics of identity' (Wendt, 1999; see also English, 2000; Herrmann 1996; Hopf, 2012; Herrmann and Lebow, 2004; Katzenstein, 1996; Lebow and Risse-Kappen, 1995; Risse-Kappen, 1994). Rather than relativities in material capabilities and shifting balances of military power determining relations between states, *identities* and *ideas* were considered paramount in understanding world politics. The end of the Cold War, a new generation of scholars claimed, was due not to a shift in the balance of power, but rather to radical changes in the thinking and identities of elites in Moscow. Due to modern forms of communication technologies and the impulses of globalization that could not be controlled by the state, new ideas filtered through the iron curtain into the communist bloc. Soviet communist party and government officials, and specialists in various functional policy areas, engaged in discussions with foreign leaders and delegations in so-called epistemic communities (for example, in the arena of arms control). These avenues for the exchange of ideas helped to change the dominant thinking on world affairs in the USSR (for a Realist critique of the Constructivist take on the end of the Cold War see Brooks and Wohlforth, 2000/01).

These scholars were indeed on to something. Finally, IR was waking up to the importance of ideas, and how these can shape identities and behaviour. Part of the problem had been the dominance of Realist theory, especially the variants produced in the United States. From Hans Morgenthau's *Politics Among Nations*, first published in 1948, through to Kenneth Waltz's *Theory of International Politics*, first published in 1979, Realism dominated the thinking of academics (and the practices of policy-makers). The fundamental assumption of Realist theory is that states operating in a system of anarchy will behave according to the logic of the balance of power, and hence, due to the fact they are all faced with the same security dilemma, domestic arrangements and ideologies are not of key importance (Mearsheimer, 2001).

It was only with the end of the Cold War, something IR theory had failed to predict, that some scholars began to focus on the role of individual leaders, ideas, and learning. But many of the works that have been produced tend to be ahistorical and/or to lack any depth and understanding of the actual power that Soviet Communism had in multiple theatres during the Cold War, or the role that nationalism played, at times working in tandem with Soviet interests, at times working against them. The Soviet Union did not collapse because the Soviet leadership suddenly saw the light of liberal democracy shining on the horizon, or "learned" through a process of deep and meaningful conversations in policy networks. It was not due to diplomatic interactions and personal relationships with Helmut Kohl, Ronald Reagan, or Margaret Thatcher, that Mikhail Gorbachev suddenly realized there was a better way forward for his country than Soviet Communism. Indeed, Gorbachev to the very end continued to believe in socialism. Although there were important changes in ideology in the late-Soviet period, many of these changes reflected a complex mix of structural and personal, as well as ideational factors. Insofar as ideas mattered, it was not that liberal democracy emerged victorious among a new generation of elites, or that a new form of humane socialism took hold in the ruling Communist Party: it was rather the power of the *national* idea that was largely responsible for the ultimate crisis of Soviet Communism, linked to a failure of the Soviet economic system.

The Bolsheviks, due to internal and external threats to their revolutionary regime, were compelled to develop two important and interrelated aspects of the new Soviet state: a federal structure based on ethnicity, and a military industrial complex. What the Bolsheviks constructed was a Soviet national security state legitimated through an ideology of international communism that was linked to the great October Revolution of 1917. Although seemingly very strong and robust, the state that Joseph Stalin built was in fact always brittle. This brittleness was not so much due to external threats from outside great powers, or capitalist "enemies of the state" from within, but from the multinational nature of the state and the inherent weaknesses of the communist political economy.

This book will show that nationalism was the catalyst for the final disintegration of the USSR, and that the dynamics between nationalism and communism were a major factor in determining the course of international politics in the previous century. These two forces were responsible for so much of the bloodshed that marked this period. Soviet Communism, based on a Marxist political philosophy, sought to go beyond the idea of the nation to create a new post-national, non-capitalist society. Many of the tensions in the second half of the century, in the Cold War era, were linked to the dialectic between these two ideas. However, states were accorded primacy in IR to such an extent that nations and nationalism and class and communism were virtually invisible. While it is the case that states are important actors, it is simply not possible to understand the rise and fall of the USSR, and its role in international politics without accounting for the ideational influences of nationalism and communism. In an age when empires were falling and the number of states was growing, nationalism was becoming increasingly significant as a force of collective identity.

The USSR was created out of a revolution in which the "national question" was a key factor linked to the then ongoing crisis in European imperialism. The USSR was created at a time when the right to national self-determination had become the normative principle for political legitimization (Shearman, 2000, p. 78). The Bolsheviks were faced with the necessity, having taken control of the Tsarist multinational Empire, of developing a federal system that recognized the power of national identities. Ultimately, towards the end of the twentieth century, the communist experiment that began at the beginning of the century was fatally challenged by a resurgence of nationalism. This book will demonstrate how Soviet communism challenged both nationalism and the traditional bourgeois capitalist state on a global scale, and yet was forced to moderate its own political structure and behaviour due to the countervailing forces of ethnicity and national identity at the local level, as well as the balance of power at the level of the international system. As an ideology initially seeking to establish a post-national society and the withering away of the state, Soviet Communism was ultimately impelled to create a national security state and to mobilize legitimacy sentiments on the basis of the nation, because the USSR failed to subvert the organizing principles of international relations. Yet international relations were, from the day the Bolsheviks gained power in 1917 right through to the end of the USSR some seven decades later, always central to the USSR's domestic revolutionary goals.

To understand the end of Soviet Communism and the demise of its global influence it is necessary to return to the origins of the USSR. It was in the Union of Soviet Socialist Republics that many of the extremes of the century, from the October Revolution of 1917, through civil war, famine, purges and the gulag, are to be found (on the Gulag see Solzhenitsyn, 1973). Anne Applebaum (2004, p. 581) calculates that fully 28.7 million citizens went through the forced labour camps. There have been controversies and conflicting interpretations over the number of Soviet citizens killed as a result of policies pursued by the communist authorities, especially under Stalin. R. J. Rummel (1990) examines the competing claims (see also Barnes, 2011). Whatever the actual figure it is obvious that practically the entire Soviet population would have been affected by the Gulag, either through direct experience or through that of a family member, work colleague, friend or neighbour. It will be shown how these experiences of war, civil war, and the gulag had a profound impact on the development of the Soviet national security state and its relationship with the outside world.

Richard Pipes refers to the Revolution that took place in St. Petersburg in 1917 as 'the most important event of the twentieth century' without which 'there would very likely have been no National Socialism; probably no Second World War and no decolonization; and certainly no Cold War, which once dominated our lives' (Pipes, 1996, p. 3). From a radically different perspective

Tariq Ali would agree with Pipes that National Socialism and Fascism were essentially reactions to and therefore fostered by the Russian Revolution and the threat of Soviet Communism. Tracing the origins of the far right in Italy and Germany, followed by Spain and Portugal, Ali stated that 'Fascism was the punishment which capital inflicted on the working class for toying with the idea of [socialist] revolution' (Ali, 1984, p. 11). Other extremes, including the killing fields of Cambodia in which more than a million people were slaughtered under Pol Pot, similarly, had their origins in the ideas that inspired the October Revolution in Russia. It was a mixture of Marxism and Nationalism, or Marxism as adapted to national characteristics, that produced the various forms of communism, inspired by October, that would later emerge.

Communism was from the outset a transformative ideology designed to radically change the world, based upon a scientific theory of class relations. It has become common to talk of the globalization of world politics in recent years: yet there has never been so potent a global idea that challenged the dominance of liberalism, the global capitalist market, and the working of the inter-state system, than that of communism, and in particular its Soviet variant of Marxism-Leninism. When Karl Marx and his close collaborator Friedrich Engels warned in the middle of the nineteenth century about the dangers facing Europe of the specter of communism there were in fact very few revolutionary communists threatening the status quo (Marx and Engels, 2002). But by the late 1940s, fully one-third of the world's population was ruled by communist parties whose leaders were inspired by Vladimir Lenin and the October Revolution. The world's largest country in terms of population (China) and the world's largest country by size (Soviet Russia) were both ruled by communist parties. One was a superpower, while the other contained the world's largest land army. Both also were at the centre of some of the most awful bloodletting in the twentieth century, especially during the early decades of their communist development.

It was not just the communist world that engaged in mass killing. As Eric Hobsbawm noted, 'during the short [twentieth] century more human beings had been killed or allowed to die by human decisions than ever before in history' (Hobsbawm, 1994, p. 12). The unprecedented slaughter in the trenches during the Great War of 1914–1918 facilitated the Bolshevik success in

1917, with the backdrop of chaos and anarchy helping to further undermine the legitimacy of Tsarist authority. Without the Great War, it is generally accepted by historians, there would not have been a socialist revolution in Russia in 1917. Pipes argued that the 'immediate cause of the Revolution of 1917 would be the collapse of Russia's fragile political and economic structure under the strains of war' (Pipes, 1990, p. 195). Orlando Figes writes that '[t]he First World War was a gigantic test of the modern state, and as the only major European state which had failed to modernize before the war it was a test which tsarist Russia was almost bound to fail' (Figes, 1996, p. 810). Sheila Fitzpatrick makes the same point: that it was the war that provided the conditions for an already vulnerable regime to collapse and for radical revolutionaries to take power (Fitzpatrick, 2008, p. 39). Whereas Figes explains the success of the Bolsheviks as partly due to a failure of the previous regime to modernize, Fitzpatrick sees the communist revolutionaries' ideology to be one of economic modernization as much as it was an ideology of revolution. It has also been suggested that the Russian Revolution should be seen as a form of "autocratic modernization," one that can be compared to Iran after the 1979 Revolution (see McDaniel, 1991). I will show that the main urge to modernization was to create the infrastructure required to create a military industrial complex for the defence of the regime and the state. Modernization was closely linked to the perceived requirements to be able to defend the revolution from hostile powers.

The horrors that nationalism was responsible for between 1914 and 1918 led to increased support for socialism and communism among peoples in the developed states. Then in the middle of the century new virile manifestations of extreme nationalism in the forms of Fascism and Nazism emerged, producing a major challenge to both liberalism and communism. World War Two and the Holocaust are linked to Soviet Communism and the Third Reich, for the central characters involved (in particular Adolf Hitler and Joseph Stalin) were in pursuit of competing utopian goals (Gellately, 2007). One of these was based on class, the other on the nation. In the end, as Martin Amis put it, 'Bolshevism was exportable and produced near-identical results elsewhere. Nazism could not be duplicated. Compared to it, the other fascist states were simply amateurish' (Amis, 2002, p. 91). Germany itself had the unenviable experience of experimenting with both of these utopian projects: Nazism under Hitler, and Communism in the German Democratic Republic (GDR) after Germany was divided between East and West following the conclusion of the war.

It was the division of Germany and the construction of the Berlin Wall in 1961 that would come to symbolize the ideological and geo-strategic components of the Cold War conflict. The geo-strategic factor inherent in the competition between the two sides was always a major component of the Cold War. Yet, it does not on its own explain the level of antagonism between the two sides, nor the form that their competition took: for this we need to understand the power of ideas. Germany was reunified in the late 1980s after people breached the Berlin Wall, moving from East to West, inspired as much by a sense of belonging to a larger German nation and to gain freedom from foreign (Soviet) control as it was to any sense of anti-communism. Indeed, in the first elections in a united Berlin, communists won the majority of votes in parliamentary elections in the eastern part of the German capital. Even in Poland, by the elections in September 2001, Solidarity failed to reach the 8per cent threshold to gain seats in the parliament, with the majority of seats being won by former communists and others in a leftist alliance. Nationalist parties also did well, marking a trend in European politics as a whole. And by this time the Communist Party of the Russian Federation (CPRF), successor to the Communist Party of the Soviet Union (CPSU), itself took on the trappings of a far-right, hyper-nationalist party (see Cox and Shearman, 2000).

The October Revolution and the World

The rise of Bolshevism provided hope and inspiration to millions of workers across the globe, while instilling fear among capitalists and political leaders of the major powers. As the world's leaders met in Paris in 1919 to finalize a post-war settlement, it was not Germany that was seen as the immediate threat to international stability, for now Bolshevism challenged the very essence of capitalist society with its radical communist ideology, with revolutionary movements gaining ground in Germany itself, in Hungary, and in the Baltic states. In the United States too, some four million workers participated in 3,600 strikes in that same year (Read, 2008). It should be noted also that the USA, the UK, and

France all sent troops into Russia to fight alongside the Tsarist "Whites" against the communists in the civil war.

The Revolution was then much more than a Russian affair. Indeed, the Revolution was never meant by its perpetrators to be limited to Russia alone. Lenin and the Bolsheviks saw Russia as the "weakest link" in a chain of global imperialism; and the October Revolution as a spark to ignite revolution in the more developed capitalist states of Europe. It was not a revolution in the name of a nation: it was made in the name of a class, with universal applicability. Pipes suggests that Lenin's advantage over his opponents on the eve of revolution 'derived from the fact that he did not care about Russia. He cared about Germany and England in the sense that, for him, as a revolutionary, they were the key countries' (Pipes, 1998, p. 45). Instead of supporting his country in the First World War, Lenin was openly calling for Russia's defeat. In the USSR the revolution was not referred to as the *Russian* Revolution, but the *October* Revolution, Great October, or the Bolshevik Revolution. The logic of the Revolution for the Bolsheviks was class conflict, and given the relative backwardness of Russia, with a small working class and industrial proletariat, and a predominantly peasant population, hope lay with workers in the larger industrialized countries, who would also revolt and hence support the development of socialism in Russia. The Bolshevik Revolution was seen as an international revolution by both those who carried it out and those who felt threatened by it.

At the turn of the twentieth century just two decades before the October Revolution there were approximately two and a half million workers in the Russian Empire, of which fully one-third were seasonally employed peasants. Three-quarters of the population, over one hundred million peasants, were engaged in farming. This theme of "backwardness" was always dominant among Russian intellectuals, and it would continue to be a central issue motivating the post-revolutionary Soviet regime, as the Bolsheviks sought to "catch up" with the West through means other than those of the capitalist market. Socialism could not be reached, nor could it be defended, without first creating a modernized, industrialized economy. With the failure of the working classes to revolt in the advanced capitalist states, and with their propensity to support the nation state, Soviet Russia was forced to adapt; by necessity it had to either give up or radically revise the original revolutionary goals and attempt to build socialism alone. Following intense internal conflict the Bolsheviks eventually chose the second path. Fitzpatrick has suggested that although industrialization and modernization were initially the means to an end, the end being socialism, ultimately the means became difficult to differentiate from the ends (Fitzpatrick, 2008, p. 10).

As this book will demonstrate, the revolutionary process in Soviet Russia took on different forms due to changing realities, both domestic and international, linked to internal power struggles and personalities. It also took on increasingly more nationalist connotations during Stalin's "Revolution from Above," inherent in the conception of "Socialism in One Country," and then later during the war against Hitler's Germany. However, it will also be argued (and this goes against much conventional wisdom) that through to the very end of the Soviet experiment, even under Stalin's Socialism in One Country, through to the "era of stagnation" under Leonid Brezhnev, to Mikhail Gorbachev's "*perestroika*" *internationalism* was a key component in the logic of Soviet Communism. Without holding its central position as leader of the wider communist world the Soviet regime always stood to lose its domestic political legitimacy and its status as a superpower. It will be shown how this adherence to communist ideology served as the seed of its own destruction. It was the inherent tensions between communism and nationalism that would be a continual complicating element for attaining the Bolshevik project. This book will argue that nationalism and communism acted as both constraining and enabling forces for the USSR, and both ideas served to compromise the natural tendencies of developing policies in traditional (i.e., Realist) conceptions of state interests in the foreign policy arena. Even though ideology tended to play a secondary role in decision-making in the foreign and security policy realms, adherence to Leninism would eventually undermine state interests.

The Revolution of 1917 created a non-capitalist alternative to the market that ultimately pitted two opposing socio-economic systems together in a global struggle for dominance. No sooner was Germany defeated in 1945 than a series of crises saw the temporary wartime alliance of the USSR and the United States spiral into adversarial relations. Crises over Iran and Eastern Europe, and a divided Germany led to the onset of a bipolar Cold War confrontation. In Asia the global bipolar confrontation resulted in real warfare, first in Korea, later in Vietnam and other parts of Southeast Asia. It will be shown how a theory of communism that originated in developed Europe and featured Europe and whose predictions related to Europe in the nineteenth century had a much greater impact in underdeveloped Asia in the middle of the twentieth century. Marxism as adapted by Lenin was seen as being entirely applicable to Third World states, as a critique of both contemporary imperialism and capitalist exploitation, and as a model for revolutionary change. The Soviet Union sought to take advantage of this phenomenon, leading directly to contest with the West (Halliday, 1983; Westad, 2007). Also hanging over the ideological and strategic conflict between Soviet Communism and western capitalism was the prospect of nuclear Armageddon, as a new balance of fear emerged with the onset of weapons of mass destruction (WMD).

Even the very idea of "the West" and the West's presentation of itself in the second half of the last century can only be understood with reference to the threat posed by the USSR. The original notion of the West was as a collection of states sharing a similar conception of a threat emanating from Soviet Communism (from "the East"). This idea of the West included countries not only in the western hemisphere and in Western Europe, but also in the Asia Pacific (Japan, Australia, New Zealand). The Non-Aligned Movement, incorporating mainly Third World states, also defined itself in relation to this global struggle between Soviet Communism (the East) and global capitalism (the West). The Third World too was a term that had its origins in the Cold War struggle (the First World comprised of the capitalist states, the Second World the communist states, the Third World the developing states of the post-colonial world). The second half of the last century saw new waves of de-colonization as Third World states gained independence through revolutions of "national liberation." Now the two main competitors for global influence, the USSR and the USA vied for influence among these new states, and regional conflicts became the most intense theatre of the Cold War. The Soviet Union developed a new conception of "socialist orientation" to describe states that were seen as moving from the *national* stage of revolution to an emergent *socialist* stage (this included states in Africa, Asia, the Middle East and Latin America). This book traces how the USSR came to recognize the powerful mobilizing dynamic of nationalism in the post-colonial Third World, and then sought to use it to help facilitate a move towards communism (through the new stage of "socialist orientation"). Conflicts in Angola, the Horn of Africa, the Middle East, Central America and Southeast Asia all brought some level of direct or indirect interventions from both the Soviet Union and the United States. By this stage the USSR and the US had been given the sobriquet of "superpower" to mark them off from other members of their respective blocs in the East and West, reflecting their much greater material power capabilities and the influence each had over their respective allies. They also represented different social, political, and economic systems.

At the end of the twentieth century Soviet Russia once more experienced new extremes, with radical, although largely bloodless, transformative revolutions taking place in Eastern Europe as a consequence of developments in Moscow. The results were an end to the Marxist-Leninist experiment that had began in 1917, the collapse of the communist bloc in Eastern Europe, the implosion of the Soviet-Russian empire/state, and the end of the Cold War, and consequently a radical restructuring in world politics. The Russian Revolutions at the beginning and end of the previous century can be seen as bookends demarcating the main transforming events in world politics of the twentieth century. Therefore, any rethinking of the twentieth century requires a reassessment of the Soviet experience and the pervasive influence that Soviet Communism had.

Rethinking History

Before proceeding further we should recognize the controversies involved in writing about history. When the Soviet Union collapsed in 1991 it was claimed that we had reached the "end of history" (Fukuyama, 1992). This was a mistaken conception of developments. What had clearly ended was not history but an era in which international politics had been marked by a bipolar conflict pitting two adversaries seeking to remake the world in their own image for both ideational and balance of power objectives. It is remarkable how quickly people forget. During the past quarter of a century I have taught in universities in the United States, the United Kingdom, Australia, and Thailand, and what surprises me is a general ignorance of, and lack of interest in, recent history among many of the new generations of IR students (of course not all). The Cold War conflict of the past century seems like ancient history to young people today, many of whom would not be able to define Cold War, and fewer would be able to identify the fifteen countries that once comprised the Union of Soviet Socialist Republics. Nor would they be able to grasp the power of Marxist ideology and the influence it had around the world. This is a problem, for it is only with an understanding of what has gone before that we can really appreciate where we are now. This is not to suggest that there is a linear path in history, or that there is a teleological historical trajectory. But we ignore history at our peril.

History is not simply the telling of a story; nor is it simply a narrative that recounts old news and events without having any contemporary meaning. It is not just a matter of reconstructing the past; it is also a matter of understanding the past and inter-preting it. It is simply not possible to understand the Russia of today, or Moscow's relations with its neighbours, without a full appreciation of the communist experiment of the Soviet period. US-Russian relations in 2015, what some see as a new Cold War, can also not be fully appreciated without knowledge of the orig-inal East-West Cold War in the previous century. This became more obvious with the East-West conflict between the US with Europe and the Russian Federation over Ukraine following Russia's annexation of Crimea in February 2014. It is not possible to understand the events in Ukraine without an understanding of the history of the Soviet communist experiment.

At the same time, re-evaluating important historical events or periods to demonstrate the victim-hood of ethnic groups, or the superiority of one type of political system over another, should not be undertaken specifically to support present-day political goals. Strong linkages between history and politics are of course inevitable. History following wars is often written *by* the victors, and then most often is written *about* the victors. However, this truism is sometimes used as a manipulative device, as a foil to write history from the supposed vantage point of the victims (Noam Chomsky's prodigious critiques of US foreign policy in the Third World come to mind). The truth is that history is a contested arena with very little agreement surrounding the most important events and periods. The classic work on defining and doing history is E. H. Carr's *What is History?* (1961) (see also

Gaddis, 2002; Swain, 2005; Tosh, 2008). There is no single view of history, and historians have always disagreed, often passionately, over the significance and interpretation of important historical events. For example in Australia, differing interpretations about European settlement, the treatment of the indigenous Aborigines, and the relevance of this history to the current politics surrounding citizenship have been so intensely argued that they have been labelled the "history wars" (Macintyre, 2003). Also history should not be a tool in the hands of political authorities to legitimize their own positions, although sadly this is often the case. Certainly in the Soviet Union the teaching and writing of history was highly politicized, creating versions of history that served deliberate political goals. This may be a tendency in other types of regimes, but at least in liberal democracies historical analysis was never tightly controlled by the state in the manner that it was in the USSR during the Cold War. Russian President Vladimir Putin has been accused of interfering in how Soviet history should be taught to children in the Russian Federation, insisting on what he says should be a more balanced (that is positive) view of Stalin's role as war leader.

As soon as the Soviet leadership under Mikhail Gorbachev loosened restrictions on censorship in the mid-1980s there was a massive outpouring of writings about the Stalin period. It was almost impossible when picking up any periodical (no matter what the title or ostensible subject matter) not to come across articles on Stalinism, the purges, the gulag, and the use of terror. Soviet peoples were seemingly hungry for knowledge, free of state interference, about their own past. However, there can be no single, correct view of past events. Primary facts are keenly contested, and this contestation was clearly manifest in the initial outpouring of analyses of the Stalin period in the Soviet Union, although it should be noted that most of the interpretations were highly critical and painted Stalin in a very poor light. This was also understandable as intellectual freedoms now facilitated the "truth" being told for the first time, as the archives were opened up (at first selectively and slowly) and memoirs were written, and democratization of the political system was underway. Although the Soviet past was laid open for more open discussion, this did not extend to criticizing Lenin—nor, indeed, did it extend at first to criticism of the incumbent political leadership under Gorbachev. The reformers were encouraging this re-evaluation of the Stalin period for their own political purposes, and this did not extend to challenging the essence of Leninism and Soviet Communism. This was another example of the political class seeking to use history for its own instrumental purposes. However, when the floodgates were opened it resulted in an outpouring of pluralism and in a resurgence of nationalism in the fifteen Soviet republics, hence undermining the intended objectives of the communist reformers.

To revisit this historical period was also very painful for many Soviet citizens, for differing reasons. Gorbachev, the last communist leader of the USSR had a fairly typical Soviet background. The son of peasant farmers, he moved through the ranks of the Young Communist League (Komsomol), went on to become a regional First Party Secretary in the Stavropol region, and then a member of the Central Committee of the Communist Party of the Soviet Union (CPSU). He eventually gained membership of the Politburo and its Secretariat, until finally being selected as General Secretary of the CPSU in 1985. Although head of the anti-religious Soviet system Gorbachev as a child had nevertheless been baptized into the Russian Orthodox Church. The baptism was arranged by his grandfather, who would later be arrested in Stalin's purges, accused of being a Trotskyist agent. The grandfather of Gorbachev's wife, Raisa Gorbacheva, was arrested in 1937 and executed for allegedly "counter-revolutionary activities" in the collective farm where he worked. When Stalin died in 1953 Gorbachev was a student in Moscow State University's Law Faculty, and recalls at the time feeling "deeply affected" by Stalin's death and nothing then was more important for him and his fellow students than lining up all night to pay their last respects to Stalin lying in state in his coffin (Gorbachev, 1995, p. 26 and 47). Even as the end was nigh, following the failed military/party/ KGB coup against him in August 1990, Gorbachev was still then expressing his faith in Leninism, stating that throughout his tenure as General Secretary he drew on 'ideas generated by Lenin's works' (Gorbachev, 1995, p. 148). This might be interpreted as a leader reluctant to let go of Leninist communist ideology due to a concern for his position, which could be seen as being dependent upon adherence to it. However, at that time (when many of his own supporters were encouraging him in this direction) Gorbachev would have done better for his own survival to jettison Leninism once and for all. Gorbachev's faith in the original goals of the Bolshevik Revolution was genuinely held to the end.

Andrei Sakharov, a nuclear physicist who helped develop the Soviet atom bomb, recalls that when Stalin died he got "carried away" and in a letter to a friend wrote 'I am under the influence of a great man's death' (Sakharov, 1990, p. 164). When he was a student at university, Sakharov notes that although he found the compulsory course on Marxism-Leninism difficult, 'it never entered my head to question Marxism-Leninism as the ideology best-suited to liberate mankind' (Sakharov, 1990, p. 36). However, unlike Gorbachev, Sakharov's faith in the system would evaporate and under Leonid Brezhnev's rule he became a leading Soviet dissident, calling for individual freedoms and democracy. A dissident Marxist historian in the Soviet era, Roy Medvedev, recalls that 'Even though my own father was repressed ... I believed in Stalin and thought he was a great leader' (Medvedev, 2009). The point here is that even Soviet intellectuals, including some of the most astute and critically thinking, did not question the system under Stalin even when it was clear that his dictatorial and murderous methods went against the central tenets of socialism. Sakharov's own family also suffered in Stalin's purges. Sakharov notes in his memoirs when reflecting upon these facts that the situation at that time was more complicated, and that he was influenced by the 'persisting revolutionary élan; hope for the future; fanaticism' (Sakharov, p. 36). It was this revolutionary hope, to create a better and more equitable world that animated most adherents to the communist cause. But it was ultimately the methods used in the pursuit of this objective that inexorably led to terror and repression.

The evaluations of the Stalinist past under Gorbachev's reformism was anything but the end of history: it marked the radical resurgence of historiography in Russia and an emerging debate about the best way forward. While it was evident that communism as practiced in the Soviet Union was in its death throes, it was certainly not a forgone conclusion that liberal democracy would necessarily take its place.

History and the Power of Ideas

Despite the horrors inflicted on its own population by the Stalinist system it is remarkable that so many people outside the USSR, with no direct material, political, or personal gains to be made, especially amongst intellectuals, continued to support Soviet Communism. Marxist ideas attracted numerous intellectuals, for they formed for them a framework to reorder society along a more equal trajectory. Marxism offered a solution to what were considered to be the inequities of global capitalism and its inherent tendency to exploit the weak and vulnerable. Again, it is incredible from our current vantage point that intelligent people continued to offer support for *Soviet* Communism even as it was inflicting terror on millions of people. There is perhaps something to learn here in relation to widespread contemporary support for terrorism in the name of Islam, which some see as a new ideology to challenge western liberal democracy and the capitalist market.

Yet, as John Gray has pointed out 'terror was practised during the last century on a scale unequalled at any other time in history, but unlike the terror that is most feared today much of it was done in the service of secular hopes' (Gray, 2008, p. 50). It should be added here that terror was also practised by the *state*. Gray argues that this phenomenon was inherent in the communist project itself, rather than being a distortion of it, and the 'use of inhumane methods to achieve impossible ends is the essence of revolutionary utopianism'. Gray argued too that if communism had been established in the United Kingdom, France, Italy, or in Scandinavia then the result would have been the same (Gray, p. 53). Given the different forms that communism took in various countries that were led by communist parties this seems an odd argument to make. It is true that the communist systems in Eastern Europe, among those countries comprising the military bloc of the Warsaw Pact, did follow the basic Soviet model—but then these countries had communism imposed upon them by Soviet tanks and were always limited in their sovereignty. This limited sovereignty would become institutionalized in the Brezhnev Doctrine following Soviet military intervention to stamp out reform in Prague in 1968. The CPSU basically had ultimate control over the fate of these states. However, Cambodia, China, Cuba, Vietnam, Yugoslavia, and other communist states, although inspired by Soviet Communism, had not followed the exact same path as the Warsaw Pact countries. It should also be pointed out the fallacy in suggesting that communism would have taken on a Stalinist nature if it had been established in the United Kingdom, France, or Italy, for these are all well-developed and not backward countries. In part Soviet Communism and Stalinism can be seen as paths to modernity and state-building in pre-industrial societies (Arnason, 1993). This could also partly explain the tendency for under-developed societies undergoing revolutionary transformations in the name of communism to eventually give rise to nationalism. If a socialist revolution had occurred in the United Kingdom, as a well-developed industrial society, it is not clear why this should then have resulted in Stalinism.

Yet it is still an interesting and seemingly puzzling fact that Western intellectuals were giving their strongest support to Soviet Communism when Stalinist terror was at its height. Paul Hollander asks why Marxist ideas attracted so many intellectuals and why so many of them continued to support the USSR even when it was clear that terror was being perpetrated. Quoting Mark Lilla he asks 'What is it about the human mind that made the intellectual defense of tyranny possible in the twentieth century?' (Hollander, 2006, p. 11). There were many key works by Western intellectuals that painted positive views of the development of a new progressive Soviet society that all managed to somehow ignore or justify the awful realities of the gulag, purges, and terror (Clark, 1960; Webb and Webb, 1937). Evidence was readily available about the forced labour camps, violence against the peasants during the collectivization of agriculture, famine in Ukraine, and the dark theatre of the show trials in Moscow. Robert Conquest in his classic work *The Great Terror* made just this point, arguing that there was no rational basis on which to accept the official version given by the Stalinist state that there was no innocent suffering, and that the Old Bolsheviks had turned into anti-communist agents of either Leon Trotsky or Imperialism (Conquest, 1968). In an interview with Michael Ignatieff the British historian Eric Hobsbawm when asked why he supported the Soviet Union in the 1930s answered: 'You didn't have an option. You see, either there was going to be a future or there wasn't going to be a future and this [the Communist Party] was the only thing that offered a future' (Ignatieff, 1994).

In his reminiscences of his days as a member of the British Communist Party (CPGB), Raphael Samuel recites how in the 1940s the communists were insulated from alien influences and how for them communism was 'the way, the truth and the life. Like earlier belief systems, it put forward a complete scheme of social salvation'. Samuel goes on to acknowledge that the 'Soviet Union was, of course, our promised land' (Samuel, 2006, 46). However, there is absolutely no evidence to suggest that these same individuals would have welcomed or supported the initiation of communist methods in their own societies. They were supporting an *idea* and then what they considered to be its best chance of success in another place, in a radically different setting. It was recognized that Soviet Communism had made detours from the true path, methods were used that were not always in line with the stated ethical stance, and that mistakes had been made—but still, many would have argued, the ends justified the means (given the specific circumstances in Russia at that time). And all who approved of the October Revolution and the goals of the Bolsheviks did so as internationalists opposed to the separation of peoples on the basis of nationality.

Isaiah Berlin stated that between 1937 and 1938 the great purges so devastated the intellectual landscape in Russia that literature emerged 'like an area devastated by war, with some splendid buildings still relatively intact, but standing solitary amid stretches of ruined and deserted country' (Berlin, 2004, p. 6). But people stuck with their beliefs due in part to wishful thinking, 'the durability and depth of commitment and faith that rest on the wish and capacity to believe—a capacity that is an integral part of human beings' (Hollander, 364). Former British Prime Minister Tony Blair's father became Secretary of the Govan branch of the Scottish Young Communist League in 1938 as the purges in the USSR took their toll. Even Doris Lessing was a true believer. It was only recently, *after* the fall of Soviet Communism, in 1993 that the British (New) Labour Party finally scrapped Clause Four of its constitution (originally written by Sidney Webb in the year of the October Revolution in 1917). This was the controversial clause calling for the *collective* ownership of the means of production. It should be noted that at no time did Tony Blair flirt with Communism (although many on the left of the Labour Party did, some of whom had Soviet sympathies). On the contrary it was Blair who fought against the radical leftists in the (old) Labour Party (the Militant Tendency amongst others) and eventually engineered the removal of the offending socialist clause from the party statutes.

A former member of the Russian royal family who fled Russia but later became a member of the Communist Party of Great Britain (CPGB), wrote in the *Daily Worker* that if the USSR is attacked, physically or verbally, then 'it is the first duty of any communist to leap to its defense' (Zinovieff, 2007, p. 317). A Croatian writer has recalled attending a Socialist Scholars Conference in New York before the collapse of Soviet Communism, where she felt that at each small criticism of "really existing socialism" [that is, socialism as practised in the USSR and the Eastern Bloc] American leftists would 'look at me suspiciously as if I were a CIA agent'. She went on to assert that '[i]t is not the knowledge about communism that they lack—it is the experience of living under such conditions. So while I am speaking from within the system itself, they are explaining it to me from without .... They see reality in schemes, in broad historical outlines' (Drakulic, 1992, p. 125). This was indeed the way outsiders viewed things. Yet there would have been very few who would ever have contemplated for a moment swapping their own positions for those of their "comrades" imprisoned in their conceptual jails on the other side of the Iron Curtain. Raymond Aron, in *The Opium of the Intellectuals,* demonstrates how "noble ideas" can lead to tyranny (Aron, 2005, p. 323). Aron saw Marxism as a secular religion, and Marxist ideology as offering intellectuals hope against what they saw as a harsh reality (here he is talking of French intellectuals such as Jean-Paul Sartre and Maurice Merleau-Ponty).

The phenomenon of western intellectuals continuing to support communist regimes during the Cold War is made all the more imponderable given the negative attitudes and harsh policies meted out to intellectuals by, for example, Stalin, Mao, and Pol Pot. Still, it is instructive to note that since the demise of Soviet Communism the two critical figures responsible for its development (Lenin and Stalin) have consistently topped polls and surveys amongst Russian citizens when asked who were the most important and impressive figures in Russian history. Now in re-evaluating their own historical past Russians have come to have a more positive view of the Soviet era and of the original Bolshevik revolutionaries, whereas intellectuals in the West have come to have a more negative view in recent times. History is what we make of it. In this history of Soviet Communism and its impact on international politics of the twentieth century I am guided by a non-ideological, non-partisan approach that stresses the tensions between communism, nationalism, and international security. However, it is useful to note how the history of the Soviet era has been and remains contentious, and can never be entirely free from political contestation.

For the political establishment in the West, Soviet Communism was perceived as a challenge and a threat, having significant effects on both domestic and foreign policies, instilling fears in the West that gave rise to McCarthy's witch hunts, but also to the development of social welfare systems. In American political discourse Soviet Communism was often referred to as "Godless communism," as for many Americans the ideological threat to Christianity was the bigger challenge than the economic threat to capitalism, or one that could more easily be employed to mobilize the masses in a deeply religious country. The anti-religious content of Marxism, on the other hand, was one of the major appeals to many intellectuals in the West who were singing the praises of the Soviet Union. Yet many dissident intellectuals in the Eastern bloc had been imprisoned, forced into hard labour, or even killed. The lucky ones escaped to external exile. It has been estimated that nearly half of the taxi drivers in Paris by the 1940s were Russian exiles (Zinovieff, 2007, p. 150).

Fukuyama's conception of the end of history was however in some way applicable, for in 1991, with the disintegration of the Soviet Union, the world had clearly reached the end of an era, and this was indeed marked by the end of more than the collapse of an Empire/state (for that is what the Soviet Union essentially was, the last of the great European empires). It marked too the death of Soviet Communism: the death of the chief ideological challenge to the dominance of world capitalism and to liberal democratic forms of government. And now that we have an end point to both the Soviet Union and its communist system, we are better able to reassess the role it played in world politics in the twentieth century and to evaluate its legacy in the twenty-first.

Here it is worth remembering that although Communism may not be the ruling ideology in contemporary Russia, it is still far from completely moribund. China, despite having been engaged in rapid development along capitalist lines for the past three decades, before even the collapse of communism in Russia, is still nevertheless ruled by the communist party. So too are Cuba, Vietnam and North Korea ruled by communist parties. In April 2008 the Unified Communist Party of Nepal (Maoist), gained power through elections to the Constituent Assembly in Kathmandu (with the Communist Party of Nepal (Unified Marxist-Leninist) also gaining a large number of seats. In some parts of Latin America, Asia, and Africa groups adhering to Marxist-Leninist principles are either fighting guerilla wars or sharing some form of political power. Hugo Rafael Chavez, President of Venezuela from 1998 until his death in 2013 (having won re-election in 2000, 2006, and 2012) was a self-described revolutionary, guided by an ideology of democratic socialism and solidarity among Latin American states in the interests of the poor and against the Washington neo-liberal consensus. Lenin and Stalin may have distorted the original Marxist principles upon which they based their policies but what they produced in practice has clearly provided others with a model for achieving their own objectives.

In the twenty-first century the experiment of Soviet Communism appears still to be attractive to some in the developing world as a useful model for modernization, just as it was in the twentieth century. It also appeals to political leaders who covet total power. Saddam Hussein was said to be a great admirer of Stalin, and modelled his regime on the Stalinist one (Coughlin, 2002, p. 47). Some would argue that Putin too has restored certain aspects of the Soviet system. Since the crisis in the global capitalist economy in 2008 there has also been political turbulence across various parts of the world, from anti-Wall Street demonstrators to the streets of Athens and across the Arab world, that indicate increasing lack of faith in the workings of capitalism. It is too early yet to bury communism as an idea, and the experience of the former Soviet Union and the rise and fall of Soviet Communism may still hold important lessons, if only about what should best be avoided in any attempt to build an alternative system to capitalism.

Western analysis of the USSR was not only politicized, in that many scholars in Soviet area studies tended either to strongly oppose or empathize with the original socialist/communist objectives, it was also divorced from what were the more influential academic debates in the IR and Strategic Studies communities. When evaluating academic work during the Cold War era—what Kal Holsti (1998) refers to as scholarship in an "age of anxiety"—this book will demonstrate why specialists failed to predict the demise of the Soviet Union at the end of the twentieth century (see on this question also Cox, 1998; Gvosdev, 2008). One of the reasons for this was the tendency, especially among IR scholars, to downplay or ignore completely the role of ideology. As will be recorded in this book, although communist ideas were based on emancipation for the majority (the "masses") the practical results of regimes seeking to implement them resulted in horrendous unanticipated consequences, but ones that were ultimately legitimated in the name of these ideas.

The anxiety emanating from the insanity of MAD (the extreme policy of mutual assured destruction) with the advent of nuclear weapons was also clearly a critical concern in the Cold War years, and hence of great interest to the IR and Strategic Studies specialists. But not having a clear understanding of the role of Soviet ideology, scholars and policy-makers could not fully appreciate the problems inherent in the communist system, and hence were unable to predict the demise of the Soviet Union. Part of the problem also was the fact that few IR scholars had ever visited the USSR, and those that did often failed to see through the veneer of the communist Potemkin village, being awestruck by the power in the inventories of nuclear and conventional weapons. Their error was to exaggerate the role of military power and to underplay the role of ideas and ideologies. They failed to see the brittle nature of the national security/ideological state. This book reassesses the Soviet experience, with particular attention paid to the significance of Marxist-Leninist ideology and the role of the Soviet state. It is revealed how Leninism eventually came to serve as a legitimizing device for political control of the Soviet communist elites, for the maintenance of a wider sphere of influence in Eastern Europe, and in relation to the global confrontation with the United States in the Cold War.

This is not to say that ideology was the only or even at all times the most critical variable, for this is clearly not the case. This book also accounts for structural factors at both domestic and international levels, in addition to the role of specific significant individuals. It was Karl Marx who stated that men make their own history, although of course qualifying this by stating that they do so only within the constraints of the material world in which they live. Systemic constraints impede the ability of even the nastiest dictators to get their way in all circumstances; yet the power of personality and the skills and ambitions of some individuals had a huge impact on the nature and the rise and fall of Soviet communism. But in the end, even the almost absolute power wielded by Stalin did not mean he could escape the constraints of the balance of power and the structure of the international system and the power of the national idea.

In the wake of the Soviet collapse, specialists in Soviet Area Studies turned away from history, focusing their attention on developments in the wider post-communist states, leading to a burgeoning literature on "transitions," mainly comparative studies of "democratization" ("transitology"). While there is a number of excellent books published by leading specialists that offer some useful narrative analytical histories of the USSR and of communism in the twentieth century (for example, Daniels, 2007; Glaser and Walker, 2007; Medvedev, 2006; Shlapentokh, 2002; Service, 2007; Volkogonov, 1999) none of them tell the story of how Soviet Communism's influence in world politics was compromised by national identities. The best work on the history of the entire communist world in the twentieth century is Archie Brown's *The Rise and Fall of* Communism (2009). Brown has produced an excellent overview for anyone wishing to gain a comprehensive story of the rise and fall of the communist systems, and the actual dramas and personal stories of the key characters. The present book takes a broader approach, focusing on the big picture and relating this to Soviet Communism's influence on the outside world and in global politics. Hopefully this book will thus help to fill a gap, providing a reassessment of the Soviet experience that gives proper attention to the ideas and practices of Marxism-Leninism, in both its domestic and its international settings, while at each stage identifying the influences of the national idea on the fate of the Bolshevik project. What this volume shows is how ideology intersected with domestic power struggles and issues pertaining to the wider "world communist movement," and structural features at both the domestic and international levels along with alternative nationalist ideologies. Insufficient attention has been accorded these important and interlinked aspects pertaining to the Soviet Union. This book therefore provides an original analysis that reinterprets the Soviet experience by taking account of key aspects that have hitherto been marginalized or misunderstood.

In Chapter 1 I trace the roots of the Bolshevik Revolution and the rise and fall of Soviet Communism, providing the necessary background for the subsequent chapters that deal each in turn with the impact that Soviet Communism had in different theatres of international politics. Chapter 2 covers the role of ideology and shows how scholarship in the West for the most part either paid insufficient attention to Soviet ideology or misunderstood its function in the realm of world politics. In Chapter 3 I examine the international communist movement, in particular the various manifestations, over different periods, of Soviet-dominated international organizations that were ostensibly designed to further the global spread of communism, highlighting how they were in fact used to further Soviet state interests, rather than to foster revolution. Chapter 4 covers the impact of Soviet Communism in the Third World (today's Global South), and Chapter 5 discusses its impact in the West, demonstrating in both cases how it then impacted on wider global politics and international security, particularly in relation to the bipolar confrontation with the United States. Each chapter shows too how Soviet Communism was consistently confronted with the forces of nationalism in both the development of Soviet internal politics and in the conduct of foreign relations. Chapter 6 gives detailed treatment to the national question in the USSR, Chapter 7 assesses issues of international security, and the Conclusion then summarizes the findings of the book, and identifies the legacies of Soviet Communism in the early part of the twenty-first century.

1

The October Revolution, and the Rise and Demise of Soviet Communism

As Martin Malia puts it, 'The Soviet socialist experiment was the great utopian adventure of the modern age' (Malia, 1994, p. 1). Yet few people could have anticipated this experiment beginning in, of all places, the Russian Empire, which at its greatest extent would be the third largest in history after the Mongol and British empires, and incorporated multiple nationalities and religions at various stages of social and economic development, but generally lagging well behind the modernized West. The Soviet Union would cover one-sixth of the world's land surface across eleven time zones from Vladivostok in the East to Kaliningrad in the West. What is also remarkable is that this radical experiment took place in the world's largest country, yet was conducted by a handful of young revolutionaries with little or no experience whatsoever of practical work, either in the public or private sectors, neither in government, nor in business. The oldest of the leading Bolsheviks at that time were Lenin himself, Leonid Krasin and Pyotr Krasikov, all just 37 years of age. Krasin played a key role as transport minister keeping the Red Army supplied during the Civil War, and Krasikov a key member of the St. Petersburg Soviet would help to draw up the Soviet legal system. The average age of the Bolshevik leaders was 34 years. The leader of the Mensheviks, L. Martov, was 34 years of age. One-sixth of the chief Bolshevik activists were under 30 years of age. Many of the communists in the Russian empire were not Russians. For example, of the delegates to the 5th Congress of the Russian Social Democratic

Labour Party (RSDLP) in 1907, only 34% were Russians: 30% were Georgians, and 23% were Jewish (Lane, 1968, p. 107).

It is common to say that Russia has an unpredictable past. There is no single historical narrative of the Russian Revolution. There is a veritable library of books on the Russian Revolution, yet as a seminal event of the twentieth century, there is no single accepted interpretation either of its causes or its consequences. There was always the official "party line" in the USSR, to which Soviet scholars and students were forced to adhere. The official line was at times revised, but there was no room for independent assessments and anyone who challenged the orthodox view did so in the clear knowledge that the consequences could be dire. The party line changed according to the perceived interests of the party hierarchy, often during internal struggles for power. Although certain individuals were written out of the drama of the revolution, and others were transformed from revolutionary heroes to "enemies of the people" (one thinks of the fates of Leon Trotsky and Nikolai Bukharin, to take just two prominent examples), October 1917 was portrayed in terms of the inevitable forces of history in line with Marxist, and later Marxist-Leninist theory. Before October 1917 socialist ideas were the preserve of 'a miniscule stratum of intellectuals and workers. After 1917 they appeared as a political possibility to millions across the world' hence the fall of Petrograd was a "universal event" (Ali, 1984, p. 17).

Introduction: Defining Revolution

When discussing any revolution it is first necessary to recognize, even in the absence of strong ideological biases, that political scientists will often dispute the meaning of important concepts. Concepts in the social sciences are "essentially contested": that is to say there is no single working definition of concepts such as "revolution" that is widely accepted. It should be noted too that political concepts are inventions of the human mind. War as an institution is a human social construction. Whilst slavery was once an accepted and acceptable social practice it is now considered to be abhorrent and only continues (unfortunately) as an illegal practice, slavery being seen as an affront to human rights. Hence, defining concepts such as revolution is never straightforward, either from a practical point of view or from an analytical one. It is the case also that often one's own preferred definition of a specific concept is reflective of political or ideological biases.

Yet there is no need to complicate matters in such a way. Revolution implies, above all, sudden, fundamental change. It has been common to talk of a revolution of rising expectations, a revolution in science and technology, or a revolution in military affairs, yet none of these phenomena meet the test of revolution, for they do not involve *fundamental* change. They may produce radical change, but not fundamental change. For example looking at political systems, if a comparison is made between the British system under Lloyd George and that under Margaret Thatcher then perhaps radical changes can be recognized. The USA under Woodrow Wilson in 1914 was radically different to the USA under Barak Obama in 2014, not least because the USA now had a black president in the White House. A comparison of Russia in 1936 under Stalin and 1963 under Nikita Khrushchev, again, fairly radical changes can be identified. In none of these cases, however, are we talking of major, fundamental, systemic changes that would warrant use of the term revolution. Those who referred to the "Thatcher Revolution" were simply misusing the term, often for ideological purposes. Revolution does not merely equate with a new government or evolutionary changes to a political system, but to a new order and systemic change, where one system is replaced by another system. A revolutionary deliberately engages in non-traditional, extra-constitutional, non-legal means (often violent) to overthrow not just the established power elite, but also to smash the political institutions and change the social relations and the economy of the country in question. Revolution means transformation, not evolution.

Revolution should also be distinguished from a *coup d'état*. A traditional coup is a sudden illegal and unconstitutional change of government usually involving the military, hence affecting the political realm in the form of a forced change in the composition of the political elite. To take one example, in Thailand between 1932 and 2014 there were some eighteen military coups; yet during this period there was no radical social change that would merit the term revolution. A revolution involves change not only in the political regime, but a transformation in the social and economic structures of society. In Russia, the October Revolution led to transformations in political elites, in political institutions, and in economic and social relations. Russian society was fundamentally transformed along a non-capitalist path of development based upon the ideas of the communist thinkers and revolutionary Marxist activists in the Bolshevik Party, as developed in particular by Vladimir Lenin. By 1980 Marxist-Leninist states accounted for fully one-third of the world's population, with communist systems in Africa, Latin America, Eastern Europe, the Middle East and Asia; and Soviet Communism was a critical factor in either inspiring or, as in the case of Eastern Europe, imposing the development of communism in each case.

IR has tended not to take revolutions seriously, or rather not to see them as critical for understanding the fundamental dynamics of interstate relations. There are two significant exceptions: Stephen Walt's *Revolution and War* (1997) and Fred Halliday's *Revolution and World Politics* (1999). Coming from different perspectives Walt and Halliday show how revolutions can have profound effects on the conduct of international politics. Although each revolution differs in specific respects they have major consequences relating to the balance of power, threat perceptions, social and ideological contestation, and wars between states. Hence, revolutions are never local events, and therefore there is really no such thing as a merely domestic revolution. The October Revolution of 1917 resulted in a major challenge to the workings of the international system, creating shifts in what Walt refers to as the 'balance of threat' with enhanced and exaggerated mutual hostilities leading to increased fears and perceptions of threat.

To return to the origins of revolution, to complicate things further, the actual participants in any particular revolution may not have the same incentives or objectives in engaging in revolution in the first place. In 1917 different groups in the Russian Empire that were engaged in revolutionary political action were motivated by similar frustrations with the established order which they wanted to see overthrown, but they did not all then share the same single vision for the future. Even among the Marxists there were serious divisions about how a post-Tsarist system should develop, and then for the ultimate victors, the Bolsheviks, there were surprises and unexpected and unintended consequences emanating from the Revolution that determined and limited their choices and hence influenced their policies. The Bolsheviks were split on the best way of achieving the objectives of the revolution once they had gained power. Ideas have consequences, but they are rarely those expected, intended, or desired by their originators. Agents, the authors and proponents of ideas are restricted in what they can achieve when faced with everyday reality. Thus, as in any revolutionary process, we have to consider domestic and international circumstances, systemic factors, as well as the role of human agency.

Revolutions have deep causes, intermediate or proximate causes, and immediate triggers. The Tunisian street trader whose self-immolation in December 2010 subsequently triggered the Arab Spring did not represent a deep cause of the revolution, but he was the immediate spark for setting off the revolutionary events across the Arab world. The deep causes of these events lay elsewhere. The deep causes of the Russian Revolution were the centuries of autocracy in which the Russian people at the bottom of the social scale were downtrodden whilst those at the top had no means through which to participate meaningfully in the political process. Going back to Alexander Pushkin's *Evgenii Onegin* many of Russia's literary giants had often taken the so-called "superfluous" man as subject in their fiction, portraying the frustrations of the educated young Russian noblemen who had no means to put their education to any effect in either the social or the economic realms. The intermediate cause was war, against first Japan and then against Germany in 1914, both highlighting and bringing to the surface the inadequacies of the Tsarist system. Then the immediate trigger for the Russian Revolution was the abdication of the Tsar, and the subsequent turmoil and struggle for power between the St. Petersburg Soviet and the Provisional Government.

Revolutionary Russia

One of the earliest, and still among the best accounts of the events leading up to the Bolshevik take-over of power in November 1917, appropriately titled *Ten Days That Shook The World*, was written by John Reed, an American correspondent in Moscow at the time reporting for the radical newspaper *The Masses*. Reed, a socialist, was partisan, a supporter of the Revolution and of the Bolsheviks (Reed, 1977). Lenin actually wrote a short introduction to Reed's book when it was published in 1919, recommending it 'without reservation' to the 'workers of the world'. Reed died from typhus in Russia in 1920 and was buried in Red Square in the Heroes' Grave, where he still lies today alongside Stalin and other former Bolshevik leaders behind Lenin's mausoleum. Although Reed had clear political sympathies for the Bolsheviks, his chronicle of the revolution is one of the most detailed available, and it brings to life, better than perhaps any other account, the drama of those revolutionary days. In the introduction to the Penguin edition of *Ten Days*, the eminent historian A.J.P. Taylor wrote: 'Reed's book is not only the best account of the Bolshevik Revolution, it comes near to being the best account of any revolution' (Taylor, 1997, p. vii).

There is no index to Reed's book, but if one had been compiled, then there would be many page references to "war." One theme running throughout the book is the question of whether or not Russia should stay in the war against Germany. From the beginning of the war Lenin and the Bolsheviks were opposed to Russia's participation. By 1917, Russia, under the strains of war, was in a situation close to anarchy, or what we would call today a failing state, a state in the throws of collapse. There were shortages of bread and the cities and the army went hungry; the countryside was in chaos with peasants becoming increasingly disenchanted; the railways and transportation system were in appalling conditions of disarray; soldiers were engaged in the third year of a bloody war against Germany with no clear end in sight or for them any obvious reason for the fighting.

The Tsarist authorities seemed incapable of providing the necessary leadership to deal with this multitude of problems. What ensued were strikes, food riots, demonstrations, the burning of manor houses, mutinies in the armed forces, increasing crime, and highly charged political groups vying for power. Without war perhaps none of this would have eventuated. As Robert Service puts it: 'Except for the Great War, Lenin would have remained an *émigré* theorist scribbling in Swiss libraries, and even if Nicholas II had been deposed in a peacetime transfer of power, the inception of a communist order would hardly have been likely' (Service, 2009, p. 26). Similarly, without that same great European conflict Hitler would not have later achieved supreme power in Germany (Overy, 2004, p. xxxvi). If the Bolsheviks had not taken power in November 1917 then the German troops could have been in Petrograd and Moscow by Christmas that same year. In the nineteenth century Russia's defeat in 1856 in the Crimean War was a catalyst for the subsequent reforms of Tsar Alexander II, including the emancipation of the serfs, and reforms in the military, legal, educational, and governmental structures. The point being stressed is that foreign wars can have unforeseen, radical, domestic consequences, and then those domestic consequences can also rebound back into the international arena. Hence, the First Word War helped bring about the October Revolution in Russia, and that in turn led to the Cold War.

In this anarchical situation Russia had become effectively ungovernable, and hence was ripe for revolution. Already in 1905, with worker discontent in the cities manifested in strikes and demonstrations, peasant uprisings in the countryside leading to killings of landlords, and rebellion in the armed forces when the crew of the battleship *Potemkin* mutinied, Russia was in turmoil. The backdrop once more had been war, this time in the Far East against Japan, a war that resulted in a humiliating defeat of the entire Russian naval fleet and with Russia ceding territory to Japan in an agreement mediated by US President Theodore Roosevelt in August 1905 (see Ascher, 1988). The war against Japan in 1905 was expected to be short and victorious and help to avert domestic revolution, or such was the hope of the Russian Minster of the Interior (Hill, 1972, p. 23). All of this demonstrated to both the Tsarist authorities and the radical socialist groups the danger (or hope and potential, depending upon one's perspective) of revolution. As Trotsky pointed out, Russia at the turn of the twentieth century comprised all stages of human development (Trotsky, 1922). Russian industry utilized the most sophisticated and technologically advanced machinery in the world, more concentrated than anywhere in Europe. Russia was the world's largest country and had the world's fifth largest economy.

However, Russian agriculture was backward, and Russia was largely a peasant society. Russia had advanced forms of capitalist production, yet the bulk of the population was made up of illiterate peasants working on the land, most of whom were practically destitute. With no legal institutions through which any of these aggrieved groups could seek to have their interests considered, unconstitutional action was the only means at their disposal. However, there was one important development during the course of 1905 that provided the Russian people with a forum to articulate their political goals: the establishment of the St. Petersburg Soviet. Soviets were created not by communist revolutionaries, but by striking workers as vehicles through which to make demands on their employers. The first such Soviet was actually founded in a textile factory in Nizhny Novgorod, but it was the Soviet in the Empire's capital that became important as the main coordinating body for the workers' strikes. Trotsky (then a Menshevik) took on the leadership of the St. Petersburg Soviet, and later, when he joined forces with Lenin, the rallying cry in October 1917 was 'All Power to the Soviets'. The Bolsheviks recognized the power and potential of organized labour taking the lead through the Soviets, whilst also coming better to appreciate the revolutionary potential of the peasants.

It was in the late 1890s when small numbers of Russian Marxists formed the RSDLP, with Lenin becoming one its leading figures. In 1903 at the 3rd Congress of the RSDLP Lenin created a split in the party based upon alternative conceptions of party organization. Lenin insisted on a small cell structure of devoted and professional revolutionaries forming the membership, whereas other delegates favoured a more traditional mass membership type of party. As a result of this disagreement the party split into two separate groups: the Mensheviks and the Bolsheviks led by Lenin. Lenin's conception of the Party was essential for the future development of the Soviet Communist system, as it developed into a centralized and disciplined one-party state.

It should of course be recalled that Marxist theory never expected proletarian revolution to first occur in a country with a largely peasant population. Revolutions either require revolutionaries to make them happen, or they create revolutionaries as a consequence of their occurrence. In other words, some revolutions take place, as it were, spontaneously with no help from organized revolutionary groups, whilst others are orchestrated and led by activists who *make* the revolution, and these can be mass-led or elite-led revolutions. What so impressed the Bolsheviks about 1905 is the spontaneous nature of the revolutionary momentum at that time and the potential revolutionary role of the peasantry. In the nineteenth century the liberal democratic westernizing socialist reformer, Pyotr Lavrov, and the anarchist Mikhail Bakunin, both believed in the revolutionary potential of the peasantry. But 1905 took the Bolsheviks by surprise. For Lenin the lesson was reinforced that it was necessary to have a group of dedicated revolutionaries prepared to lead the revolution, because the masses on their own could not do so.

In every case the situation has to be ripe for revolution, otherwise, whether mass- or elite-led, revolutionaries will fail in their objectives. In the case of Russia in 1917 the situation was indeed ripe for revolution. The masses were intent on revolutionary change in both the countryside and the towns, with groups of professional revolutionaries ready to take advantage of the situation. The background then to the Russian Revolution was complex, for on the one hand the bulk of the population in the countryside wished to own their own land, whilst many workers in the factories wished to have control over their enterprises. The educated classes and the nobility were torn between various prescriptions for Russia's future ranging from a restoration of the Tsar through liberal constitutionalism and parliamentary democracy, to anarchism, socialism (in various guises) and Great Russian nationalism.

However, it should be stressed that the October Revolution was not a nationalist one. Although some ethnic groups took advantage of the emerging anarchical situation to seek autonomy from the centre, the revolution was undertaken in the name not of nations but of classes. Russians, Georgians, and other nations came together in what they perceived to be a struggle to liberate the peoples of all nationalities from an authoritarian system that subjugated them all. The rallying cry that brought them together was for bread, peace, freedom and justice. The Bolsheviks offered peasants land, workers control over their factories, and peace and a future free from insecurity.

The so-called situation of "dual power" emerged following the abdication of the Tsar in February 1917, although in reality the Russian state was left with no effective power at all, as the Provisional Government under Alexander Kerensky's leadership and the Petrograd Soviet issued countermanding and contradictory, opposing decrees. The Provisional Government had been established after the Tsar abdicated, and the intention of the government was to convene an elected constitutional assembly to draft a new constitution. The Tsar had been forced to abdicate following mass demonstrations, strikes, peasant uprisings, and clashes with the authorities in the capital during which many soldiers defected to the opposition. The Petrograd Soviet became an arm of the Bolsheviks under Trotsky's direction and eventually the Bolsheviks, in the name of the Soviets, overthrew the Provisional Government in October. As had been promised elections were held for a constitutional assembly on 12 November, but in January 1918 the Bolsheviks, who had failed to gain a majority of votes, forcibly disbanded it. The Bolsheviks received just over 9 million votes (25% of the total) less than half of the 20,900,000 votes (58%) gained by the Socialist Revolutionaries. Lenin and the Bolsheviks were not willing to let the fate of the Revolution rest with a western-type parliamentary assembly, with Lenin stating that 'a republic of Soviets is a higher form of demo-cratic principle than the customary bourgeois republic with its Constituent Assembly' (quoted in Lee, 2003. p. 98).

Lenin was the principle figure in pushing for the Bolshevik take-over of power in October 1917. Soon after overthrowing the provisional government in the name of the Soviets, Lenin con-fided to Trotsky 'from persecution and a life underground, to come so suddenly into power ... it makes you feel giddy' (quoted in King, 2008, p. 42). Pipes writes that viewed from the perspec-tive of history 'one can only marvel at their audacity. None of the leading Bolsheviks had experience in administering anything, yet they were about to assume responsibility for governing the world's largest country' (Pipes, 2003, p. 139). However, understanding the Bolshevik's motives and commitment to what they considered to be a scientifically-grounded theory, one can readily comprehend their audacity: armed with superior knowledge and an ideological commitment that went beyond any idea of country they set out to change not just Russia, but the world. As Volkogonov points out whilst Lenin, for example, would describe himself as Russian for the purposes of bureaucratic paper work when filling in forms, in his outlook he was an internationalist, one for whom revolu-tion and the Party "were to be immeasurably more precious than Russia itself" (Volkogonov, 1994, p. 8).

Lenin had actually not been in Russia for the previous ten years, during which time he had been developing his ideas on two related levels of analysis: an internationalist level in which he adapted Marxism to account for the global nature of capitalism in the epoch of imperialism, and at the Russian state level with his conception of how the communist party should be organized. He considered the putsch against the Provisional Government not as an end in itself, but rather the beginning of *world* revolu-tion. October was designed as the first shot in the larger war for communism, representing the interests not merely of the small Russian working class, but of the workers of the world. In Marx's famous words all the workers of the world had to lose were their chains; well, Lenin saw the Bolshevik seizure of power as breaking the first major link in the global chains that suppressed the workers in the more mature capitalist states. The Bolsheviks had, it was assumed, ignited the spark that would set off socialist revolutions in Germany and other western capitalist countries. Lenin's idea of the Bolshevik party was one that should be centrally controlled and secretly organized in small cells of disciplined revolutionaries. Lenin had effectively adapted Marx's theory of the capitalist state, which was linked to an economic determinist view of the future, to account for what he saw as the workings of the global capitalist system in which he stressed the role of the individual revolutionary, thereby following a more voluntarist conception of revolution.

The Russian Revolution also coincided with a shift in the international balance of power, with the United States emerging as a dominant transatlantic power. It was also a period in which imperialism as a system of international politics was being challenged both ideologically by leading political figures among the Great Powers and practically by indigenous forces in the colonies. The role of American President Woodrow Wilson symbolized both of these forces, for he was not averse to using US power to influence the future of Europe after the Great War, nor in providing strong support for the right of nations to self-determination. Wilson stated to a joint sitting of the US Congress in February 1914 that self-determination was not a 'mere phrase', but an 'imperative principle of action' (Talbot, 2008, p. 152). This principle had potentially far-reaching consequences for Russia, for the first (and, as it turned out, the last) census that the Romanov dynasty ever took of its people revealed that Russians accounted for less than half of the total population of the Empire (Empire Census, 1897). And what Trotsky had noted concerning the tensions involved in the stark social differences in the population was made all the more complex by the vast array of different nationalities.

A state that included Great Russians and other Slavs, Georgians and other peoples from the Caucasus, and Turkmen and other Muslim nations of Southwest Asia, seeking to develop the new Soviet person was a little like trying to form a union between Norway and Afghanistan. Indeed, as will be covered in more detail in Chapter 6, the Communists were confronted with the nationalities problem from the outset, despite the revolution being made in the name of the international proletariat, as many of the national groups took advantage of the revolutionary situation to seek independence for themselves. Ukrainians, to take one important example, declared an independent republic twice in the twentieth century: in November 1917, during the First Russian Revolution, and again in 1991, during the Second Russian Revolution.

Ukraine was always a key part of the Empire due to its geostrategic location, its industrial base, its abundance of natural resources, its agricultural produce, and its military might, as well as the important historical and cultural connection to Russia as the origins of the first Russian state in the ninth century. Whereas Ukraine failed in its attempt to gain independence at the beginning of the century, it had succeeded by the century's end. The reasons for this are covered in detail later. However, as events in early 2014 would reveal, Ukraine remained divided about its identity and its political orientation. With demonstrators in Kiev in opposition to the government's refusal to sign a cooperative agreement with the European Union, Russian President Vladimir Putin interceded at the last minute by offering a deal to supply Ukraine with oil and gas at discounted prices, whilst also providing an economic aid package. Russia was still reluctant to see Ukraine integrate with the West. Putin wished to include Ukraine in a new Eurasian Union, along with other former republics of the USSR. This crisis quickly led to the Russian Federation annexing Crimea and to rebellions in the eastern part of Ukraine, with ethnic Russians there also wishing for either more autonomy from Kiev or for incorporation into the Russian Federation.

The Russian Revolution can be viewed as a crisis of modernization; and then later, as we shall see in the next chapter, the communist system as developed by Stalin can also be seen in terms of development and modernization. The Russian Empire had become by the beginning of the twentieth century the fifth largest industrial country in the world. Yet, this modernization was set against the backdrop of a largely agrarian society and an authoritarian system that denied the sorts of opportunities for political development that had grown hand-in-hand with modernization in the West. Russia's best chance for a bourgeois parliamentary path had been stymied after the revolutionary events of 1905. Furthermore, the vast bulk of infrastructure projects and a majority of heavy industry was either financed by foreign capital and/or owned by the Russian state. In the Tsarist state there was no outlet for the increasing demands of modern society.

Civil War and Its Aftermath

Establishing a parliamentary democracy was never Lenin's intention or promise. Having forcibly disbanded the Constituent Assembly the Bolsheviks were faced with strong internal opposition, from organized monarchists, wealthy landowners and the richer peasants, and minority non-Russian nationalities. Landowners were forced to give up land to the peasants, in the cities the wealthy were either forcibly removed from their stately homes or forced to share with other tenants as their large houses were transformed into communal flats, with housing committees established to form new residency rules for occupants now sharing bathroom and kitchen facilities. These communal apartment blocks were designed to overcome shortages of accommodation for the peasantry and the working class, and were seen by the Bolsheviks as 'a microcosm of Communist society. By forcing people to share their living space, the Bolsheviks believed that they could make them more communistic in their basic thinking and behavior' (Figes, 2008, 179).

The ensuing civil war also saw limited foreign intervention from a number of states, including the United Kingdom and the United States, France, and Canada, fighting against the Bolsheviks on the side of the Whites. In July 1918 President Wilson sent a small American military force into Arkhangelsk in northern Russia to guard allied supplies to the port from shipments through the White Sea, and these were also used to assist Czechoslovak Legions fighting against the Bolsheviks. According to the official Soviet view, the civil war attracted foreign intervention because the October Revolution was the start of a 'world socialist revolution', and hence a blow against 'world imperialism' (*Bolshaya Sovetskaya entsiklopediya*, 1969, p. 78). The Tsar and his family were executed by the Bolsheviks in July 1918, not out of simple revenge, malice or to instil fear, but rather, as with execution of Saddam Hussein in Iraq in December 2006, to demonstrate to the mass public that there could be no return to the immediate past and a restoration of the old order.

Here it is necessary once more to mention the importance of nationalism to complete the picture of the civil war, that element that was largely ignored in Western scholarship. As already noted, the Russian Revolution can only be fully explained in light of the mass killings and destruction of the First World War. Another consequence of the war, unanticipated at the time and little appreciated subsequently for its impact, was a growth in national awareness among colonial peoples. I will return to this in subsequent chapters, but it is worth noting here that the civil war was not strictly a "class war," but a complex mix of political, socio-economic conflicts and wars of national liberation. Inside the Russian Empire the Bolshevik seizure of power and subsequent conflict between Whites and Reds, between monarchists and socialists, were seen by many national groups as an opportunity to break free. Amongst those who fought, some more fiercely than others, for liberation were the Estonians, Finns, Latvians, Lithuanians, Poles, and Ukrainians. From a Marxist perspective this was not surprising, as Lenin and the Bolsheviks recognized that anti-Russian nationalism was always a possibility among educated urban bourgeois elites.

National movements emerged in the countryside too, and not only in the western-most parts of the Russian Empire, but also among Muslim groups in the Caucasus and Central Asia. It was considered that peasants, opiated by religion and mysticism, were only concerned with narrow parochial issues, unable therefore to be mobilized in support of wider collective nationalist interests. This was a misperception that Lenin initially held in 1917, and would be held still by Gorbachev in the 1980s, as the last Soviet leader considered any problems in the regions could be resolved simply by the correct personnel polices. Nevertheless, Lenin was sufficiently aware of the importance of the national question when developing the federal structure of the Soviet state, based as it would be on the principle of national identity.

Stalinism, Terror, and the Purges

The uncompromising and violent nature that characterized the Soviet Communist system under Stalin can be explained at least in part by the years of struggle for survival in the period 1914 to 1920, a period marked by the most atrocious bloodletting in which countless numbers of Russians were killed or maimed. There is also a marked tendency for extreme ideologists to resort to organized, institutionalized violence and terrorism in pursuit of their goals. This has been the case with Nazism, Communism, Islamism, and Nationalism. Post-revolutionary societies also continue, once the regime is established, to engage in a kind of defensive paranoid militarism. Communist revolutionaries considered it necessary to operate in secret cells, to be tightly disciplined, and to engage in terrorist acts against the Tsarist state authorities, given the realities of the subversive system in which they had to operate. Hence, years of clandestine political activities, the use of terrorist methods, experiencing the carnage of trench warfare, followed by civil war, it is not surprising that the Soviet system was prone to continued militarism.

The Civil War was a major formative experience for the new leaders, and the Red Terror tactics they had used to ensure the revolution survived, went some way to establish the institutional, psychological, and cultural nature of the new regime. For example, the Cheka, the Soviet secret police (forerunner of the KGB) that would become a household name not just in the USSR but throughout the world, was initially organized with unrestricted powers just two months after the Revolution. The head of the Cheka, Felix Dzerzhinsky, himself of Polish origin, recruited large numbers of non-Russians into the new organization, especially Latvians, because they were considered to be tough and disciplined, and would also know the best ways to control the ethnic minorities.

Merle Fainsod found that many of the party and soviet officials in the Smolensk region were Red Army soldiers who during the Civil War were subject to communist indoctrination and discipline, and were 'rewarded with appointments to leading village posts or were launched on careers as members of the district governmental, Party, or police hierarchy' (Fainsod, 1958, p. 452). For many 'the ends justified the means, and it was the Civil War that turned revolutionaries into dictators' (Getty and Naumov, 2010, p. 22). Russia had suffered enormously during the early part of the twentieth century, with famine, epidemics, civil war and two world wars, with no family left unscathed, so it should not be surprising that there would be a tendency for a hardened regime to emerge.

Between 1921 and 1922 thousands of starving people turned to cannibalism, with one man convicted of the crime of eating children noting in his defence that 'In our village everyone eats human flesh but they hide it. There are several cafeterias in the village—and all of them serve up young children' (quoted in Figes, 1996, p. 777). Around one quarter of all peasants at the time were starving, and famine was the biggest cause of death. More people died of famine between 1921 and 1922 than were killed in the recent world war and in the civil war combined. In that one year some seven million children had suddenly been turned into orphans, living rough in railway stations, derelict houses, and rubbish dumps. Many of them died, with the survivors turning into alcoholics, drug addicts, prostitutes, beggars and petty criminals. As with children in similar circumstances in parts of contemporary Africa, many became child soldiers on both sides of the civil war, coming to see killing as a normal part of everyday existence. Again, estimates vary, but perhaps some ten million Russian citizens lost their lives as a direct result of the civil war, and death was such a common occurrence that people became inured to it and dead bodies lying in the street attracted no attention (Figes, 1996, p. 774). Milton Leitenberg (2006, p. 9) has estimated that adding in the deaths during the war against Poland to those of the civil war, between 1918 and 1922 12.5 million Russians lost their lives, roughly equal to all battlefield deaths among all combatant countries during the First World War.

The early part of the twentieth century had already brought great suffering and death to Russia in wars against Japan in 1905. At the battle of Mukden 500,000 men were in battle, marking at that time the largest battle in modern military history. The Russians lost 90,000 men to the Japanese. Then Russia experienced the horrors of trench warfare in what was then the bloodiest of all wars, with Germany between 1914 and 1918. Now Russians found themselves fighting one another in a vicious civil conflict that ranked as one of the bloodiest conflicts of the twentieth century.

The militarized culture necessitated by war ultimately helped to fashion the nature of Soviet Communism, showing here another significant influence of war on society. Coercion and violence are what help define a civil war, and the very idea of "enemy of the people" that was employed to devastating effect by Stalin in his later purges was a product of the Russian Civil War. By the end of the Civil War some 5 million Russians were serving in the Bolshevik Red Army, with many of the leading figures going on to gain influential positions in the communist party and state hierarchy and taking with them an uncompromising militancy. In Chapter 7 it will be shown how this affected the institutional development of the national security state.

Mass repression under Stalin was not designed simply to protect the Soviet state from external and internal enemies, but became a 'constitutive part' of Soviet state policy (Shearer, 2003, p. 113). In the absence of mass popular support, state suppression and state violence became necessary instruments to ensure compliance with Communist control (Getty and Naumov, 2010). Given how many people were subject to arrest, imprisonment, torture, forced confessions, labour camps, and execution, it is not credible to argue that under Stalin it was mainly party officials who were subject to the terror and purges. As Solzhenitsyn notes in his record of the Gulag system, even during the time most often associated with an assault on the old party elite (1937–1938) so many millions were arrested that party and state officials 'could not possibly have represented more than 10 percent' of the total (Solzhenitsyn, 1973, p. 29). As many people died as result of Stalinism, in some of the higher estimates, than the current entire combined populations of Albania, Armenia, Austria, and Australia.

One has to see the development of Stalinism in the context of the failure of October to ignite proletarian revolutions in the West. Winston Churchill once compared power struggles in the Kremlin to bulldogs fighting under a carpet: stating that outsiders can hear the growling but it is only when one sees the bones flying from underneath the carpet that it is obvious who won (Churchill, 2011). With the failure of revolutions to break out in the western democracies the new Soviet state at the end of the Civil War had no option but to reassess the way forward. This actually led, one might posit inevitably enough, to a number of competing options among the new elite, and many bones were to fly from underneath the carpet as a consequence.

Trotsky's path was for a "permanent revolution," to continue to work towards world revolution. This became the main opposition to Stalin's alternative, which was to build "socialism in one country." Trotsky argued that 'the completion of the socialist revolution within national limits is unthinkable ... The socialist revolution begins on the national arena, it unfolds on the international arena, and is completed on the world arena. Thus, the socialist revolution becomes a permanent revolution in a newer and broader sense of the word; it attains completion only in the final victory of the new society on our entire planet' (quoted in Knei-Paz, 1979, p. 152). Stalin's own conception of socialism in one country arose in a polemic against Trotsky to counter the idea of "permanent revolution." This can be evidenced by the fact that just after Lenin's death, in *The Foundations of Leninism* (early 1924) Stalin rejected the notion of socialism in one country: 'For the final victory of socialist production, the efforts of one country, particularly of a peasant country like Russia, are insufficient; for that the efforts of the proletarians of several advance countries are required' (quoted in Stalin, 2014). Later that same year in his *Problems of Leninism*, Stalin argued the exact opposite case. The switch was due largely to his struggle with Trotsky, but it had profound implications.

Stalin, as will be detailed in Chapter 2, developed a cult of personality to legitimize his rule. This veneration of the great leader and interpreter of the Leninist doctrine, as Stuart Rees puts it, required its antithesis: 'Oppositionists charged with Trotskyism, Zinovievism, Bukharinism, were anathematized as apostates, heretics, and schematics' (Rees, 2003, p. 37). Employing terror and purges, executions and forced exile, persecutions and forced labour, Stalin eventually managed to defeat his opponents and enemies and in the process established a personal dictatorship and a cult of personality. It was during this period (from the late 1920s through to the mid-1930s) that Stalin forced upon the USSR a new system whose chief characteristics (achieved with great suffering) were the following: collectivization of agriculture, rapid industrialization, state controls over the arts and sciences, and state planning in the economy with the establishment of five-year plans for most all aspects of economic life. Due to Stalin's "Revolution from Above" the USSR would come to have the world's second largest economy after the United States. The Soviet Union became the world's largest producer of oil and gas, ferrous metals, and minerals, and accounted for the world's largest output of coal. In terms of population the USSR with 287 million ranked number three in the world behind the less-developed countries of China and India. In terms of military power the USSR had achieved rough strategic parity with the USA in the nuclear realm by the 1970s, following Stalin's early development of the bomb immediately following war with Germany.

World War and Its Aftermath

The war against Nazi Germany had the effect of uniting the Russian people in support of the state, and hence solidifying and legitimating the Soviet communist system. The state was ostensibly, officially, one of a "new type" as Stalin's regime sought to inculcate a sense of pride and patriotism, and the development of a "new Soviet man" whose sense of identity would be beyond class and nation. There were said to be no significant class antagonisms, nor any conflicts of identity as all ethnic groups were viewed as part of a single unified collective. There were still recognized distinctions based on an individual's origins relating to social, economic, and cultural factors, but these were not conflicting divisions. There were social categories (worker, peasant, intelligentsia) but there were no longer now, officially, any antagonistic classes.

Yet the reality was very different to these official constructs. Stalin and the ruling CPSU had always been wary of foreign influences, even as they claimed the Russian Revolution to be international. As will be demonstrated in Chapter 3, the Soviet leadership sought to control international communism more out of fear of outside influences on the Russian people and for national security reasons than for any high internationalist ideals (although there were always those in the party who were true believers in international socialist solidarity). Many of the foreign communists who sought refuge in the USSR from suppression at home ended up as victims of Stalin's terror campaign and purges. Stalin was possibly responsible for killing and victimizing as many German communists in Russia, who had fled to escape Nazism, as had Hitler in Germany itself.

Also, all Soviet citizens had an "internal passport" in which it was compulsory to list one's nationality. "Soviet" was then not a nationality, but a designation of citizenship. And some nations were clearly more equal than others within the borders of the Soviet state. Russians, notwithstanding Stalin's Georgian origins, played the lead role in all areas of life, political, economic, and cultural. Stalin invoked previous heroic figures from past Russian history, such as Peter the Great, to help mobilize the Soviet people in their epic struggle against Germany. He was appealing more to former Russian imperial sentiments than he was to a new Soviet post-national unity. Indeed, Stalin mistrusted the nations in the Caucasus to such an extent that he had them deported en masse to the far eastern regions of the USSR, into the Kazakh steppes (see chapter 6).

However, Soviet Russia emerged from the war against Germany (1941–1945) with its population ready to make more sacrifices following the awful devastation inflicted on the USSR during those years, and also with its international reputation enhanced given the fact that Soviet troops did most of the fighting and the Soviet people most of the suffering and making the most sacrifices to defeat Nazism. Soviet Communism also emerged substantially strengthened with the development after the war of communist regimes in Eastern Europe (albeit mostly imposed by the USSR after liberation from Nazi rule). The USSR was now a major power in its own right, with impressive industrial capacity for renewal, control over a large part of Eurasia, and a formidable (if weary and battered) fighting machine. And within a few short years after the US dropped the Atom bomb on Japan it had also developed its own atomic capability. The wartime alliance between the Soviet Union and the western democracies in the common fight against German Nazism very quickly gave way to mistrust, suspicion, mutual fears, and the onset of what came to be termed the "Cold War." Perhaps at no other time than immediately following defeat of Hitler did Soviet Communism enjoy such international favour.

Although the population had suffered terribly during the war, by the time Stalin died in 1953 Soviet citizens justifiably felt a sense of pride at gaining victory over Nazism, giving revived respect and faith in Soviet Communism. This would later be enhanced when Yuri Gagarin became the first man to orbit the earth in April 1961. When Stalin died, despite his direct responsibility for the mass murder of innocents, the majority of Soviet people went into genuine and deep mourning. Yet at the same time it was hoped that his death would mark an end to arbitrary rule and fear of a knock on the door in the middle of the night. Within a short time these hopes were being realized with Nikita Khrushchev's more liberal approach.

From Khrushchev to the Era of Stagnation

Nikita Khrushchev may have lacked a higher education and sophistication—the Russian artist Ernst Neizvestny once said

Khrushchev was the 'most uncultured man he had ever met' (quoted in Taubman, 2004, p. 211)—but it was the new Soviet Communist Party leader that would give more freedom to the artistic community than they had enjoyed since the early heady days of the October Revolution. After Khrushchev's death his family commissioned Neizvestny to design his tomb at Novedevichy Cemetery. At the 20th Party Congress in 1956, in a speech which lasted four hours, Khrushchev denounced Stalin's cult of personality and promised to bring the party back in line and to return to Leninist norms. This marked an end to terror as a tool of political control and many innocent victims of Stalin's purges were posthumously rehabilitated (this did not include Trotsky or Bukharin) and people were released from the labour camps.

Khrushchev nevertheless continued to maintain Soviet control over the communist bloc, putting down an uprising in Hungary in 1956, and suppressing opposition in East Germany and Poland. The Soviet Union was now the head of the Warsaw Treaty Organization (WTO), a military alliance pitted against the North Atlantic Treaty Organization (NATO) led by the United States. Khrushchev also ventured into the Third World, extending Soviet influence into the Middle East, South and Southeast Asia and the Caribbean. It was the crisis surrounding Soviet missiles being placed in Cuba in 1962 that helped to undermine Khrushchev's domestic standing. His tendency to engage in piecemeal and destabilizing reforms in the party, his failed reforms in agriculture, and his self-aggrandizement brought him down in a peaceful but forced removal from office in 1964 by the other members of the party elite. Alexander Tsipko referred to Khrushchev as not so much a Leninist as a Stalinist himself, a 'dogmatic Marxist, convinced that capitalism was headed for an early and unavoidable economic collapse' (Tsipko, 1990, p. vi). Although Khrushchev did indeed predict that capitalism would face a general crisis and bragged about the Soviet Union overtaking the West in standards of living, he was not so much a dogmatic Marxist as a fairly straightforward believer in the promise of Marxism-Leninism. He should be remembered principally for removing the worst features and excesses of Stalinism. His own fate is testament to this: rather than being shot he was provided with a dacha and a pension and permitted to live a fairly normal life until he died in 1971 (although his activities were closely watched by the KGB).

Leonid Brezhnev, a dull apparatchik succeeded Khrushchev as party leader in 1964, and his priority domestically was not to rock the boat, but to give stability to the system (in the West this was termed the "stability of cadres"). In foreign affairs Brezhnev was motivated to improve relations with the United States and the West. This was due to a number of factors that together warranted a loosening of Cold War tensions. First, with the Sino-Soviet split the CPSU leadership was concerned about the possibility of war with its Chinese neighbour, and having Washington on side would help to balance things in Moscow's favour. This stimulus for what came to be termed *détente* was based on the structural logic of the balance of power in international politics. The split with China itself (this is covered in some detail in Chapters 3 and 4) was also partly due to structural factors, domestic concerns, and to a smaller extent ideological differences and personality conflicts.

The second incentive for Moscow to engage in *détente* with Washington was fear of an escalating arms race spiralling out of control that could result in nuclear Armageddon. The Cuban missile crisis of 1962 provided an earlier lesson of such dangers. There was a sort of mood matching in both capitals on this issue that encouraged moves toward managing the nuclear arms race.

A third factor pushing Brezhnev to improve East-West relations was the desire to import western technology and goods, given that the Soviet system, due to its ideological rigidity in relation to the political economy, was unable to produce such goods itself. Brezhnev was a cautious leader, and he was reluctant to engage in any form of radical economic reform that would involve lessening state control over production, recognizing that this could have a deleterious effect on the stability of the political system. So, instead of domestic economic reform to stimulate economic production and to improve the technical level of industry, Brezhnev relied on importing western technology and goods. One telling fact that starkly reveals the inadequacies of Soviet production in consumer goods is that by the end of the Brezhnev era the entire Soviet communist bloc countries together exported less manufactured goods to Organisation for Economic Co-operation and Development (OECD) countries than did Malaysia on its own. Members of the CPSU still had to operate within the code, the paradigmatic constraints of Marxism-Leninism as had been laid down over the previous decades, favouring heavy industry over manufacturing consumer products.

A fourth factor that led to improved relations with the West in the early 1970s was linked to Brezhnev's personal motivations; he used détente as his own independent policy marking him off from other challengers to the leadership in the Communist Party as he sought to solidify his power. *Détente* became central to Brezhnev's goal of maintaining his own leading position in the Party and to reinforcing his authority (see Breslauer, 1982).

There was a limit to how much the leadership could veer from official Marxist-Leninist ideology. This was particularly true in relation to foreign relations. It was necessary for any revisions of the code to be presented in terms that fit within the Leninist canon. The ideology had inspiring features: many Soviet citizens continued to believe in the radiant future that was the promise of October. However, the ideology also had restraining features, preventing people from branching out beyond specified basic orthodox assumptions. For a Soviet communist to openly take issue with the fundamentals of Leninism regarding the role of the United States in world politics would have been akin to a member of Al Qaeda today openly confronting official assumptions about the role of Israel in the Middle East. It would have been just as difficult for Osama bin Laden to suddenly convert to western liberal democracy, as it would have been for Brezhnev to embrace the capitalist market.

Yet *détente* did challenge contemporary notions in Soviet ideology that saw the US as an aggressive neo-imperialist militaristic power; hence it required justification in Leninist terms. It was considered that the international class struggle would continue, but the logic of nuclear weapons implied the need to co-exist with the class enemy. Khrushchev was the initiator of the concept of peaceful coexistence, something made imperative due to the logic of mutually assured destruction; and now the Brezhnev leadership sought a new type of relationship with the United States to manage the nuclear arms race. Hence the class competition would be conducted in other areas short of war. There was much opposition in the CPSU leadership to engaging in *détente* with the United States, for there was a fear of becoming dependent on western technology and of the ideological contamination that might occur not only in the USSR but also, and perhaps more worryingly, in the East European communist states.

What prevented the Soviet leadership from being forced into more seriously contemplating domestic market reform were the huge deposits of natural wealth with which the USSR was endowed. It has become common in more recent times to refer to the Russian Federation as an "energy superpower." As it would later for Putin, these abundant riches allowed Brezhnev to maintain levels of economic growth sufficient to improve the living conditions of most citizens. The fortunes of Soviet Communism in fact were closely correlated with the rise and fall in the prices of these commodities. It was the very high prices of oil following the war in the Middle East in 1973 that helped save the Soviet economy at that time, for even with the massive sums of foreign currency that oil exports provided, still the Brezhnev leadership was forced to look to the United States and Western Europe for economic and technological assistance. Gorbachev would not be so fortunate when it came to his tenure as Soviet leader, as it coincided with a dip in oil prices, which surely was a major factor in explaining the motivations for domestic economic reform, and hence the end of Soviet Communism.

The End of the Soviet Communist System

Michael Mandelbaum asserts that 'The end of Communism came when the political equivalent of its customers, the constituency for its product, the people it governed, ceased to believe in it' (Mandelbaum, 2002, p. 53). There is some evidence to support this argument, as it was clear that in the late-Soviet period citizens in the USSR began to clearly recognize that there was a discrepancy between official Communist Party propaganda and everyday reality. As the world became more global and interdependent the Kremlin leadership found it impossible to stem the flow of information from and about the outside world penetrating the iron curtain. Foreign media networks, such as the BBC World Service, the Voice of America, and Radio Liberty, broadcast programs in the Russian language directly into the USSR, and many people tuned in, particularly among the intelligentsia.

Foreign tourists to the USSR brought with them evidence of the superiority of western capitalist consumer products, as well as stories that did not match the portrayals of life in the West that people had been fed by the CPSU. Younger generations of state and Party officials and academics had become more mobile in the Brezhnev era, with some being allowed to travel overseas in the course of their work. Although it was still only a minority of citizens who were allowed to travel outside Soviet borders, many of those who did established networks through which they gained different perspectives on life and politics and culture. Whilst all of this is true, the argument that this somehow led to a sort of cognitive dissonance in the body politic and hence a legitimacy crisis for Communism in the face of the superior example of capitalism and liberal democracy, as Mandelbaum and others have claimed, does not add up. There is much impressive empirical data and memoir literature to show that although ideology fell into crisis under Gorbachev, among both the masses and the elites in the late-Soviet period many still believed in the idea of communism.

Most accounts of the late-Soviet period overlook the fact that reformist ideas began to take hold in the higher echelons of the Soviet Communist Party leadership before Gorbachev came to power. It has been suggested that Yury Andropov, head of the KGB, and not Gorbachev 'was instrumental in bringing about a liberal evolution of the Soviet system' (Konchalovsky, 2011). Ideas for more liberal reforms originated in the KGB in the 1960s, and also within the heart of the CPSU Central Committee apparatus, pushed by Andropov and other like-minded personnel. Andropov was in a better position to appreciate the problems inherent in Soviet society than anyone else, but still he acknowledged in the early 1980s that 'We are ill-informed about the society in which we live' (Vodolazov, 2004, p. 82). Clearly, centralized control over the arts and sciences, and tight controls over freedom of expression, had the negative effect of preventing the authorities from properly appreciating public sentiments, for people were not able freely to express their views, desires, and priorities.

As the drama was unfolding of contested ideas and policies in the late 1980s the common interpretation in the West pitted hardline conservative CPSU apparatchiks against the liberalizing Westerners. The main villain among the party ideologues was Yegor Ligachev who was viewed as an old-fashioned communist hold-over who wished to revert to the bad old Stalinist days. It is true that Ligachev eventually became strongly opposed to many of Gorbachev's policies, yet it is incorrect to make this simple dichotomy between the good reformer (Gorbachev) and the bad reactionary (Ligachev). Ligachev was himself in favour of reform when Gorbachev came to power in 1985, and like Gorbachev at that time he supported reform to save the Communist system, not to bury it. Ligachev himself had no reason to idolize the Stalinist past, as his own family suffered the consequences of high Stalinism. His father-in-law had been executed in 1937 following a short trial in a Stalin terror tribunal, and in his memoirs he recalls how his family was subjected to the stigma of being branded an "enemy of the people." He also writes about the time that he himself, twelve years later, in 1949, was falsely accused of belonging to a counter-revolutionary Trotskyist organization (Ligachev, 1996, p. 10). It was only in 1961 that this blot on his official record was removed, enabling him to work in the central party apparatus.

During the era of stagnation under Brezhnev, Ligachev could see plainly that the system was not working effectively and that change was necessary. He recalls that after Brezhnev's death and the succession of Yuri Andropov to the top communist post: 'I, like many other provincial Party secretaries was impatient for change, uncomfortably aware that the country was headed for social and economic disaster' (Ligachev, 1996, p. 16). The fact is that Gorbachev brought Ligachev from the provinces to serve in the Politburo as an ally in reform, hence they began in 1985 on the same side. It was only later, when Ligachev believed perestroika and glasnost had gone too far that he began to warn Gorbachev about the dangers he perceived of rising nationalism leading to separatism and a threat to the USSR's territorial integrity.

The history of this late Soviet period needs an important corrective, for most interpretations focus on the deliberate and positive role that Gorbachev played in what is seen by many to have been a careful, and comprehensive plan to bring about a Soviet form of socialist democracy. This is simply untrue. Gorbachev helped to unleash forces that would lead to radical change, but it was in a direction he himself did not expect, and ultimately over which he had no control. For much of his tenure Gorbachev floundered and often seemed somewhat lost as events unfolded around him. As president of the United States, George Bush (the 1st) was astounded by Gorbachev's lack of knowledge regarding basic economic principles of the market, and his National Security Adviser, Brent Scowcroft found that 'he either did not recognize or grasp the depths of the reforms required' (Bush and Scowcroft, 198, p. 494). An expert on agricultural policy during his early years in the Soviet leadership Gorbachev's memoirs contain tortuous detailed accounts of the minutiae of farming policy.

His own limited experiences, his narrow educational background in the Soviet system, and his lack of any real understanding of how civil society or the economic market actually worked, left him often with no clear ideas of how to proceed. The conception that he had a grand plan, which included the tearing down of the Berlin Wall is simply wrong.

This is not to deny or denigrate the critical role Gorbachev played in allowing the Soviet Union to expire peacefully, without mass loss of life, nor his key role in facilitating democratic reform. Although we can never know, it is surely likely that with a different leader in the Kremlin when the tumultuous events of the 1980s unfolded a more violent ending easily could have ensued. Indeed, Ligachev criticized Gorbachev for the very thing that the world can be grateful for: refusing to send in Soviet troops to stamp out opposition in the national republics, to try and save the Union as it was falling apart. In the end Ligachev's commitment to preserving the USSR overrode his reluctance to use force. Gorbachev was simply not willing to inflict violence on his own people.

Gorbachev was not a visionary, but rather found himself in a position of power at a moment when structural and systemic dynamics were pushing the USSR in different directions, buffeted by both endogenous and exogenous forces. In the end Gorbachev was buffeted within a tide of events brought about by a "diverse confluence of circumstances" over which he had little control (Vodolazov, 2004, p. 80). Many would come to see Gorbachev as having been responsible for bringing Russia to its knees—a metaphor often used by Putin at this time—as economic crisis followed the collapse of the USSR. Russia experienced in the 1990s the deepest and most rapid economic collapse of any state in modern history, worse even than the Great Depression in Europe of the 1930s.

The level of Gorbachev's popularity was demonstrated in the Russian presidential election in 1996 when he gained only 0.5 percent of the vote (less than the Beer Lovers Party received in the Duma elections the previous year). Gorbachev's delusions are clear from the statement he made on the last page of his memoirs (published in 1996): 'My trips around the country, my talks with my fellow-citizens and their reaction to my speeches, together with many letters I received, convinced me that the country needed Gorbachev and that inspired me to participate in the 1996 presidential campaign' (Gorbachev, 1996, p. 695). Whereas

Lenin, Trotsky, Bukharin, and Stalin had credentials as revolutionaries, with theoretical works and practical goals, and strong-
willed determination to achieve them, Gorbachev was brought
up in the Soviet bureaucratic system, and it clearly showed in his
approach to reform.

Leonid Shebarshin, a senior KGB official who was very briefly
acting head of the organization after the August coup attempt in
1991, would berate Gorbachev for being a traitor to the USSR
as a result of his 'self-adoration and naivety' (quoted in Andrew
and Gordievsky, 1993, p. xv) Opinion surveys have demonstrated
consistently that the Russian people continue to have a poor opinion of Gorbachev as the last leader of the USSR. Asked in 2011
to name the "most outstanding Russian" of all time Gorbachev
did not figure at all: top of the poll was nineteenth-century poet
Alexander Pushkin, followed by Peter the Great, Stalin, Lenin,
then Putin, in that order.

However, there was indeed an alternative ideational or ideological challenge to Soviet Communism that eventually helped
to undermine the legitimacy of the ruling Communist Party
and the idea of a World Socialist System. This ideological challenge did not come from liberalism or free market economics,
as Mandelbaum and Fukuyama and others claimed. It came in
the form of nationalism. It was not so much changing polarity
in the international system that caused shockwaves in the World
Socialist System, but the Poles in the Gdansk shipyards. Stalin
once famously inquired facetiously how many military battalions
had the Pope, thereby dismissing the idea that Catholicism could
pose any threat to communism. Yet in the 1980s a Catholic Pope
forged what was in effect a political coalition with a Catholic
American president, Ronald Reagan, in support of a Polish trade-
union movement that was challenging the incumbent communist leadership. In 1980 the independent trade union movement
Solidarity was formed in Poland, in the shipyards in Gdansk.

Under the leadership of Lech Walensa (who would go on to
become post-Communist Poland's democratically elected president) Solidarity not only engaged in industrial action for higher
wages and better conditions, but began to challenge the political
legitimacy of the regime and hence the communist system. It was
not any natural sympathy for the industrial action of the working
class that motivated Reagan, an American president noted for his
antipathy to organized labour, it was the prospect of undermining

the legitimacy of communism that provided the motive to support Solidarity. In the end Ligachev's warnings to Gorbachev would prove to be prescient, as the virus of nationalism, as Ligachev perceived it, would spread throughout the wider Soviet bloc, to the USSR itself.

War in Afghanistan

Another factor causing domestic and foreign problems for the Soviet leadership was again linked to war. In December 1979 the USSR invaded Afghanistan. This came as a major surprise to US President Jimmy Carter, who immediately re-evaluated his views about the Soviet leadership and his policies towards Moscow. This was the final nail in the coffin for *détente* and Brezhnev's so-called "peace programme." Carter instituted a major increase in US defence expenditure, designated the Persian Gulf a region of American strategic interest, and openly supported dissenters to the regime in the Soviet Union. He also instituted a boycott of American athletes from the Olympic Games in Moscow in 1980.

Yet, some six months before the Soviet invasion, as acknowledged later by Robert Gates, who at the time was Director of Strategic Evaluation in the CIA, the US intelligence services were already secretly supporting the mujahedeen guerrillas in Afghanistan (Gates, 1996, pp. 146–147). Carter's National Security Adviser, Zbigniew Brzezinksi, acknowledged in an interview in 1998 that Carter authorized secret aid to the mujahedeen in support of their struggle against the incumbent Soviet-backed regime on July 3, 1979. Asked if in retrospect he regretted this Brzezinski was nonplussed, saying on the contrary it was an "excellent idea," recalling that he wrote to Carter at the time saying 'We now have the opportunity of giving to the USSR its Vietnam War'. Further into the interview Brzezinksi was asked if he did not regret having given support to Islamic fundamentalists and the consequences of giving arms to future terrorists. Brzezinksi answered with a question of his own: 'What is more important in world history? The Taliban, or the collapse of the Soviet empire? Some agitated Moslems or the liberation of Central Europe and the end of the Cold War' (quoted in Johnson, 2004, pp. xiii–xiv).

As noted earlier, foreign wars can have major impacts on both domestic politics and broader international relations. The Soviet war in Afghanistan did have some influence in the internal policies of the USSR under Gorbachev. For Gorbachev ending the war was the right thing to do practically for internal reasons, economically and politically as it was becoming costly in terms of expenditure in funds and lives lost.

The war was unpopular, and as a result of Gorbachev's liberalization of the media, it was also being more openly criticized with groups forming to oppose the war. Ending a war that he did not start also provided Gorbachev with an opportunity in the international realm, fostering improved relations simultaneously with both China and with the West. But the war did not, as Brzezinski claimed, bring an end to the Cold War and the liberation of Central Europe. The dynamics that brought these about had little if anything to do with US support for Islamic fundamentalists. The real long-term consequences of this support led to the attacks on the United States on September 11, 2001, and the subsequent "war on terror." The USA and the CIA helped to create the monster that would blow back to threaten American security leading eventually to the wars in Afghanistan and Iraq. Al Qaeda, as with the original Leninist conception of the Bolshevik Party, saw itself as a vanguard movement for the Muslim world. It engaged in terrorist acts and violence to achieve its objectives in an asymmetrical struggle against the state, developed a rigid doctrine, and saw itself as the head of an international Islamic Jihad. It was undertaking a holy war as opposed to a class war. The mujahedin themselves considered their victory over the USSR to be the beginning of the rapid end of communism across the rest of the Soviet bloc, with one leading figure, Burhanuddin Rabbani, leader of the mujahedin party boasting 'We saved the world because Communism met its grave here in Afghanistan' (Braithwaite, 2002, p. 330). Rabbani served as President of Afghanistan from 1992 until 1996, when the Taliban took power. After 9/11 he became temporary President between November and December 2001. Rabanni was killed by Taliban suicide-bombers ten years after 9/11, in September 2011. Niall Ferguson is one among many observers who today see Islamism as the successor to Marxism as a challenge to Liberalism, stating 'If you actually read what Osama bin Laden says, it's clearly Lenin plus the Koran. It's internationalist, revolutionary, and anti-capitalist rhetoric is more of the left than of the right' (quoted by Daniel Dreznev). The Soviet experience in Afghanistan, insofar as it helps to explain the collapse of the USSR, shows that the war provided increased pressure on the Kremlin to further reform the political system. It was certainly not the key to understanding the collapse, but was an important element. It was more of an inter-mediate factor than a deep one or a trigger for bringing the Soviet system down.

Conclusion

Following the collapse of Communism in December 1991, Russia found itself in multiple transitions: from empire to nation state; from a political economy based upon state socialist planning to one based upon the market; from a single party totalitarian sys-tem of rule to a pluralist democratic system of governance; and from a single and official ideological belief system to multiple and competing conceptions of the future. As a consequence of the collapse of communism the Soviet Union had simultaneously lost its belief system, its sense of identity, its empire, and its status as a superpower. One remarkable fact worth noting here is the one thing that saw little change: the representation of the political and economic elites. In the mid-1990s still more than eighty percent of political elites in Russia consisted of people who were members of the CPSU, with over half of those having held high execu-tive office in the Party. Further, two-thirds of the new capitalist business elite in 1993 had previously belonged to the Communist Party (Lane and Ross, 1998).

Such a continuation of the elite shows how self-perpetuating the system of elite rule had developed after, and partly as a con-sequence of, Stalin's purges of the 1930s. The political elite of the 1980s owed its characteristics to the events of the 1930s, and, going against Marxist theory, much of the Communist elite managed to carry over its privileged position into the capitalist post-Soviet era. It is also a fact that many members of the old CPSU retained their belief in the Communist system and many ordinary citizens continued to support them. This was reflected in the very strong showing for the Communist Party of the Russian Federation (CPRF), the successor party to the CPSU, in both parliamentary and presidential elections in the decade following the collapse.

Until the end, those in the highest positions of power, includ-ing Gorbachev the reformer himself, remained faithful to the long-term cause of building socialism, the original objective of those who made the Revolution in 1917. Perhaps by this stage not many Soviet Marxists had a sophisticated understanding of Marxist theory, but the ones in control of the Party nevertheless sought to put its basic principles into effect. Yet, from the very beginning of the Soviet system, to stay in power the Communist Party leadership required a cowed and obedient population and hence could not afford to loosen the controls over society. Once this happened the floodgates were opened and the system very rapidly disintegrated as people joined forces in a variety of civil associations demanding ever more political freedoms. The force of such groups was especially potent among those based on ethnicity. Boris Yeltsin, who Gorbachev initially brought into the central leadership from the provinces to manage the construction department of the CPSU, would eventually himself use the institutions of the Russian Federation (first the reformed Russian parliament, then the new elected presidency) in a power struggle against the last leader of the Soviet Union.

In the final analysis it is perhaps more accurate to refer to the end of the Soviet system than it is to the end of Communism as an idea. The CPRF as the successor to the CPSU actually came very close to gaining power in what were essentially open and free elections in the immediate post-Soviet period, and the party remains strong today. Also, communist parties in many other countries still represent a vital fabric of the political scene, and the experience of Communism in the former-Soviet Union continues to offer lessons for contemporary thinking on the way forward for many of them, as well as still being an attractive model for development for some in the Third World. A new radical politics has arisen also out of what some see as a more general crisis of capitalism resulting from the global financial crisis of 2008. A new global anti-capitalist movement has emerged, perhaps the seeds of a new anti-market international movement that contemporary leftist groups will eventually seek to build upon. I will turn in the next chapter to look more closely at the functions of ideology in Soviet politics and to evaluate theories of Soviet Communism.

2
Soviet Ideology and Theories of Soviet Communism

In this chapter I evaluate Soviet ideology, and how it was over-determined, underplayed, or misunderstood in Soviet Studies. There is a number of factors as to why Soviet Studies got Soviet Communism so wrong, and in many ways the answer is to be found in its actual origins, for from the very beginning it was always a highly politicized subject. Soviet Studies as a separate field was not established until the 1950s. There had naturally nevertheless always been a strong interest in the Russian Revolution among intellectuals, journalists, and academic specialists. The Bolshevik Revolution of 1917 clearly had its adherents among radical leftists outside the Russian Empire, and some of the early works in the West were written by those who were strong supporters of the communists' goal of creating a socialist society, such as the book by Reed referred to in the previous chapter, or the work of Sidney and Beatrice Webb. In other words, one of the problems at the outset was that much of western analysis of the Soviet system was itself ideologically motivated. Martin Malia suggests that Soviet Studies was the 'most impassioned field of the social sciences' (Malia, 1994, p. x.). Someone once said that researchers in the natural sciences stand upon one another's shoulders, whereas, proverbially speaking, political scientists tend to stand upon each other's faces! This was perhaps more true of Soviet Studies than it was in any other area of the social sciences.

Archie Brown defines communist systems with reference to six features under three headings: political, economic, and ideological. The political system is defined by a monopoly of power held by the Communist Party and by democratic centralism as the organizing principle. The economic system is defined by non-capitalist ownership of the means of production and the dominance of a command economy. The ideological system is defined by a declared goal of attaining communism and the sense of belonging to a wider international communist movement (Brown, 2009, pp. 105–110). The monopoly power of the CPSU was enshrined in Article 6 of the Soviet Constitution that was enacted in 1977 under Brezhnev's leadership, where it stated clearly that 'The leading and guiding force of Soviet society and the nucleus of its political system, of all state organizations, is the Communist Party of the Soviet Union' (Constitution, 1977, p. 21).

Any definition of the Soviet Communist system must logically begin with reference to the ideological and political goals of the Russian Revolution. Communism as both idea and practice is central to the defining features listed by Brown. If we do not appreciate these, then it is not possible to understand the system that developed. There is no need to go into the complex details of Marxist or Marxist-Leninist semantics, although it is necessary to understand the fundamentals pertaining to Soviet Communism. Despite the dense and often tortured prose of some Soviet Marxist literature, the essentials of the ideology are very straightforward and easy to outline. Having stated this, it should be stressed that Marx left behind an ambiguous legacy, which bred deep divisions between his communist descendants. Divisions within the Left were often more bitter than conflicts between the Left and the Right of the political spectrum. Francis Wheen writes that: 'Marxism as practiced by Marx himself was not so much an ideology as a critical process, a continuous dialectical argument; Lenin and then Stalin froze it into dogma' (Wheen, 2005, p. 101). But Marxism was manifest in many forms, including rival sects such as Trotskyist, Stalinist, Maoist, Marxist-Leninist, Eurocommunist, or followers of Castro, the Frankfurt School, Gramsci, and others. Lenin and Stalin did not so much freeze Marxism into dogma as adapt it, due to the requirements of the post-Empire domestic setting and the external setting relating to the balance of power. It is necessary also to consider this within the context of competing views among the original Bolsheviks linked to a struggle for domestic political power among ambitious individuals. Yet, despite the major differences within the various branches or sects that invoked Marx, they all shared the fundamental assumptions of the Marxist critique of capitalism.

The differences were more over how to arrive at what was largely a shared preferred destination: a communist society in which to each according to needs and from each according to their abilities. One of the main features of the system, perhaps its central defining characteristic, is the absence of the capitalist mode of production. The system was a non-market (anti-market) system in which the party-state controlled the means of production. This developed not out of any desire of a crazed bunch of dictators wishing to hold onto power for its own sake. On the contrary, power was taken in October 1917 in the name of the international working class for idealistic goals.

The Changing Role of Ideology in the Soviet System

In this section I will first define what is meant by ideology, before evaluating how the field of Soviet Studies defined the Soviet system. To simplify, all ideologies are "isms": Communism, Liberalism, Conservatism, Fascism, and Nazism, to list the principal ones. It should be noted that not all "isms" are ideologies: terrorism is not an ideology, but a tactic, often employed for a strategic political purpose. This political purpose might then be linked to a broader political ideology. The Jewish Stern Gang engaged in terrorism (a tactic) in the name of Zionism (an ideology) in the middle of the twentieth century, and the Irish Republican Army employed terrorism in the name of nationalism at the end of that century. At the beginning of the twenty-first century, Al Qaeda and other groups in the name of Islamism are using terrorism in pursuit of their goals. Lenin's elder brother was executed for terrorist activities, and the Bolsheviks too used it as a tactic before the revolution in the name of socialism. Discussing ideology's origins in an "ology" links it directly to other fields of study such as sociology, psychology, biology, zoology, etc. Ideology is linked to the study of political ideas, hence the term Ideaology. Antoine Destutt de Tracy originated the term in the aftermath of the French Revolution as he sought to create a science of ideas (see Heywood, 2007, p. 6; Eatwell and Wright, 1999, p. 4). Ideologies are not philosophies. Ideologies are ideas and principles *designed to be implemented.* Ideologies are oriented to a specific goal. Socialist thought and ideas and practice first developed in the West, in France, Germany, and Britain among radical groups and intellectuals. However, it was only with the victory of the Bolsheviks in October 1917 that Marxism would become the dominant ideology and a guide for action and the making of policy in the world's largest state.

When discussing this question it should be stressed that Marxist-Leninist ideology was not produced originally to legitimate the political system and its policies. The system and policies were designed to fulfil the ideological goal of creating communism, hence putting into practice the ideas developed by Marx and adapted by Lenin. It was only later that systemic structural factors worked to reverse this linkage, with an entrenched bureaucratic party elite coming to manipulate the ideology in part to maintain its privileges and to legitimate its hold on power. However, it was the rise of Soviet Communism and the challenge it posed to capitalism that turned the twentieth century into an ideological struggle between East and West. The Cold War was in essence an ideological conflict between two socio-economic and political systems, in addition to being a traditional Great Power competition reflecting the global balance of power. Differences in ideologies, as both sides in the Cold War sought to remake the world in its own image, complicated the normal workings of a balance of power system, making it much more difficult to manage. Liberalism and the capitalist market faced an existential challenge.

Lenin was perhaps the first *globalist* thinker, expanding Marx's work on capitalist development, what effectively we would now call case studies—detailed studies of specific cases from which to make generalizations. The problem was that the cases (the development of capitalism in Germany or England) by definition had limited applicability in radically different settings, such as that in Russia. Lenin's first major work was an empirical assessment of the development of capitalism in Russia (Lenin, 1970). For Lenin, Russia's relatively backward and uneven development and predominately rural economy did not make an argument for a specific form of Russian agrarian socialism, as called for by the revolutionary Populists of the time. Capitalist development in Russia, Lenin noted, was mainly by western investors, thereby explaining the absence of an indigenous industrial and financial class. And foreign capitalists relied on a repressive state apparatus in Russia to ensure their investments were secure.

Lenin supported the development of large-scale industrial production in Russia, as this would create a revolutionary proletarian class that would challenge the capitalist order. In his theory of imperialism, Lenin would claim to have identified the "highest," and hence the final stage of capitalism: global imperialism (Lenin, 1963). Russia now was seen not as standing alone, nor as a former political colony of the western powers, but as part of a global capitalist system.

However, Marx did not leave a clear blueprint for how a future communist society would function and Lenin and the Bolsheviks, following revolution and war, were faced with the need to quickly develop the institutional infrastructure and policies to ensure the survival of the regime. Again, it is mistaken here to criticize Lenin for steering away from liberal democracy, because he had never promised to institute it in the first place. On the contrary, Lenin was always critical of bourgeois democracy, seeing it as a mechanism to ensure the continued subjugation of the masses. He considered the state as 'a product and a manifestation of the *irreconcilability* of class antagonisms' (Lenin, 1977, p. 10). For Lenin the state was an organ of class rule and one of oppression of one class by another. Writing in 1917 after the abdication of the Tsar, but before October, Lenin in his treatise *The State and Revolution*, advocated, in the event of a socialist revolution, the destruction of the apparatus of state power (Lenin, 1977, p. 12). Lenin intended to write a final chapter to *The State and Revolution* in which he would have considered the experiences of the Russian Revolutions of 1905 and February 1917, but, as he stated in the postscript, this was interrupted by the *October* Revolution. Lenin stated that he would have to put off the writing of this part for a long time but adding: 'It is more pleasant and useful to go through the "experience of the revolution" than to write about it' (Lenin, 1977, p. 114).

Perhaps the single most important feature of Soviet Communism was the goal of abolishing private property. Marx and Engels stated in the *Communist Manifesto,* first published in 1872, that: 'the theory of the Communists may be summed up in the single sentence: Abolition of private property' (Marx and Engels, 2002, p. 235). In this regard the main priority after the Revolution was to maintain control over the "commanding heights" of the economy. This was quickly done by nationalizing key industries, including coal, oil, iron and steel, chemicals and textiles. Clearly it was necessary to create a new bureaucratic structure to manage and direct these state-controlled industrial enterprises, hence a state apparatus was required. For Lenin this was to be a temporary requirement, as a dictatorship of the proletariat would use the state for the interests of the industrial proletariat and the development of a new socialist society. Only after exploitation was completely abolished, when there would no longer be antagonistic classes, would it be possible for the state to "wither away."

One of Lenin's most important works was *What Is To Be Done*, first published in 1902 (Lenin, 1973). The subtitle of this pamphlet was *Burning Questions of Our Movement*, and the two burning questions for Lenin concerned on the one hand *ideology* and on the other *organization*. Lenin argued that 'Without a revolutionary theory there can be no revolutionary movement', and in Russia at that time there could be no effective revolutionary movement without a disciplined, centralized party led by intellectuals as the vanguard of the working class (Lenin, 1973, pp. 28–29). Hence, for Lenin, '*the role of vanguard fighter can be fulfilled only by a party that is guided by the most advanced theory*' (Lenin, 1973, p. 29 emphasis in original).

For Lenin, writing in 1920, a vanguard was necessary to help raise the class consciousness of the working class and to lead the broad masses who, he stated, were still then 'for the most part, apathetic, inert, dormant and convention-ridden' (Lenin, 1976). Many scholars (and many more opponents of Lenin) have misinterpreted *What Is To Be Done*, taking certain parts out of context, or taking the wording of certain parts too literally as representing a fundamentalist view of centralized leadership and a lack of faith in the working class. Rather, it can be argued, Lenin has been misunderstood or deliberately misrepresented (see Lih, 2006). It was not Lenin's intention to create a bureaucratic dictatorship, let alone a system with a single dictator at its apex. Lenin was, rather, genuinely concerned that without a dedicated vanguard of critical, capable individuals, the working class would be tempted to compromise with the capitalists against their own real interests (as perceived by the Bolsheviks).

Lenin's objective was to save the revolution and inspire the workers into eventually taking over class leadership in the interests of the entire people. This stance was already apparent in his earlier writings, in which he was concerned about the necessity to develop the political consciousness of the working class. In *What Is To Be Done* Lenin famously takes issue with the "amateurishness of the economists," those on the Left who were advocating reform, of mobilizing class consciousness through mass political organization and trade union activism. One interpretation of Lenin's polemic against the economists states that whereas they were advocating democratic means of achieving socialism, with faith in the working class's long-term prospects for gaining power through reformism, Lenin was an elitist who wanted to install a personal dictatorship through a conspiracy of a small elite.

In reality, as the recent re-evaluations of Lenin's thought and writings and life shows, Lenin was more of an idealist whose intentions were to inspire the working class to take leadership themselves (Lih, 2011). Lenin's intentions became distorted as a result of civil war, internal political wrangling, and external circumstances. Writing about the revolutionary momentum of the Arab Spring in 2011, Henry Kissinger noted: 'You cannot judge the outcome of a revolution by the proclamations of those who made it', going on to remind us that: 'Secondly, those who make it rarely survive the process of revolution' (Kissinger, 2011). However, it is important to remember the original proclamations of those who made the Russian Revolution for it would otherwise be impossible to follow and understand events that subsequently unfolded. Nationalization, Five Year Plans, forced industrialization and the collectivization of agriculture, would all be inexplicable if we did not have a clear appreciation of the goals of the original revolutionaries, and the heated debates in the early years between them about the best means of achieving their objectives. Stalinism would make no sense outside the context of the Russian Revolution and the revolutionaries' original Marxist project.

Just four years after the Civil War the party and state bureaucracy in the Soviet Union numbered around four million. Trotsky argued that the "bureaucratization" of the Soviet state was due to the "degeneration" of the Communist Party. Trotsky wrote: 'Under the guise of a struggle with the Opposition, there occurred a sweeping replacement of revolutionists with *chinovniks* [minor state bureaucrats from the Tsarist era]. The history of the Bolshevik party became a history of its rapid degeneration' (Trotsky, 1936). Simon Sebag Montefiore claims that: 'Far from being the colourless bureaucratic mediocrity disdained by Trotsky, the real Stalin was an energetic and vainglorious melodramatist who was exceptional in every way' (Montefiore, 2004, p. 2). Stalin was "super-intelligent" according to Montefiore, an intellectual who avidly read history and literature, a revolutionary committed as a "Marxist fanatic" to building Soviet Communism. Stalin was "married to Bolshevism" and sacrificed his own personal happiness to "political necessity" (Montefiore, 2004, pp. 4, 13). Stalin may not have had any "proper" work experience, but he was nevertheless a workaholic whose goal was to both gain ultimate power for his own ambitions, and to carry on with the work set by the October Revolution of creating a socialist system.

However, Stalin's strategy in seeking to achieve this, in the face of capitalist encirclement, was to build up Soviet industrial infrastructure as first priority. Vincent Barnett makes the sensible point that for Marx a socialist economy 'had absolutely nothing to do with industrialization. Socialist planning was supposed to be about improving the quality of all human life by means of overcoming exploitative social relations starting from an advanced capitalist economy, not manufacturing vastly more iron and steel by means of a tyrannical forced labour system starting from a backward semi-feudal peasant-dominated economy' (Barnett, 2006, p. 462). However, it is difficult to see what other option Stalin had if he wished to save the revolution than to build up the instruments necessary to ensure its defence, which required not carrots and potatoes, but iron and steel. Stating this is not to give support or credence to the methods Stalin used; but it is really to state the blindingly obvious: If the USSR did not modernize then its chances of survival in the face of the forces opposing it would have been close to zero. Marxist-Leninist-Stalinist ideology was a major motivating factor in a clear lineage giving rise to the Soviet communist system that eventually developed.

Culture, the Arts, and Religion

The "Cultural Revolution" that was part of Stalin's campaign of creating socialism through state-led industrialization and collectivization, as Pavlova puts it, 'played a utilitarian role by laying the foundation for the universal ideologization of the people and oriented them to serving the interests of state power' (Pavlova, 2001, p. 80). The Soviet Communist Party maintained tight control over the arts and literature, fearing that a free expression of ideas would undermine the legitimacy of the system. Lenin was aware of the power of literature, himself (along with a generation of Russian radicals of his generation) being influenced by Chernyshevsky's novel *What Is To Be Done* (from which he took the title of his 1902 pamphlet). Indeed, Lenin said of the novel: 'It completely reshaped me. This is a book that changes one for one's whole life-time' (Priestland, p. 75). Lenin in fact cited Chernyshevsky more often than any other writer—more than 300 times—in his collected works (Volkogonov, 1994, p. 76). Lenin read the novel *five* times, and modelled himself on the hero, the young, disciplined, idealistic, and determined revolutionary Rakhmetov (Rappaport, 2009, p. 6). Fedor Doestovesky's novel *Notes from Underground,* published one year after Cherneshevksy's book in 1864, was a direct rebuttal of its main ideas (on Doestoevsky's polemics with Cherneshevsky see Offord, 2002). A tight link between literature and politics had long been a feature of Russian society.

Later Lenin would admit to German communist Klava Zekin: 'I am incapable of considering the works of Expressionism, Futurism, Cubism, and other "isms" the highest manifestation of artistic genius. I do not understand them' (Volkov, 2008, p. 73). According to Lunacharsky's memoirs, 'Lenin tried to shut down the Bolshoi and Maryinsky theatres several times, reasoning that the opera and the ballet "were a piece of purely bourgeois culture"' (Volkov, 2008, p. 73). In contrast, in his youth, Stalin, although less formally educated that Lenin, was an avid consumer of literature, film, and theatre. In his youth he had himself written poetry. As Volkov notes, Stalin was more of a "connoisseur of high culture" than Lenin (Volkov, 2008, p. 95). Although Stalin organized tight state control and censorship of the arts and the media he wished nevertheless to transform the illiterate masses and to make them cultured (*kulturny*). This was achieved in an impressively rapid timeframe, but it was a narrow notion of cultured, for the imposition of "socialist realism" in the arts and the absence of foreign travel or contact with other cultures left the population ignorant of world literature and art. Stalin employed the press, literature, and the arts to create a new discourse that reflected Soviet Communism as now defined by Stalin himself (see Brooks, 2000).

One factor that threatened the Soviet system from within was organized religion. Marx had considered religion tied to the state as a powerful tool of exploitation, as a means of keeping the masses in check. The Bolsheviks were very much aware themselves of the powerful forces of Russian Orthodoxy amongst the mass of peasants that comprised the bulk of the population, and how the Church had long been linked to the previous Tsarist regime. Hence, it was deemed critical to undermine what was seen as the pernicious influence of Russian Orthodoxy, and indeed of Islam and other religions of the minority nations comprising the USSR. Churches were demolished, closed down, or transformed into buildings providing different services. The Kazan Cathedral on Leningrad's most famous central avenue, Nevsky Prospekt, was handed over to the Soviet Academy of Sciences and turned into the Museum of the History of Religion and Atheism: 'The greatest testament to atheism in all the Soviet Union and perhaps the world' (Marsh, 2011, p. 110) (the Cathedral was returned to the Orthodox Church after the collapse of communism in 1991). The most important Orthodox Church in Moscow, the Cathedral of Christ the Savior, was demolished by Stalin in 1931. The plan was to construct where the church once stood a huge monument to Soviet Communism to be named the "Palace of Soviets," with a massive bust of Lenin on top. In the end, war with Germany and floods from the Moscow River prevented construction, and Khrushchev eventually turned the site into the world's largest outdoor swimming pool (a replica of the church was rebuilt on its original grounds and opened for services in 2000).

Cemeteries were transformed into parks or sports grounds, priests were arrested, believers were intimidated, and atheistic propaganda was targeted at the young in schools, in the Young Pioneers, and in the Young Communist League. The potential power of religion in post-October Russia can be gleaned not only from the clear continuing influence of the main Orthodox Church, but the fact that as *Pravda* noted in 1921 there were more members in the Baptist Youth Organization than there were in the Young Communist League (Marsh, 2011, p. 110). To help dilute religious belief, new Soviet rituals were established to replace traditional ones linked to the Russian Orthodox Church. Many of these had a focus on Lenin, lying himself in the sacred tomb in Kremlin's Red Square. There were also rituals associated with initiations into the Young Pioneers, the Komsomol, the CPSU, the Red Army, and festive rituals surrounding state registration, for example, of births and marriages (see especially Lane, 1981, 1984).

By the 1970s the revolutionary component of Soviet ideology was clearly no longer the single key motivating factor in Soviet behaviour. Under Brezhnev in 1971 the new concept of "Developed Socialism" was officially proclaimed. This was an acknowledgement that Khrushchev's stated expectations of over-taking the West with a full-scale construction of communism were not about to be realized any time soon. The transition to full-scale communism was now put off to the far distant future, as laws of economic and social development would involve a long historical process. This was not to abandon communism (this would not be possible for reasons to do with domestic political legitimation) but rather to accept that the path was a long one, and that meanwhile the USSR had achieved an important new stage towards the final goal. This concept was reinforced in the revised Brezhnev constitu-tion of 1977 in which also the "leading and guiding" role of the CPSU was concretized.

Although it was necessary for members of the CPSU to have some familiarity with the basic canons of Marxism-Leninism, few by this stage, in the Brezhnev era, had a deep knowledge of, or were able to contribute anything to, Communist ideology. It was oblig-atory for officials to have their offices lined with Lenin's collected works, but few could now do more than quote a few essential lines off pat when justifying their policies and, more importantly, jus-tifying their own incumbencies. Although the study of Marxism-Leninism was compulsory for all students in the USSR, few took it terribly seriously, many found it complicated or uninspiring, and it was by the Brezhnev period seen for what it was: state prop-aganda designed to instil a sense of loyalty to the regime, being so recognized thereby having the opposite effect. Whereas Islamists can quote verbatim from the Koran, and many do have deeply held beliefs that following the prescriptions of Islam is their duty, many Soviet communists towards the end of the twentieth cen-tury merely paid lip service to Marxism-Leninism. It was evident from private conversations with Soviet officials that few had read the tortured and complex prose of Marx's *Das Kapital*. As an undergraduate at Oxford former British Prime Minister Harold Wilson, as was customary at the time for many students, toyed with Marxist ideology, but he found the long and dull and (for him) impenetrable writing too much to carry him past the first few pages of *Das Kapital* (of some 1,400 pages). Later Wilson would note with pride that he had never actually managed to get beyond 'that whacking great footnote on the second page' (quoted in Ziegler, 1993, p. 18). The founding father of Russian social-ism, the creator of the RSDLP, Plekhanov, admitted that in his Marxist study group people could not read *Das Kapital* because it was simply too difficult (cited in White, 2001, p. 23).

As noted above, Soviet ideology was adapted to justify changes in approach and policies. Ideology was a significant factor in policy formation because of the requirement to always be seen to be in accord with the original socialist goals of the Bolsheviks. In the one party system that developed, adherence to the basic tenants of a non-capitalist path of development was essential for the continuing legitimacy of the regime (for the role of ideology in international affairs see Light, 1988). In the end the ideology was difficult to throw off entirely, but nor was it sufficiently malleable to survive radical change. This made it impossible to successfully reform the Soviet Union, for once the ideological glue holding it together *had* started to come unstuck with Gorbachev's reforms it led to serious cracks in the system, filled ultimately by alternative ideologies of nationalism. The church too made a rather spectacular comeback with the death of Soviet communism, with very large numbers of Russian citizens either returning to the church or discovering it for the first time. Yet, for the entire Soviet period Marxism-Leninism could not be jettisoned as it became central to the very identity of the Soviet state, a necessary instrument for the political leadership to gain support for its centralized control, and until the end those at the apex of the system, for whatever mix of reasons (some ideological, some personal) continued to maintain their basic faith in the non-capitalist path. Ideology in the USSR was inescapable whether at school, at work, or even during recreation. All Soviet citizens grew up being imbued with the basic tenets of Marxism-Leninism, even if they had little real interest or any sophisticated knowledge of its more complex features, they were clearly very much aware of its most simple basic assumptions (and its restrictions on their personal lives). This ultimately was part of the problem when it came to trying to reform the system, for what did become manifestly clear to the majority of citizens was that communism had not delivered on its promises and was unable to compete with global capitalism in providing a higher standard of material living as well as a better quality of life generally.

Totalitarianism: Comparing Soviet Communism with Far Right Ideologies

Here I will turn to some of the dominant approaches in Soviet Studies and how they conceived both the system and its ideological foundations. Much ink and oxygen were spent on discussing the USSR as a "totalitarian state," with comparisons most often made between Soviet Communism and German Nazism. It is worth spending time on this question for it was so critical to the debates of the period following the Second World War, and in rethinking the international politics of the twentieth century revisiting this issue is useful for evaluating the respective natures of the two ideologies that challenged Liberalism in the middle of the century. It was this temptation to compare Stalin with Hitler and the two "totalitarian" systems that prevented a true understanding of either one. The essential difference was that Soviet Communism was always of the Left and was anti-capitalist and internationalist, whereas Nazism (and Fascism) were effectively of the right and were corporatist and nationalist.

The defining characteristics of a totalitarian system were most often enumerated according to the "six-point syndrome" (Shapiro, 1972, p. 18). The six defining points are: (1) an officially regulated chiliastic ideology; (2) a single dominant party led by a dictator; (3) terroristic police control; (4) party monopoly control over all effective means of mass communication; (5) party monopoly control over all means of effective armed force; and (6) party monopoly control over a centrally directed economy. These are very close to Brown's defining characteristics listed above. By the 1960s "totalitarianism" was a term of common currency, one that the average interested observer of current events would have at least been aware of. Up until that time it was the most influential paradigm in Soviet studies (see Siegel, 1998). Any student of Soviet Studies would have been familiar with the term.

The term was first coined by Benito Mussolini who employed it in the mid-1920s to describe the fascist system that he had himself created, referring to the "totalitarian state" (see Shapiro, 1972, p. 13). Although its origins relate to fascism in Italy, the conception of the totalitarian state was further developed to incorporate German Nazism, and Soviet Communism. Hannah Arendt produced the first major work that set out to define a totalitarian system, in which she outlined why, in her view, such a system was incapable of change or reform (Arendt, 1951). The key text was published in the mid 1950s at the height of and reflecting the politics of the Cold War (Friedrich and Brzezinski, 1956). The concept was attractive because it offered a simple (some would argue a simplistic) means of both defining a particular type of political system and a framework for comparison. Klause von Beyme saw the concept as a move towards "empirical comparative politics" (Beyme, 1998, p. 40).

Adolf Hitler did not use the term to define the authoritarian system he developed in Germany, and Stalin only used the term to describe fascist regimes. Soviet officials considered the western tendency to apply the term to the Soviet Union as being politically motivated as part of Cold War anti-Soviet propaganda. Indeed, this was for the most part the case, as many journalists and politicians who were critical of Soviet Communism frequently and deliberately used it as a term of abuse, implying that the Soviet system was rotten. It was then certainly the case that in the policy-making world the term came to have very negative connotations. Fascism was a (fairly) coherent ideology (if also ultimately a flawed one) yet eventually in common discourse it too became a term of abuse. It is still widespread practice today to use the term almost indiscriminately against one's political opponents. In February 2014, in Bangkok, Caracas, and Kiev anti-government protestors, in each case, were condemned as "fascists" by their enemies. Although it was the case that some far right nationalist groups were among the protesters, such hate-filled distorted descriptions of those leading the opposition groups did not serve to ameliorate the problems. Teachers, traffic wardens, hotel porters, security guards have all at times been called "fascists" for simply carrying out their duties. As George Orwell noted long ago: 'The word Fascism has now no meaning except in so far as it signifies "something not desirable"' (Orwell, 1946). Whereas initially Orwell volunteered to fight in the Spanish Civil War to "fight against fascism," in the end he said he was fighting for "common decency" (Orwell, 1989, p. 47). Orwell is famed for his satires on Stalinism in his two novels *Animal Farm* and *1984*, the latter clearly influenced by Zamyatin's novel *We* banned by Soviet censors in 1921.

Also in more recent times the threat from radical Islamism has predictably been accorded the unhelpful label of Islamo-fascism, both in academic circles and in the political arena. Christopher Hitchens wrote after 9/11 that 'the bombers of Manhattan represent fascism with an Islamic face, and there's no point in any euphemism about it' (Hitchens, 2001). The term totalitarianism, although not as widely used as fascism, nevertheless also developed strong political, negative connotations, and as such was ultimately unhelpful in assisting a better understanding of what were essentially different types of authoritarian systems (i.e., Fascism,

Nazism, Communism). To equate Soviet Communism with Fascism and Nazism does not hold up to scrutiny. It is not logical to compare the Holocaust with the Great Terror and the Gulag (see Naimark, 2010), despite the horrible nature of both (see Snyder, 2011). One is the premeditated planned slaughter of an entire race, the other a product partly of revolution and civil war and in great part the neurosis of Stalin. It is akin to comparing the planned killing of innocents in the Holocaust to the dropping of Atom bombs on Hiroshima and Nagasaki and equating this to the inherent nature of a certain type of political system. Leninism can be seen as a utopian internationalist ideology of inclusiveness. Lenin, in Volkogonov's words, 'was an internationalist cosmopolitan, for whom the revolution, power and the Party were to be immeasurably more precious that Russia itself' (Volkogonov, 1994, p. 72). In contrast, Hitler's Nazi ideology was based on racial superiority and a hatred for Jews and homosexuals. The nation, defined in terms of biology (not by culture as with Italian Fascism) was seen as the natural embodiment of the state.

The fact that the Bolshevik leadership included a number of different nationalities demonstrates that, at least at the outset, it was far from racist. Stalin himself was a Georgian. Of the twelve members of the Central Committee of the party in October 1917, five were Jewish. The Politburo that led the revolution that month contained three Jews out of its total of seven members. Poles, Germans and members of other nationalities also played significant roles in the early years of communist power. Hitler, on the other hand, held a deep belief that there was a global Jewish conspiracy to dominate the world, and that Bolshevism was a front for gaining this objective. Although Leninism was an internationalist ideology the Soviet state did not engage in aggressive expansionist policies by dint of its ideology: the capitalist system would fester from within. In contrast, the Nazi state was inherently aggressive, militaristic, and expansionist, based on an ideology that mixed ideas of racial supremacy with geopolitics. A critical difference between Communism and Nazism was that for the former the economic sphere was central and the abolition of private property fundamental, whereas for the latter the private market should be responsive to the interests of the state.

Lenin's writings eventually became almost sacred, with his successors being obliged to justify their politics with a relevant sprinkling of quotes from his works. The year before the Soviet collapse there was estimated to have been 6,453 million copies of Lenin's writings in 125 different languages, as Volkogonov puts it this was 'perhaps the only area of abundance achieved by the Communist effort' (Volkogonov, 1994, p. xxx). Yet, some scholars from among both those critical and those more sympathetic to his life and work, acknowledge that Lenin frequently changed his mind and that some of his writings were either unfinished, first drafts, or simply polemics in a fight over policies (Pipes, 1998; Lin, 2011). Lenin was a committed Marxist, but he was also a tactician, someone willing to modify his views to achieve what was realistically possible in the short term, rather than blindly following an ideological doctrine in pursuit of a distant Utopia. Hitlerism was less flexible in many fundamental ways. We should not forget too that in the end German Nazism and Soviet Communism fought each other in the bloodiest war in world history. It is also worth reiterating that the eastern half of Germany moved from one form of "totalitarianism" (Nazism) to another (Communism) between 1933 and 1945, and that what developed after 1945 in the German Democratic Republic was very different to the Germany of the Third Reich in the previous decade.

As the historian Richard Overy notes, the temptation to compare Nazism with Communism, and Hitler with Stalin, has been compelling (Overy, 2004, p. xxxi). With two countries undergoing radical change whilst espousing different ideologies during the same historical period, with each responsible for mass death and destruction, assessing the regimes similarities and differences is a potentially useful exercise in comparative political analysis (see Tismaneanu, 2012, for a recent analysis). Any comparison of what gave rise to the two regimes would need to account for war. Both "lost" the First World War in the sense that they did not achieve their objectives; both were forced to give up territories as they sued for an armistice, and both came out worse off than other participating states. In addition, the aftermath of war brought hyperinflation, and a legitimacy crisis in their respective political systems, fuelling resentments among the people.

Both Germany and Russia became isolated from the international community. Overy, in his comparative study of Hitler and Stalin, states 'To recognize that the two dictatorships were products of a particular set of historical conditions reduced the temptation to see them only as monstrous historical caesura' (Overy, 2004, p. xxxvii). One cannot ignore or forget the terrible mass suffering inflicted by the Stalin regime on the Soviet people—it has been estimated that between 1929 and 1953 some 18 million people passed through the Gulag system, and another 6 million suffered forced internal exile to Siberia and the deserts of Kazakhstan. All together it has been calculated that the total number of forced labourers in the Soviet Union came to 28.7 million (Anne Applebaum, 2004, p. xvii and p. 581). Stephen Courtois (1999, p. 4) provides figures for different parts of the communist world for those who died (what he terms "rough approximations") as a direct result of communism:

Country or Region	Deaths due to communist crimes
USSR	20,000,000
China	65,000,000
Vietnam	1,000,000
North Korea	2,000,000
Cambodia	2,000,000
E. Europe	1,000,000
L. American	150,000
Africa	1,700,000
Afghanistan	1,500,000

These numbers are, it should be stated, contentious. Wendy A. Goldman has evaluated recent archival material that she claims shows earlier estimates of arrests and executions in the period 1927–1928 had been highly inflated. For example, she found that original estimates suggested that between 7 million and 20 million people had been arrested, whereas in fact new figures show that it was around 2.5 million people who were arrested for normal criminal transgressions as well as political crimes. She goes on to argue that the figure given commonly by historians of the number of executions, at around 7 million, were grossly off the mark, with the correct number being roughly one-tenth of that estimate (Goldman, 2007, p. 5). A reasonable argument could also be made that capitalism was responsible for millions of deaths too, in Southeast Asia, Africa, Latin America, and Korea (see Perrault, 1998). However, the fact remains that whichever figures one employs and no matter the methodology used, the number of deaths that can be directly attributed to communism is huge.

One of the common features of the totalitarian model relates to the role of the leader. Mussolini, Hitler, and Stalin all enjoyed dictatorial powers, each developed a cult of personality, and each designed mechanisms to thwart anyone challenging his power. The cults of personality were however different in each setting, designed to help legitimate the system through appeals to historical, national, and cultural traditions. In each case, ideas, institutions, events, and policies were linked to the great leadership qualities of the Fuhrer, Duce, or General Secretary to create a bond between the leader and the wider masses. It was, as noted above, this aspect of the Soviet system under Stalin that was the brunt of Khrushchev's criticism at the 20th Party Congress. It was common among Soviet specialists to refer to Max Weber's typology of the three different methods of political authority: traditional, rational-legal, and charismatic when discussing Stalin's personality cult (Weber 1958 (original 1919), also see Rigby, T.H. and F. Feher (eds) 1982; Holmes, 1993). Basing authority and legitimacy on tradition (given the revolutionary break with the old regime) or rational-legal authority (in the absence of functioning plural political institutions) was a complicated affair in the USSR, hence Stalin developed a system based at one and the same time partly on fear of and yet love for the Great Leader, as if acting out a script written by Machiavelli in *The Prince* (1988). Note also the role Lenin played throughout the entirety of the Soviet system as a cult figure, immortalized not only in narratives of his past great feats, and the iconic status of his writings and speeches, but also the fact that he remained (and remains) in mummified form in the heart of the ancient Russian capital, in the Kremlin, to which people still make pilgrimage. Stalin's cult, which developed after Lenin's death was in large part based on him being portrayed as the natural heir to Lenin, and the continuer of Lenin's grand project of building communism. The cult of Lenin was created to legitimize his successor.

Despite Khrushchev's denunciation of Stalin's cult of personality within a short period of his own tenure as leader he too would develop a personality cult around his leadership, based in large part on his stated objective of returning to the proper path first hoed by Lenin. The main horrors of the gulag and the terror in Soviet society might have been mostly dispensed with as a means of ensuring compliance following his death, but each of Stalin's successors nevertheless eventually came to have a cult of personality develop around himself. One of Yeltsin's main criticisms of Gorbachev's leadership would be what he considered to be too centralized a system of power around the dominant leader. It is the case also that Gorbachev sought to legitimate his leadership by the stated goal of a return to Lenin's principles and ideas of the early 1920s. Certainly one can identify too in the post-Soviet era a *Putin* cult of personality. This demonstrates perhaps that such a focus on individual leaders is not inherent in "totalitarian" systems, nor unique in Russian history to the Soviet era.

Part of this mysticism surrounding the dominant leaders, and Soviet communism as an ideological and cultural force, as Berdyaev put it long ago 'was deeply indebted to Russian Orthodoxy' (quoted in Rees, 2003, p. 7). Certainly all "totalitarian" regimes of the twentieth century sought to instil loyalty from the masses through cults of personality and attempts to control most aspects of society legitimated through these cults—but each was substantially different from the other partly based on their different histories, cultures, and the radically different objective circumstances pertaining at the time in each country. Although officially denying the importance accorded the individual from a Marxist class perspective after the Revolution, the Bolsheviks were so concerned about a cult forming around the Tsar and his family that they had them executed. They were shot in the cellar of the house where they had been imprisoned, one year after the Revolution.

It is important to note that despite the fact that totalitarianism had lost its dominance in the field of Soviet Studies by the late 1960s, it nevertheless always retained its status as a descriptor of the Soviet communist system by dissidents in the Eastern bloc. Also, following the demise of Soviet communism totalitarianism came back into vogue amongst many academics in the West and now also among large numbers of scholars in post-Soviet Russia. (see Siegel, 1998). In a sweeping denunciation of the system he once served, Alexander Yakovlev, former Politburo member and close associate of Gorbachev describes how Soviet communism had total control over all aspects of society, the personal and the public, from the clergy to the factory and the classroom, no element of society was free (Yakovlev, 2002). Gorbachev in later years referred to his days as a student, and the school system 'which played an enormous role in forming our ideas about the world' and that he grew up to believe that 'socialism for us ... was something for which there was no alternative' (Gorbachev and Mlynar, 2002, p. 17). As a young student in his final high school examination Gorbachev chose to write an essay on 'Stalin— our combat glory, Stalin—the elation of youth,' for which he received the highest mark in his class and which 'was held up to school graduates for some years as an example to be followed' (Gorbachev, 1995, p. 47). An excellent portrayal in novel form of the psychology of a communist leader in the Soviet bloc as it was being dismantled is found in Julian Barnes' *The Porcupine* (1992). In his retirement Gorbachev read or reread the Marxist classics and it was only with the 'greatest difficulty' that he eventually came to accept that Lenin too was responsible for the horrors that are more associated with Stalin (Braithwaite, 2002, p. 73).

Irina Pavlova, Senior Research Fellow at the Institute of History of the Russian Academy of Sciences, in a review of Western interpretations of Stalin's Russia of the 1930s, argues that contemporary historians who criticize the totalitarian model of Stalinist history in effect have 'turned into apologists for the regime' (Pavlova, 2001, p. 73). For many historians in the West who employed a social approach to the Stalin years what was impressive, and would have been counterintuitive for those holding a rigid statist and political approach that focused on the Moscow elites and Stalin himself, was the fact that many officials in the regions outside Moscow demonstrated initiative in carrying out certain policies. This included what appeared to be the arbitrary use of tyranny and repression. Yet the fact remains that for the most part it was directives that came from the central CPSU apparatus in Moscow that set the general line, and any dissent from these central strictures, or any significant manifestations of independence among regional leaders was swiftly and mercilessly dealt with. Liquidating "enemies of the people," the struggle against the Kulaks, the harassment of the Orthodox Church, and the attacks on wreckers and anti-party groups were all instigated by the Stalin leadership in the Kremlin. Stalin and the Communist leadership in Moscow directed the whole enterprise thereby imposing what many saw as a revolution from above. Insofar as there was any leeway for local initiative at all it was allowing limited manoeuvre within the confines of centralized commands to the titular nationalities. And then only so long as they adhered to the essential dictates handed down from Moscow. There existed no institutional structures separate from the state through which any disagreements or opposition or alternative points of view could be aired and aggregated, notwithstanding some leeway in the national republics.

Richard Pipes argues that it was a natural evolution for Leninism to merge into Stalinism and for Bolshevism to develop into totalitarianism. Despotic rule was required for the communist regime to cling on to power (Pipes, p. 39). Pipes argues that 'Soviet totalitarianism ... grew out of Marxist seeds planted on the soil of Tsarist patrimonialism' (p. 127) One of the key structural problems with the Soviet Communist system was the absence of any institutionalized method of leadership succession, creating a seriously dysfunctional weakness at the heart of the system. The method of an orderly form of leadership change involving competition in democracies creates space and opportunities for new leaders with fresh policies to gain power with competitive elections providing them with the legitimacy, authority, responsibility and accountability essential for the smooth and effective process of governing. Yet even in democracies leaders tend to be concerned more about their own careers than they are for the greater good of the wider population. The next election and the desire to get elected (or re-elected) is the key determinant of their policies, and not the next generation. As a recent study demonstrates, it is inherently a human trait—in *all* types of political system—for leaders to rationally pursue policies to keep themselves in power in any way possible within the institutional and structural constraints they might face (de Mesquita and Smith, 2011). It might not be a perfect system, but as Winston Churchill once commented in a speech to the House of Commons, democracy is the best of a host of much worse alternative forms of government. With no method or accepted process for selecting a new leadership the Soviet system was prone to instability and leadership crisis in the event of the death of the incumbent dominant leader.

Also, the absence of an orderly process for leadership succession can feed an incumbent leader's paranoia that there is always someone plotting in the wings to remove him. This seemed to be particularly the case with Stalin. Listing the number of people that Stalin had murdered due to fear of challenges to his leadership would fill too many pages of this book, but just to mention a handful of key figures will provide the picture required for an understanding of his paranoia: Trotsky, killed in Mexico by Stalin's agents; Bukharin, shot after one of Moscow's show trials;

Kamenev too was shot, along with his wife, one of his sons, his brother and sister-in-law, with his second son spending years in labour camps and prison and exile. Even those that were spared themselves lost members of their family in the terror: Molotov's wife served in the gulag, Khrushchev's daughter was imprisoned by Stalin, as were two sons of Anastas Mikoyan (Hochshild, 2003, p. 97). Khrushchev himself was fortunate to escape becoming a personal victim to Stalin's purges, for when he was a student on a worker's training program in 1923 he briefly flirted with an anti-Stalinist Trotskyist opposition group (Taubman, 2003, p. 57). Referring to the terror and the use of torture under Stalin, Martin Amis wrote that: 'He tortured, not to force you to reveal a fact, but to force you to collude in a fiction' (Amis, 2002, p. 33). Or, as David Shearer puts it, mass repression became 'more than a means to fight the state's enemies. Under Stalin, it became a constitutive part of Soviet state policy' (Shearer, 2003, p. 113).

As noted, by the time of Brezhnev's rise to power the Soviet system atrophied due in part to *too much* stability of cadres, as Khrushchev's successors in the Kremlin made a pact that there would be no more turbulence in the higher echelons of the party apparatus. This then led to the "era of stagnation," as safety of tenure (for the most part, if the boat was not rocked) led to inertia. Khrushchev was unusual in being forcibly removed from power in 1964, and not dying in office as all other leaders in the USSR eventually did, from Lenin, through Stalin, and then Brezhnev, Andropov, and Chernenko. Gorbachev of course didn't die in office, but the system he led *did* die, thus his position does not really undermine this essential feature of the Soviet Communist system. This all goes to show how important constitutionally binding electoral mechanisms are for changing political leadership, to ensure peaceful and effective changes in governments and policies. Elections many not be sufficient, but they are essential for democracy and enhance the prospects for political stability (notwithstanding events in, for example, such disparate parts of the world as Ukraine and Thailand in early 2014).

Again, it is interesting to recall how, once the Soviet Union had collapsed (or had been dismantled) that many former communist leaders in Russia and elsewhere in Eastern and Central Europe began themselves to use the term totalitarianism to describe the communist system. This was to continue along with the existing earlier tendency to politicize the term. It has in effect become, like fascism, a term of abuse rather than a term of analysis, therefore it is no longer one we should take seriously in contemporary assessments of the former USSR. Before leaving the topic of totalitarianism one might conclude that if the term is still useful to describe a Stalinist-type communist system then it would be more applicable to the system that still exists in North Korea, rather than the communist systems that remain in Cuba, Vietnam, or China. And even in the case of North Korea we should qualify this by recognizing that it is totalitarianism with "national characteristics." A more recent variant of totalitarianism is that inherent in the fundamentalist anti-liberal forms of Islamism represented by such groups as Al Qaeda.

Modernization Theories and the Behavioural Turn

Archie Brown wrote a short critical, concise survey of the field of Soviet Studies in 1974, in which he noted that in the 1960s approaches to Soviet politics 'began to change rapidly' connected to the so-called "behavioral revolution" (Brown, 1974, p. 9). A major landmark in the field of Soviet Studies was the publication of Merle Fainsod's book *Smolensk Under Soviet Rule* in 1958 (see also Fainsod, 1953). Fainsod's work was based on the Soviet party archives that were discovered during World War Two in Smolensk. This marked the beginning of a move to more empirically oriented studies of Soviet Communism. There was much controversy, however, when, following Fainsod's death, Jerry Hough revised his text on the Soviet system, radically changing much of the content and analysis to make the USSR appear a much more pluralistic system than that originally described by Fainsod. The change in the title perhaps said it all, as Hough retitled the book from *How Russia is Ruled* to *How the Soviet Union is Governed* (Hough and Fainsod, 1979, see also Hough, 1969). Clearly the assumption was that whereas perhaps in the 1950s Russia had a "ruler" who ruled, in the 1970s it had a government that "governed."

In the 1970s a new academic approach was applied to the study of Soviet Communism and the wider communist bloc. One main impetus for this new approach was to trace what was seen as the historical, cultural factors that influenced the development of the communist systems. The Soviet system was seen as a natural outgrowth of Russian authoritarianism. Yet the Russian Tsarist bureaucracy, as impressive as it may have been, was very much smaller than its Soviet counterpart. Whereas the Soviet state sought almost total control over all aspects of ever day life, the Tsarist authorities were concerned principally with those aspects perceived to have direct bearing on the political process at the top. There was censorship under the Tsars, and, as Orlando Figes has noted 'Nowhere has the artist been more burdened with the task of moral leadership and national prophecy, nor more feared and prosecuted by the state', than in Russia. (Figes, 2002, p. xxvii). In an article entitled 'How We Support Talent', published in a St. Petersburg newspaper in March 1905, the author writes: 'We drove Pushkin to a suicidal duel. We sent Lermontov to face bullets. We sentenced Dostoevsky to hard labour. We buried Chernyshevsky alive in a polar grave. We exiled one of our greatest minds, Herzen. We expatriated Turgenev. We excommunicated and denounced Tolstoy. We expelled Rimsky-Korsikov from the Conservatory' (cited in Volkov, 2008, p. 23). This all took place before the Bolsheviks took power, hence one can perhaps trace the manifestation of strict censorship in the realms of politics, literature, music and the arts generally to an existing political culture going back centuries.

However, under the Tsars the state was not ubiquitous in every area of the arts and sciences. Civil society may not have flourished to the extent that it did in nineteenth century Western Europe, but under the Tsars there were independent publishing houses, private schools, religious freedom, and the right to travel overseas. Marx's works were translated and published in Russia (admittedly because the censors did not consider his theories applicable to the Russian Empire). The Tsars did not engage in mass executions or ethnic cleansing, nor did they establish a huge network of concentration camps—all features of Soviet Communism. Ultimately there was nothing in the private life of the Bolsheviks themselves that escaped the gaze of the Soviet Communist Party leadership. A public culture developed under the Soviet Communist system in which each member was obligated to reveal his or her inner self to the greater collective good. This was unique to the Bolsheviks. As Figes put it 'there was nothing like it in the Nazi or Fascist movements, where the individual Nazi or Fascist was allowed to have a private life' (Figes, 2008, p. 37).

This Bolshevik requirement to devote the entire private self to the cause was found neither in German National State Socialism, Italian Fascism, nor in the former Tsarist system. Such a phenomenon would only be witnessed again with the Chinese Cultural Revolution, although in a different form. Hence, although there were those who argued that the USSR was a reincarnation of the Tsarist system, and that Soviet Communism was just another version of Tsarist absolutism, it is necessary to note these important differences. The decade before the Revolution in Russia did show some small moves towards democracy and the potential for development along these lines, with Russia moving slowly but seemingly inexorably towards a more progressive path. Some consider that Russia at this time, in the decade before the Revolution, was growing a dynamic civil society with the country moving towards the rule of law and plural politics (see, for example Dowler, 2010).

With the failure of the October Revolution to ignite revolution in the more developed capitalist states, one might argue that the revolution's true purpose became one of rapid modernization. Barrington Moore had identified three paths to modernization: the bourgeois revolution leading to liberal democracy; a conservative revolution from above leading to fascism; and a peasant revolution leading to communism. Tim McDaniel in a comparative study of revolutions in Russia and Iran suggests a fourth path: a path of 'autocratic modernization' (McDaniel). For some, Stalin's repression was viewed as a terrible method, but nevertheless an effective means of rapid industrialization that once achieved would create changed social and political relations, leading to growing pluralism (see, for example, Johnson 1970). As the post-Stalinist USSR was seen to become more pluralistic as a result of modernization there was even talk of convergence between capitalist democratic systems and communist centralized ones (on this see Meyer, 1970).

Modernization theories, in contrast to totalitarianism, emphasized the sphere of economics and the determinant effects of technology on social relations and hence the political system (see Rostow, 1960). The processes of industrialization would result in both capitalist and communist countries eventually converging in their political, social, and economic systems, as increasing interdependency would lead to shared values and interests. There was thought to be a modernizing imperative that would impact on all systems in which total control by a one-party communist system would become dysfunctional. Pavlova, however, argues that such interpretations are wrong, for they ignore the fact that the main goal of Stalin and the Communist Party in the 1930s was 'not the modernization of Russia ... as many Western historians think but the building of socialism' (Pavlova, p. 79). To transform the economy along socialist lines, in the face of anarchy, chaos, and opposition, it was deemed necessary to employ repressive measures to mobilize the population to perform the herculean task of rapid industrialization and the collectivization of agriculture.

There is a large literature on the role of state bureaucracies, yet many argued that this literature did not apply to the Soviet Communist system due to the nexus between the party and the state and in particular the dominant role of the individual dictator, especially in the Stalin years. As Pipes put it, the Soviet bureaucracy came to constitute a separate "caste" that 'placed its collective interests above not only those of the population at large but those of the Communist cause that they nominally served' (Pipes, 2003 p. 43). Later Pipes used the term "class" to describe this new bureaucratic elite. This class, what had earlier been deemed a "new class," had a shared interest in maintaining the system for its own vital interests (Djilas, 1957). The survival of the system was necessary for them to continue enjoying the privileges that it provided to them. As time went on these included: access to special medical facilities, holiday resorts, retail shops with consumer goods not available to the wider population, and many other privileges, leading one scholar to talk about 'relative poverty' in the USSR (Matthews, 1978 and 1986). This new Soviet communist vanguard represented a self-perpetuating elite.

Perhaps the most widely cited Soviet specialist of his generation, Jerry Hough, used positivist methodologies to test hypotheses about politics in the Soviet Union. Hough also employed theories of legitimacy derived from the works of Max Weber and Talcott Parsons, with a clear working assumption that the Soviet regime enjoyed genuine legitimacy and mass loyalty (Hough, 1997). What made this particularly problematic was the simple fact that positivism requires observable data and it was next to impossible to gain access to any that was transparently reliable about or from the USSR. Science without data cannot be science. Although Hough in his work was attempting to apply the scientific method to a study of the USSR (and following the contemporary trend in comparative politics and the wider social sciences) his analysis demonstrated a poor grasp even of the methodology. His definitions were stretched, and at the end of the day Hough's plural actors, the KGB, the CPSU, the Military Industrial Complex, all shared fundamental and essential interests. The KGB, for example, was explicitly from its origins an arm of the party and not the state, something clearly emblazoned on all KGB documents. Its role was not to defend the state in the first instance, despite its name (Committee of State Security) but to defend the Communist Party—although of course it was not really possible to separate the two, as party and state were fused.

Also influential at this time were the works of Gordon Skilling and Franklyn Griffiths, who sought to demonstrate that plural groups each with their own often contending interests existed under Soviet Communism, mainly based on occupational or professional affiliations (Skilling and Griffiths, 1971). Each of these "interest groups" in fact represented much more of a single collective group with shared, and not contested interests, than independent actors with an ability to "pressure" the leadership through interest articulation and aggregation. There were "party-restricted" occupations, those that basically required membership of the CPSU, even if this was not always written in official treaties (see Rigby, 1968; Hill and Frank, 1986). These occupations incorporated all senior positions in state bodies, including all Soviets, ministries, executive committees, administrative committees, and directors and leading personnel in state enterprises (factories and farms) and key posts in the armed forces. All state and civil institutions were in practice controlled by the Communist Party; from trade unions to the military and even the Orthodox Church. These institutions were in essence what some called "transmission belts" for the CPSU, structured in such a way to ensure they performed their roles in the interest first of the Party. The Party set agendas and controlled personnel appointments through what was termed the *nomenklatura* system, in which the Central Committee apparatus had a list of all important posts in party and state bodies and then a list of candidates suitable for filling them.

Francis Fukuyama also argues that Sovietologists underestimated the importance of civil society and overestimated the power of the totalitarian model (Fukuyama, 1993, p. 223). Fukuyama claims that the totalitarian model's fundamental problem that kept it from foreseeing the end of the Soviet regime was its dismissal of civic culture, or civil society, and the pressures this would have on the system. For Fukuyama it was a proto-civil society that eventually pressured the one-party regime to engage in liberal reforms. There is however little evidence for this (and Fukuyama does not cite any). Whether or not it was the case that many individuals in the USSR were unhappy with their own personal situations (it would be incredible if that were not the case; there is no such thing, surely, as a totally satisfied population in any political system), there were no civic groups that posed a threat to the regime. One recent study of everyday resistance in Soviet life demonstrates that many citizens dealt with their displeasure about the regime through individual acts of resistance, such as the telling of a joke to friends, or writing a letter to the authorities (see Kozlov, Fitzpatrick, and Mitrovenko, 2011). Some criticism was not only permitted, but was actually encouraged, so that the regime could both get an appreciation of any dissent over policies and weed out officials not performing their jobs. This was neither a reflection of civil society, nor a challenge to the system itself. It was reform from above that created an altered situation that resulted in forces that would eventually undermine the system. And then it was not so much new civic forces pushing for change that were critical in what followed, but rather the old communist elites who quickly dumped Marxism-Leninism for nationalism as a mobilizing ideology. Ignored in all of this talk of pluralism, interest groups, and emergent civil society in the former Soviet Union was any reference to ethnic groups, nationalist tensions, and the fact of empire (taken up in Chapter 6).

It is true that there were those who dissented from the official party view in many issue areas, especially amongst intellectuals in the world of the arts. This should not be surprising, as by definition for art to flourish freedom of thought is necessary. Yet here too for the most part people conformed, due to natural human survival instincts, and worked within the parameters set by the party. An excellent fictional portrayal of the dilemmas faced by artists in the Soviet system can be found in the contemporary novel by Olga Grushin, *The Dream Life of Sukhanov,* about a talented painter who compromised his art to ensure that he enjoyed the good life and one free from risk of the Gulag (Grushin, 2006).

Of course there were also true believers in the Soviet Communist cause in the former Soviet Union, yet it was manifestly evident for anyone who visited and knew the country well, certainly from the 1970s, that perhaps the majority of minor officials from the younger generations who espoused Marxist-Leninist ideology did so in large part out of a predilection for their own personal safety, or a desire to further careers and increase material gain, rather any deep conviction to Soviet Communism's central tenets. As was clearly demonstrated by the treatment of those who dissented from the communist scriptures handed down from above, opposition to or criticism of the regime carried very serious risks. Dissidents were hassled by the KGB, pronounced insane and incarcerated in lunatic asylums, imprisoned, sent into internal exile, or, in some cases, expelled from the country. It was certainly easier and less dangerous to conform to the system. Furthermore, of course, many people were direct beneficiaries of this system under what was now officially termed "developed socialism." Under Brezhnev's "stability of cadres," following the tumultuous and turbulent Stalin years, and the uncertainty of the Khrushchev era with its constant party reorganization and radical shifts in policies, a kind of pact was created in which the central party leadership would refrain from constant purges, terror campaigns, or radical reformism, and hence provide the population with a secure stable environment in which to go about every day life. As noted in the previous chapter Khrushchev's secret speech was a major turning point in the Soviet communist world, but it did not challenge or criticize the fundamentals of the political system, and failed to produce any rethinking in Soviet communist ideology. Khrushchev was careful to restrict his criticism to Stalin's personal crimes and not to permit this to evolve into a wider critique of the ideological foundations of the regime that Stalin had constructed.

Conclusion

In the final analysis it can be determined, that however much the original Bolshevik Marxist ideology had been adapted, and no matter the extent to which it was stretched to fit the purpose of legitimating the incumbent CPSU leadership and the Soviet system, from October 1917 through to 1991 Soviet Communism was in ideological and systemic contestation with Liberalism. The fact that experience after the revolution turned out to be so very different from that anticipated according to Marxist-Leninist theory, did not lead to an immediate crisis in ideology. The communists could not admit that they were wrong for, as Pipes put it: 'To admit to being wrong would threaten to unravel the whole theoretical foundations of their regime, since it claimed to be scientifically correct in its parts' (Pipes, 2003, p. 42). As traced in this chapter Marxist-Leninist ideology became more than a body of political thought—it became the guide to political action, the basis for political identity, the source of beliefs, norms and political and cultural discourse, and provided the myths and symbols that helped the Soviet elite maintain its legitimacy.

It was noted that the origins of the concept of totalitarianism was linked to a comparative study of Fascism, Nazism, and Communism. The similar historical, social, and economic backgrounds leading to the establishment of Nazi and communist regimes were also noted. It has also been shown that there were very important and clear differences, some relating to means, some to objectives, and some to political cultures, between these different ideologies. It should be stressed, whatever the eventual form it took, Soviet Communism was designed as an instrument to achieve social progress for all, irrespective of nationality; Nazism on the other hand was an ideology whose goal was linked to progress for a particular race of people. German Nazism was a self-proclaimed *national* socialist enterprise; Soviet Communism was always in its stated objectives an *international* socialist project. Due to the multiple roles that Marxism-Leninism came to play in the USSR it became obligatory from the very beginning, and remained so until the very end, as it adapted to changing domestic and international circumstances, for the USSR to play a key role in the wider international communist movement. This issue is dealt with in detail in the next chapter.

3

Soviet Communism and the International Communist Movement

As noted in previous chapters, Soviet Communism by definition was always perceived in international as opposed to national terms. Within three decades of the October Revolution one-third of the world's population lived in states whose regimes were directly influenced by Lenin's model of the ruling communist party. At one point in the twentieth century 3.5 billion people—more than half of the world's entire population—lived under some form of communist influence. Marxists rejected the idea of the nation as a natural outgrowth of cultural or ethnic identity, seeing it rather as tied to and serving the interests of the capitalist mode of production. Therefore, nations would not be eternal or long-lived, but would disappear with the end of the capitalist mode of production and those living under communism would be part of one common international, or post-national community. Nationalism after all was a social construction, a form of identity that did not exist before and was invented during the French Revolution and then gaining traction during the industrial revolution. A socialist revolution therefore was expected to result in strengthened identities reflecting a new mode of post-capitalist, socialist production. Rejecting the concept of political practices being defined by, and state legitimacy being linked to the "nation," Marxists had always prioritized class as the main determinant of human relations seen in international terms. The concept of communism on an international scale did not then originate with the

Bolsheviks or the Russian Revolution in October 1917, but goes back to the origins of the Marxist critique of capitalism.

The First and Second Internationals

Although it was the case that by the mid 1940s a large portion of the world's population was living under some form of communist regime inspired by Marxism, it was also the case that at that time the communist world was very much centred in, and for the most part controlled by, the Kremlin. To see how this eventuated it is necessary to go back and trace the origins of communism as a worldwide movement. This was first given institutional structure with the founding of the First International— the International Working Men's Association—at a meeting in London, in September 1864. Marx and Engels played important roles in both the practical organization of the International and in developing its ideological underpinnings. Embodied in the First International was the idea of international proletarian solidarity, and support for workers in all countries in their struggles against capitalism. However, this First International never really offered a coherent programme due to its rather eclectic membership, incorporating anarchists and various socialists representing often radically opposed viewpoints. It was disbanded in 1876.

It was the Second International, founded in July 1889 on the centenary of the storming of the Bastille that was more significant in creating an effective international grouping bringing together leading Marxists from various countries, although the German Social Democrats under Karl Kautsky played the leading role. Lenin would later clash with Kautsky over the most appropriate means of achieving socialism, with Kautsky advocating the parliamentary path, and Lenin the revolutionary. This Second International was disbanded in 1916 as its members fell into disagreement about whether the workers in each of the belligerent countries during the First World War should continue to fight for their countries, or, as Lenin advocated, turn their guns on their own governments in the name of the international proletariat. This was another example of the power of the nation, as opposed to a shared identity based on economic class as a mobilizing factor among the masses as they continued to fight for country, and not international socialism.

After the Bolshevik Revolution the Soviet Union would eventually seek to ensure, through a variety of means, that the CPSU would become and would remain head of the international communist movement. Initially, however, this was neither desired nor anticipated, for the hope and expectation in 1917 was that the October Revolution in "backward" Russia would ignite revolutions in the more advanced industrial countries in the West, and hence Soviet Communism would play an important but ultimately subsidiary role in the construction of world communism. Lenin perceived the First World War as an imperialist war, and in the midst of this war he considered that revolution in Russia would stimulate proletarian solidarity among all belligerent countries. In the *Communist Manifesto* Marx and Engels made it clear that they viewed Germany as the country where revolution would most likely take place, for compared to England or France it had a much more developed proletariat, hence the bourgeois revolution in Germany 'would be but the prelude to an immediately following proletarian revolution' (Marx and Engels, 2002, p. 88). Trotsky clearly stated that: 'Only the victory of the proletariat in the West would protect Russia from bourgeois restoration and assure the establishment of socialism' (Trotsky, 1964, p. 140). Lenin had lamented some five months after October that the expected German Revolution had not come as anticipated on the heels of the Russian Revolution, and 'an absolute truth, is that without the German Revolution we shall perish' (Fischer, 1951, p. 219). The young Bolshevik leaders never envisaged that after revolution in Russia they would eventually be forced to work within the framework of an international system of sovereign states that had been established by the bourgeoisie. They had never for a moment seen the world in terms of interstate relations in the classical realist manner, but rather they saw themselves as the 'advanced guard of Marxist science and revolutionary progress' (Service, 2011, p. 62). *The Communist Manifesto* famously ended with the call for 'workers of all countries unite!' Unfortunately for the Bolsheviks, following world war and the October Revolution, this did not come to pass as expected.

The Third International

In March 1919 the Bolsheviks founded the Third International, which came to be known as the Comintern. The Comintern was designed to achieve through all necessary means the overthrow of the bourgeoisie and the establishment of an international Soviet republic, as a transition towards the abolition of the state and the creation of world communism. The establishment of the Communist International was in part designed 'to win support among left-wing radicals in the West for the revolution in Russia and to spread it worldwide' (Gellately, 2007, p. 345). British Trotskyist John Molyneux judged the years of the Comintern, between 1919 and 1923, as representing the 'highest point reached in the history of working class political organization' (Molyneux, 2008). The Comintern was designed to promote *world* revolution, acting as a support-group, propaganda instrument, and ideological guide to encourage workers in all countries to unite in overthrowing the capitalist order in the name of socialism. Trotsky referred to the Third International as the 'General Staff of the World Revolution', and Leading Bolshevik figures were appointed to the Executive Committee, with Grigory Zinoviev, a close associate of Lenin, being made President (he served as head of the Comintern until 1926). For the next few years after the Comintern's founding Zinoviev 'lived in a revolutionary dreamworld in which Bolshevism was about to conquer Europe and sweep across the planet' (Andrew and Mitrokhin, 2005, p. 2; see also Carr, 1982). This militaristic jargon should not lead one to the conclusion that the Soviet Union was pursuing an aggressive expansionist foreign policy. Fascism and Nazism were expansionist ideologies. Although they adhered to an internationalist ideology, Soviet Communists for the most part never believed that it was desirable, or even possible to export revolution. By definition socialism could only come about through the inherent contradictions within capitalism, and not directly from outside military forces. Although, in the event of proletarian revolutions occurring elsewhere, it was considered to be the responsibility of the Soviet communist party to provide assistance to the extent that it could.

Although Russians were dominant in the leading positions of the Comintern, communists from other nationalities were represented—for example in the first years of its existence John Reed served on the Executive Committee, as did Hungarian, French, Dutch, Norwegian, Swedish, Yugoslav, Polish, Finnish, Korean, and Chinese nationals. Reed died in Russia of typhus whilst engaging in full-time activity for the Comintern. A leading member of the right opposition against Stalin, Nikolai Bukharin, replaced Zinoviev (a leading member of the left opposition) and served as head of the Comintern for two years. Then the Bulgarian Georgi Dimitrov took over as secretary general of the Comintern, remaining in that post until Stalin disbanded the organization in 1943.

Stimulated by events in Russia, there had been some promising but ultimately disappointing revolutionary movements in parts of Europe, including the establishment in Hungary of a Soviet Republic, on 21 March 1919. However, this was to last only nine months, collapsing after Budapest was occupied by Romanian troops. This was the first communist government to be established in Europe after the Russian Revolution, and its rapid demise was a lesson to Lenin that the Bolsheviks needed to rethink their strategy in relation to international communism and world revolution. At the time, although the communist leaders of the Hungarian Revolution called for military assistance from the Bolsheviks in their struggle against foreign and local anticommunist forces, Lenin was unable to oblige due to the ongoing civil war in Russia. Nikolai Bukharin wrote his famous *ABC Of Communism* in 1919, and it is clear at that time he saw the revolutionary struggles in Finland, Austria, and Germany, in addition to Hungary, as portending the demise of the bourgeois states and the victory of the international proletariat (Bukharin, 1966, p. 127). Communists did briefly take power in Munich, in April 1919, when Russian-born German Jew Eugene Levine established the Bavarian Soviet Republic. Munich was a one-time home for Lenin during his years in exile, and at the time of the communist takeover Adolf Hitler resided there too. With the bloody collapse of the communist uprising and the execution of Levine just a few weeks later, this marked the end of Lenin's hopes for communism in Germany, and helped to stimulate the rise of the German Nazis eventually under Hitler's leadership. Yet still, speaking at a meeting with German, Polish, Czechoslovak, Hungarian, and Italian delegates to the Third Congress of the Communist International in July 1920 Lenin was optimistic that Europe was, as he put it, 'pregnant with revolution' (Lenin, 1976, p. 324).

It should not be surprising that the Bolsheviks were, in the wake of October, enthusiastic and initially optimistic about the prospects for revolution elsewhere, for if a relatively small group of communists could successfully topple the Tsar and bring the Russian Empire to an end, then surely, it was considered, it should be much more likely that organized worker parties in the West could take power from capitalist regimes in crisis. The greatest hope for the spread of revolution throughout Europe was in the summer of 1920, during Russia's war with Poland, a war that Richard Pipes claims to have been 'one of the most decisive in all of history' (Pipes, 1996, p. 67). Socialist and one-time member of the Peoples Will, a revolutionary movement that sought to overthrow the Tsar, and fervent Polish nationalist, Josef Pilsudski led a Polish army in a fight for independence from the Russian Empire during the First World War. Pilsudski had earlier been arrested along with Lenin's brother Alexander Ulyanov for his membership of the group that planned to assassinate the Tsar in 1887. Ulyanov did not ask for clemency, and was shot. Pilsudski served five years hard labour in Siberia. The Central Powers proclaimed Poland's independence in November 1916, which was officially ratified in Warsaw after the war, in November 1918. During the Russian civil war Pilsudski fought initially on the side of the Reds, seeing them as the lesser evil than the Whites, who wished to restore a Russian empire that would be supported by the West. Pilsudski would later form an alliance with Ukrainian nationalist Simon Petlura to help Ukraine establish independence from Russia, providing yet another example of how national identity triumphed over class solidarity.

Following Pilsudski's invasion of Soviet Ukraine, with Polish forces occupying Kiev in May 1920, Russians rallied, similarly stimulated more by nationalist sentiments, to repel the invaders. It was at this point that Lenin and the Bolsheviks held great expectations that the German Communist Party could gain power. Bukharin, writing in the communist party newspaper *Pravda,* anticipated that the momentum of the Soviet army would inspire revolution beyond Poland to Paris and London. It was not only communist parties in the international communist movement that supported the new Bolshevik leadership in its struggle with Polish nationalists. Although the war did not carry the socialist revolution to London, the British Labour Party, meeting in the British capital for their annual conference in 1920 passed a resolution calling for a general strike if the British government intervened in any way on the side of the Poles. This did not prevent Soviet sources from condemning the British Labour Party for its reformism and "toadying" to the capitalist classes (see Bowker and Shearman, 1990). In the event the Poles fought back, and with the signing of the Treaty of Riga between Poland and the Bolsheviks in 1921, made considerable territorial gains, including the incorporation of parts of Lithuania, Belorussia and Ukraine into an expanded Polish state. This marked not only a huge military defeat for the new Soviet state, but also a big blow to hopes for spreading communism to the advanced capitalist states in Western Europe. It was also yet another lesson regarding the powerful forces of nationalism.

The Comintern as an Instrument of the Soviet State

It was at the Second Comintern Congress in 1920 that the Russian Bolsheviks began to centralize international communism under Soviet control. It was at this Congress that Lenin established 21 conditions that had to be met before fraternal socialist parties could gain membership of the Comintern (Lenin, 1920). These conditions included an obligation for individual parties in Europe and America to engage in 'illegal activities' to further the class struggle, and a duty to support any Soviet republic in its struggle against counter-revolutionary forces. A two-thirds majority among aspirant parties was necessary for membership of the Comintern, and the last condition stated that any members who opposed any of the conditions should be expelled from the party. Lenin at the time had also drawn up restrictions on intra-party dialogue and tightened centralized control over the party apparatus through a rigid imposition of the principle of "democratic centralism," a principle to which applicant parties should adhere to gain membership of the Comintern. Lenin considered those features emanating from the experience of the Bolshevik Revolution to be applicable to the wider international socialist community. Lenin was responsible for preventing open debate within the ranks of the Soviet party, thereby undermining pluralism and democratic development at home and alienating a large number of fraternal parties overseas, which had the effect of undermining the potential of the Comintern to gain wider influence abroad. This was the same year that the Independent Labour Party (ILP) was formed in the UK and its leaders made an official application to join the Comintern. However, the response from Moscow 'was such a fierce and abrasive condemnation of the ILP and its leaders that much support was alienated' (Jones, 1977, p. 6). Although the Communist Party of Great Britain (CPGB), established in 1920 from an amalgamation of small Marxist groups had miniscule electoral support, it became the officially accredited representative of the British working class in the Moscow-controlled Comintern.

Due to Soviet attempts at disciplining fraternal communist parties many foreigners became disillusioned. Freda Uttey, a young British leftist representing the Socialist Clubs in British Universities, first went to the USSR in 1927. She married a Russian CPSU member and stayed for six years in Stalin's Russia. She had been brought up in the socialist tradition, Bernard Shaw and Sidney and Beatrice Webb were family friends, and her father had once spoken from the same platform as Friedrich Engels. However, Uttey soon became disillusioned with the Soviet communist system, later comparing it to the Nazi regime in Germany (Uttey, 1940, p. 4). Uttey's communist Russian husband was shot in Vorkuta, one of Stalin's infamous labour camps. Lenin's 21 conditions for membership of the Comintern split other leftist parties, leading soon after to the establishment of the French and Spanish Communist Parties in 1920, and the Italian Communist Party in 1921. Lenin therefore can be seen as a splitter, preventing the establishment of a cohesive and strong and truly international communist movement.

During his attendance as a delegate to the 1921 Communist International Congress in Moscow, Bernhard Reichenback of the Communist Workers Party of Germany (KAPD) recalls that anyone who expressed an opinion that differed from the official Russian position 'remained isolated' (Reichenback, 1964). Reichenback stayed in Moscow (in the Hotel Lux, of which more below) for six months, and during this time he said it was possible to spend half a year in Moscow without even being aware of Stalin's existence. By 1921 even the most optimistic Soviet communists recognized that socialist revolution would be confined to Russia itself. The KAPD withdrew from the International in that same year. Such experiences of foreign communists in Stalin's Soviet Union were common, and reflected in part the regime's fear of the influence of alien nationals on the stability of the system. The great hope for socialist revolution may have initially been placed on the German working class, but now their representatives were forced to play a secondary and largely compliant role under Moscow's leadership.

It was soon after these events that Stalin developed the concept of "socialism in one country," and the Communist Party of the Soviet Union in pursuit of this objective sought to ensure its control over the wider international communist movement. Whilst in theory articulating an internationalist policy, Stalin's Russia was in practice now imposing total control over foreign communists in the service of the Soviet state. As Trotsky would state of Stalin's attitude towards the Comintern: 'He profoundly believed that the task of creating socialism was national and administrative in nature. He looked upon the Communist International as a necessary evil which should be used as far as possible for the purposes of foreign policy' (Trotsky, 1964, p. 191). Stalin never once addressed a Comintern congress, and apart from the wartime trip to Tehran he never went abroad outside the Communist bloc. Stalin may have been largely invisible, but his influence was omnipresent.

The Kremlin's control over the foreign communist parties became 'administratively, psychologically, and in many instances financially—virtually complete and unchallenged' (Dallin and Firsov, 2000, p. 17). The level of control the Comintern had over fraternal communist parties was demonstrated in 1937 when under instructions from the Comintern (in effect from the CPSU) the Polish Communist Party was dissolved. Not all fraternal communist groups were willing to follow blindly the line handed down from Moscow. There were inevitably some dissenting voices within the councils of the Comintern. For example, the influential Peruvian socialist, Ronaldo Mariategui refused to adhere to instructions from the leader of the Comintern's South American Secretariat in the 1920s, a time when the Soviet Communist Party leadership had little faith in the prospects for proletarian revolution in that part of the world. The Comintern's strictures were for advancing the formation of an Indian Republic in South America, modelled on its similar proposals to establish Black Republics in the southern United States. However, Mariategui dissented from the strictures handed down from the Comintern, favouring a more traditional Marxist approach based upon class, but one which should be adapted to native indigenous conditions (see Becker, 2006). Despite disagreements and some dissent in the ranks of fraternal communist parties the CPSU held tight control over the basic line and polices of the Communist International.

One of the problems of being at the centre of world communism for Stalin was that this did actually require dealing with foreigners. Stalin was not a great cosmopolitan, and certainly had not been a seasoned traveller like the other early Bolsheviks who had lived in exile in various parts of Europe, and who had mastered several foreign languages whilst living there. In its early years the Comintern was led by those intellectual, multilingual Bolshevik internationalists later to perish in Stalin's purges (including Bukharin and Zinoviev). But it was not only Soviet citizens who would perish in the purges, as Stalin's fear of foreigners extended also to foreign communists. As Archie Brown notes, after Stalin's death life became more predictable and tolerable yet 'paradoxically, there were almost certainly more true believers in a radiant future during the worst years of mass terror than forty years later' (Brown, 2004, p. 489). Much of the reason for this would have been not just a commitment from foreign communists to the internationalist cause, but also a faith in and respect for Stalin and the Soviet state in combating fascism in Europe.

With the leading institutions of the Communist International based in the USSR, the CPSU was able to control both the personnel policies of many foreign communist parties, and their political programs. Many communist leaders were not able to operate openly in their own countries, and hence took temporary refuge in the USSR. Many foreign members of the Comintern were housed in the Hotel Lux on Gorky Street, Moscow's central avenue leading up to Red Square and the Kremlin (in 1990 the avenue was given back its original pre-revolutionary name of Tverskaya Street). Residents of the Hotel Lux included leading communists from various parts of the world. Many ended up becoming victims of Stalin's terror and purges, whilst others, more fortunate, returned home to become communist leaders of their native countries. Some of the communist figures that had been accommodated there included the Bulgarian and former head of the Comintern Dimitrov, who became the first communist leader of Bulgaria in 1946 (he died in 1949). Another resident of the Lux was Ho Chi Minh, who was President of the Democratic Republic of Vietnam between 1945 and his death in 1969. Ho became a committed activist and agent for the Comintern immediately after leaving the USSR. Other residents included Antonio Gramsci, founder and first leader of the Italian Communist Party, and Palmiro Togliatti, leader of the Italian

Communist Party between 1927 and his death in 1964 (taking over from Gramsci, who had been arrested and imprisoned by the fascist government in Rome).

Many of these foreign communists studied Marxist theory and Soviet political economy at one of two special universities that had been established in Moscow for the purpose: the International Lenin School (mainly for Europeans and North Americans) and the Communist University for Toilers of the East, colloquially referred to as the Stalin School (principally for communists from colonial and post-colonial countries). The first head of the Peoples Republic of China, Lin Shaoqi, studied at the Stalin School, as did Tran Phu, the first ruling General Secretary of the Communist Party of Vietnam. Lin was accused of right-wing deviationism in the late 1960s and was a victim of Mao's Cultural Revolution in China, but was then rehabilitated in 1980 by Deng Xiaoping, another graduate from the Stalin School. Graduates of the Lenin School included Josep Tito, Wyladyslaw Gromulka, Erich Honeker, and Harry Heywood, the black American communist activist (who had also earlier studied at the Stalin School). As David Priestland put it, 'Communist activists ran into each other in the cold showers', adding that it was in these 'unpromising circumstances' that Earl Browder, the American Communist Party leader first met Tito. (Priestland, 2010, p. 125). Boleslaw Bierut, who attended the School of the Comintern in Moscow in 1925, became an agent of the Soviet Military Intelligence Service (GRU) in 1931, and finally became head of the Polish United Workers Party between 1944 and 1947. Beirut spent most of the war against Nazi Germany in the USSR.

Other leading communist officials from other countries who spent time in exile or studying or working in Moscow before taking up leadership positions in their own countries included Czechoslovakia's Klement Gottwald (Communist leader in Czechoslovakia 1948–1953); Matyas Rakosi (leader of the ruling Communist Party in Hungary 1945–1966); Vulko Chernenkov (leader of the ruling Communist Party in Bulgaria 1949–1954); Walter Ulbricht leader of the ruling Socialists Unity Party in East Germany 1950–1971); and Kim Il Sung (leader of the ruling Workers Party of Korea 1948–1972). Blas Roca, head of the Cuban Communist Party before the Revolution in 1959 spent time in the USSR working on the Moscow metro. Kim Jong Il, who succeeded to the leadership position on his father's death in

1972, was thought to have been born in the Soviet Union, near Khabarovsk.

Patrice Lumumba University in Moscow was also an institution where many future communist leaders from the Third World were educated. Originally named the Peoples' Friendship University when established in 1960, it was renamed to commemorate the Congolese independence leader who was executed on January 17, 1961. One of the most famous students of the university was Ilich Ramirez Sanchez, better known as "Carlos The Jackal," who became the most notorious terrorist in the world in the 1970s. He engaged in daring terrorist acts in support of a Palestinian homeland. A committed Marxist-Leninist he was thrown out of the Venezuelan communist party and expelled from Patrice Lumumba University for his radicalism and failure to follow strict centralized party discipline. It was essential for students, at least in the seminar room and in their public discourse to follow the Marxist-Leninist line handed down from the USSR. This was another effective means of the USSR maintaining its control of the wider international communist movement, for these party institutions helped to train loyal communists with aspirations for leadership in their home countries, whilst also providing an opportunity to weed out the ones considered undesirable for such positions by the Kremlin.

One can perhaps make some loose comparisons with these institutions and the Madrasas in Pakistan and Afghanistan that helped to train radical Islamists in their anti-West campaigns in more recent times. As with leftist groups Islamist groups have also been divided. However, those from across the world who were schooled in Islamist camps did not have reason to fear for their own safety during their training programmes, at least not from their hosts or instructors. In contrast, those who had been provided with rooms in the Lux Hotel it turned out had very good reason to fear the proverbial knock on the door in the middle of the night, as numerous of them disappeared into Stalin's gulag. Many of them were in fact at much greater risk than their Soviet comrades, and it was only a minority that did not receive a visit from the secret police in the early hours of the morning (Andrew and Mitrokhin, p. 4). A German film, *The Lux*, released in 2011, (with elements of farce and drama) is based on real characters and real events at the hotel on Gorky Street during this period. The hotel was renamed the *Zentral'naya* in 1954, and ceased to be a hotel for international communists.

The Rise of Fascism and the Soviet Response

In 1921, the same year that Lenin instituted NEP, the Communist Party of the Soviet Union called upon other communist parties to form united fronts with other parties rather than calling for immediate revolution. Then in 1928 Stalin imposed an "ultra-left" policy on the Comintern calling for direct action and preparations for a violent revolutionary struggle (although not with any Soviet military support). This period, which prevented leftist groups from forging alliances with social democrats and non-communist trade unions lasted until 1934, when a "united anti-fascist front strategy" was introduced. During the ultra-leftist phase, democratic socialists and other groups on what we might call the "soft left" were chided as "enemies of the working class" and "social fascists." With the rise of the far right in Europe in the early 1930s, Stalin instructed the international communist movement to participate in "popular fronts," forming coalitions of the willing with other anti-fascist groups, to counter the influence of the far right. In effect the Comintern was being used to help ensure the survival of bourgeois liberal democracies in their struggle against fascism. Soviet instructions to the international communist movement were to join forces with other anti-fascist groups to seek representation through the ballot box, rather than following the Bolshevik model of revolution. Stalin's priority was preventing the victory of fascists, rather than fostering socialist revolution in Europe. However, it was during this period perhaps that the Soviet system held its greatest appeal to a wide range of radicals and other idealists whose bond was not so much pro-communism, as anti-fascism. But the united-front strategy came too late, as Germany had already seen Hitler's successful rise to power, due in part, it was widely assumed, to the failure of the left to have previously united in an electoral bloc.

By 1924 the conception of international communism was revised from that originally established by Marx and the First International in 1864 in support of the international proletariat, to become an instrument to support the interests of *Soviet* Communism. The Comintern instituted a "Bolshevization" campaign to ensure other communist parties modelled themselves institutionally on the CPSU and ideologically on Leninism (as decreed by the USSR). Priestland states that: 'In practice, this meant that communist parties were increasingly transformed into tools of Soviet foreign policy' (Preistland, p. 124). Basically the main duty of an international communist was to do everything to assist the development of communism in Russia. Therefore, despite the development of "socialism in one country" under Stalin, the communist parties of other countries were still expected to remain loyal to the CPSU in Moscow. They could not pursue their own brands of socialism in one country but rather were to be guided by instructions from the Soviet party.

The first military intervention the USSR conducted in a non-contiguous country was also against a fascist far right regime, in Spain during the civil war between Franco and the Republicans (1936–1939). Working through the Comintern Stalin approved the creation of International Brigades (such as the one Orwell fought with, as noted in the previous chapter) and the mobilization of support for the anti-fascist forces. However, direct participation of the USSR was limited, and was in response to and legitimated by German and Italian material support for Franco, including aircraft, tanks, and personnel. The motive then was not principally solidarity with the internationalist left, but what was again considered to be a struggle against a strengthening geopolitical threat to the Soviet state.

It was during this period that Trotsky, now in foreign exile, also came back to further haunt Stalin. Following the civil war in Spain in 1938 Trotsky founded the Fourth International, a group of revolutionary Marxists who were critical of Stalin's popular front policies, which were viewed as reactionary and bowing to the forces of nationalism, rather than class. In the previous chapter reference was made to the one-time dominance of totalitarianism (and its subsequent use by former communists themselves)—and it was the Trotskyist's of the Fourth International who first saw similarities between Nazism and Stalinism in the 1930s. As its name implied, this organization was designed to compete with and hopefully supersede the Third International, which was viewed more as an organization pursuing Soviet *state* interests, rather than one representing the real interests of the international working class. Trotsky's influence amongst western intellectuals is interesting, especially given many of them would later turn to the radical right. Former members of Trotskyist groups included some of those in the United States who would later become very influential in American neo-conservative circles. Many of the contributors to the neo-conservative periodical

The Public Interest, established in 1965, had once flirted with Trotskyism, being heirs to Jewish-American leftist intellectuals. Priestland (p. 520) suggests that the neo-conservatives can be seen as 'Trotsky's revenge' on the USSR. Some of the neoconservatives in the Bush White House in 2003 were once Trotskyist leftists— what some would perhaps call the "Trotskycons" (see Jeet Heer, 2003). The neoconservative experiment was played out in the war against Saddam Hussein in Iraq. It is certainly the case that the United States under George W. Bush pushed an aggressive foreign policy that sought to export liberal democracy through military means, making it in practice far more internationalist and revolutionary than the former USSR had ever been.

To the incredulity of the communist world, in August 1939 the USSR signed a non-aggression pact with Nazi Germany. This was very difficult to justify in ideological terms, or in terms of international communism. As head of the Comintern, Dimitrov was struggling to find the best approach in justifying this radical about-turn in Soviet policy. In early September Stalin received Dimitrov (along with Molotov and Zhdanov) where the head of the international communist movement was told that fraternal communist parties were to be instructed that it was now their responsibility to undermine imperialism in general, and the western democracies in particular. The Comintern directive that was rushed out the next day described the war as imperialist and unjust and and: 'The international proletariat can under no circumstances defend fascist Poland, which refused the assistance of the Soviet Union and which oppresses other nationalities' (Dallin and Firsov, 2000, p. 152). As a result of the Nazi-Soviet Pact, Soviet troops regained territories in the Baltic and in East-Central Europe that had been lost during the First World War, and Poland was divided between Germany and the USSR.

The pact with Hitler created only breathing space for Stalin, to prepare for the time when Germany might turn its guns eastwards against the USSR. This eventuated with the German invasion of June 1941. During the ensuing war the USSR was to take the brunt of the fighting in Europe on the Eastern Front, and Soviet troops would be responsible eventually for ensuring Hitler's defeat. The Battle of Stalingrad was the beginning of the end for Nazi Germany, and the Soviet Union under Stalin's wartime leadership was widely viewed, quite correctly, as the key force in defeating Hitler's troops and saving Europe from having fascism imposed upon it. This resulted in rising sympathy for the suffering of the Soviet people during the war, along with an increasingly positive appreciation of the relative strengths of the Soviet communist system after the war, as much of Europe lay devastated. This was not a boost for international communism as such: it was rather a major boost for the reputation of the Soviet communist system and the Soviet state. Many were inclined to feel solidarity with the Soviet people, the Soviet state, and the Soviet model, rather than any separate fundamentalist belief in Marxism or international communism, although of course there were always those who did continue to hold this belief.

International Communism, the World Revolutionary Process, and the World Socialist System

The "world revolutionary process" was a concept developed in the Soviet Union after the Second World War, with the advent of new communist regimes in Eastern Europe, and the anti-imperialist movements in the Third World challenging western capitalist states in their struggles for independence. The term "Eastern Europe" only came into usage after the Second World War and designated not a geographical area, but that part of Europe under communist control. No longer was the USSR practically alone as the only communist regime, as it had been since 1917 (with the single exception of Mongolia, see Table 3.1.). The USSR remained very much the centre of the system, having come through the travails of revolution, civil war, war against the Nazis and the great turbulence and suffering of the Stalin years. The three basic components of the world revolutionary process were the "world socialist system," comprising states led by communist parties (the "socialist commonwealth") and other communist-ruled regimes; the non-ruling communist parties in the rest of the world, along with radical trade unions and other groups sympathetic to the communist cause; and finally the national liberation movements in the Third World with the potential to develop a socialist orientation. All three components were linked into the wider world revolutionary process due to their antipathy and opposition to imperialism and global capitalism. Here I will cover the most important component of the world revolutionary process: the ruling communist party regimes, for these

Table 3.1   The world socialist system

Country	Establishment of Communist System	Member of CMEA* (year joined)	Member of Warsaw Pact
Albania	1944	1949 (to 1961)	Yes (until 1968)
Bulgaria	1946	1949	Yes
China	1949	not a member	No
Cuba	1959	1972	No
East Germany	1950	1950	Yes
Hungary	1949	1949	Yes
Laos	1975	1986 (observer)	No
Mongolia	1924	1962	No
North Korea	1945	not a member	No
Poland	1945	1949	Yes
Russia (USSR)	1917	1949	Yes
Vietnam	1975	1978	No
Yugoslavia	1945	1964 (associate)	No

* The Council for Mutual Economic Assistance. The non-communist states gaining observer status of CMEA were: Finland (1973); Iraq (1975); Mexico (1975); Nicaragua (1984); Afghanistan (1986); Ethiopia (1986); South Yemen (1986).

formed the nucleus of the international communist system. The national liberation movements and states of socialist orientation will be covered in the next chapter on the Third World.

The Soviet Union had dissolved the Comintern in 1943, a step deemed to have been the 'most remarkable departure from revolutionary communism' ever made (Priestland, 2009, p. 206). Stalin pushed for the dissolution of the Comintern during war with Germany in part to stress the national (i.e., patriotic, Soviet) nature of the struggle. Stalin made himself a Marshal of the USSR, adopted a new Soviet national anthem, and began to glorify the names of former pre-revolutionary Russian military leaders. In addition, by dissolving the Comintern the Soviet Union was also making a gesture to the U.S. as the two states were becoming close military allies in the common fight against Nazism. The functions of the Comintern were collapsed into a new organization. This was the Department of International Information (Dallin and Firsov, 2000, p. 255). In 1947 yet a new international organization was established, named the Communist Information Bureau (Cominform), which was an attempt to recreate some semblance of an international communist organization (in addition to the USSR and the new communist states of Eastern Europe, the French and Italian communist parties were represented). The Cominform's main activity was publishing materials that propagated those views that its members shared, and in part to counter U.S. Marshall aid to Europe, particularly as some East European countries were tempted to make applications to join the European Recovery Project. During its very first meeting Zhdanov gave his famous two camps speech, widely seen at the time as the USSR's declaration of a new type of ideological war against the West. Zhdanov told the Information Bureau that the world was now split into two antagonist camps, and it was the duty of the fraternal communist parties to unite in countering 'America's aspirations to world supremacy' (Zhdanov, 1947, reprinted in Procacci, 1994). Zhdanov talked of a US "strategic plan" for world domination and an ideological struggle against the USSR. It was therefore, again, the responsibility of the international movement to counter American hegemony to save the Soviet communist state. The Cominform was dissolved in 1956 as a gesture to reconciliation with Tito (Yugoslavia had been expelled from the organization following Tito's split with Stalin in 1948).

It was after the defeat of Hitler and the relative rise in the power of the USSR and the spread of communism throughout Eastern Europe that tensions between the US and the Soviet Union rose to such a level that the term Cold War was used to describe the relationship. As one observer put it: 'In intellectual terms the Cold War was a competition between two ideologies, Marxism and Liberalism, that had a great deal in common. Both were Enlightenment ideologies that looked forward to a universal civilization. Both interpreted history in reductive terms, viewing technological and economic development as primary and religion as a secondary factor of dwindling importance' (Gray, 2008, p. 42). Whatever similar starting points they may have had in western political thought and in terms of their overall goals of economic modernization, both sides nevertheless represented competing versions of political economy and governmental structures, as they became engaged in what was in effect an existential struggle in which only one side could emerge victorious. Though they saw one another as mortal enemies they differed chiefly on the question of which economic system was best suited to achieve the modernizing goals they shared. In addition, and some would say more to the point, there was the geopolitical competition based upon shifting power relations following the defeat of Germany and Japan and the demise of the European empires. The bipolar structure of power determined that the USSR and the USA would become adversaries due to the security dilemma. From a realist perspective, competition for global influence would have materialized irrespective of the differences in the two protagonists' domestic arrangements and ideologies.

It was, however, during the Cold War that the "spectre of communism," especially in the view of the U.S., did eventually come to haunt Europe in a serious way. With the advent of the world socialist system, and in the face of economic dislocation and wartime devastation, with high levels of unemployment and millions of refugees, Western Europe was seemingly ripe for radical leftist politics. It was not the idea of international communism that threatened the West, so much as the potential influence of spreading Soviet influence, as the Kremlin now controlled the wider "socialist commonwealth" of East European communist regimes. In order to counter this threat the United States provided aid in the form of the European Recovery Project, colloquially named the "Marshall Plan" after its architect, the US Secretary of State George Marshall. The Plan was designed to counter the appeals of a non-capitalist path of development, particularly given the strong mass appeal of the communist parties in France and Italy after the war, and to extend America's sphere of economic and political influence. But it was also designed as part of a wider package of policies to "contain" the Soviet state based on the logic of geo-politics and the balance of power. Hence, the Cold War was at one and the same time an ideological struggle, a competition over ideas, *and* a classic geo-political struggle relating to material power. Soviet communism and the Soviet state were central in each sphere, the ideological and the material.

Following the Second World War Soviet Communist influence spread throughout the eastern and central part of Europe. Many of the former communist party leaders who had been exiled in Moscow took over the reigns of power in some countries, and in most cases communism was imposed upon Eastern Europe by Soviet tanks rather than being independently achieved through the ranks of local communist cadres. The communist-ruled regimes that were also members of the Council for Mutual Economic Assistance (CMEA) were officially part of what was referred to as the socialist commonwealth of nations (see Table 3.1). Stalin established the CMEA in January 1949 to integrate the economies of the communist bloc, with the aim of gaining self-sufficiency and independence from the market economies of the West, and partly in response to the Marshall Plan, which was seen as an instrument of American imperialism. Pressure from Stalin discouraged those states in Eastern Europe that were tempted to consider joining the Marshal Plan (including Bulgaria, Czechoslovakia, Poland, and Romania). The plan was designed to aid post-war development in Europe and to discourage both communism and hyper-nationalism, both strong possibilities given the economic and social devastation caused by the war. The USSR, with by far the strongest economy of the communist bloc took the lead in decision-making, and the CMEA effectively became another arm of the Soviet state. It was yet another instrument to ensure Soviet control over the communist states of the Eastern bloc.

There was also a military alliance that the Soviet Eastern bloc established, in May 1955, incorporating all East European communist regimes with the exception of Yugoslavia, which had broken with Moscow in 1948. This mutual defence treaty (see Table 3.1) was again a direct response to developments in Western Europe: the incorporation of West Germany into the North Atlantic Treaty Organization in 1955. Albania did not participate fully in the Warsaw Pact following the Sino-Soviet split in 1961, and withdrew from the Treaty completely in 1968. Although China was never invited to join the Warsaw Pact, at one stage after the Communist Revolution in 1949 the USSR and the People's Republic of China did establish a bilateral security alliance. This proved to be relatively short-lived, with a crisis in relations in the 1960s almost leading to war over border skirmishes and ideological divisions in 1969. Hence, although continuing on a non-capitalist path of development, and remaining theoretically part of the wider world socialist system, China at this time broke away from the Soviet sphere.

Eventually, following President Nixon's overtures, China effectively formed an anti-Soviet alliance with Washington in a triangular balance of power. Here again is a further example of the power of nationalist, statist, and geopolitical forces that overrode any conceptions of belonging to a wider international socialist community. The splits inside the world socialist system with Yugoslavia, Albania, and China all gaining independence from the Soviet sphere of influence, provided clear evidence of this. In addition there was a number of crises within the tighter Soviet-controlled "socialist commonwealth of nations," as first the East Germans (1953), then the Hungarians (1956) and finally the Czechoslovakians (1968) all sought to gain increasing autonomy from Moscow and to follow a more liberal (and national) form of socialist development. In 1956 and again in 1968 Soviet troops were used to put down these popular uprisings.

The intervention in Prague by Warsaw Pact troops in 1968 was officially justified in Moscow as having been required to protect threats to socialism. Therefore the intervention was justified in internationalist terms, relating to socialist solidarity. This came to be known as the Brezhnev Doctrine, or a doctrine of "limited sovereignty." This can be contrasted with the later doctrine of the "responsibility to protect" (R2P) that NATO would use to justify interventions in Kosovo and Libya. Ostensibly following a similar logic, of states forfeiting their sovereignty if incumbent regimes cannot or will not prevent systemic abuses or threats to order, it becomes the responsibility of the wider international community to intervene for 'humanitarian purposes', with express authorization from the UN Security Council (UNSC). There are many serious problems with the idea and practice of the responsibility to protect, as it could be used to justify limited sovereignty in many murky circumstances thereby undermining the bedrock of international relations (state sovereignty), as states intervene for ulterior purposes whilst simultaneously invoking the doctrine. NATO's intervention in Kosovo did not have UNSC approval, and hence was as illegal as the Soviet intervention in Prague in 1968; and the intervention in Libya went far beyond the UNSC's remit by engaging in regime change and removing Gaddafi from power.

It is instructive to recall that President Medvedev, at the time of the short war between Russia and Georgia in South Ossetia in 2008, justified the Russian military intervention with reference to the responsibility to protect. Looking back at the former USSR the Soviet regime justified its own interventions in the communist bloc as being necessary to save socialism from being undermined. In fact it was a mechanism to ensure continued Soviet control. There is no moral equivalence between the Brezhnev Doctrine and the R2P: the R2P was designed to protect against mass abuses of human rights, whereas the Brezhnev Doctrine's objective was to maintain Soviet state power that clearly undermined the rights of others. Yet one can, I think, nevertheless see the inherent dangers involved in adopting doctrines justified on the basis of a collective good that interferes with and undermines sovereignty. The Brezhnev Doctrine was first outlined in an article in the Communist Party newspaper *Pravda* in September 1968, which gave the right to Moscow, as head of the socialist commonwealth, to use military force to ensure compliance if satellite states veered from the Soviet version of socialism. The Doctrine would be extended to Afghanistan with the Soviet invasion in 1979, when the head of the KGB (later to succeed Brezhnev briefly as General Secretary of the CPSU), Yuri Andropov, was 'convinced that Afghanistan, like Czechoslovakia eleven years earlier, was threatened with "ideological sabotage" and that only Soviet military intervention could prevent the "overthrow of socialism"' (Andrew and Mitrokhin, 2005, p. 399). Ten years later it would be abandoned by Gorbachev, when in March 1989 he stated that fraternal communist parties would resolve their tasks in accordance with their own traditions and values, with the USSR respecting their sovereignty. This came to be called the Sinatra Doctrine (after the song *I Did it My Way*; i.e., now members of the world socialist system could do it their way).

The Warsaw Pact became a vehicle not for the common defence of its members, nor a means of collective security: rather it was a military organization used by the USSR to serve two functions: first, to deter NATO from encroachments in the Eastern bloc, and second to discipline and where necessary enforce compliance to Soviet objectives amongst WTO members. Whereas NATO was a voluntary organization of equal partners (at least in status, if not in stature), the Warsaw Pact was very much an organization that was tightly controlled by the USSR, representing the interests of the Soviet state.

The Thaw, the 20th Party Congress and International Communism

Three years after Stalin's death Khrushchev presented his "secret speech" to a closed session of the CPSU Central Committee, in which he catalogued Stalin's crimes against the Party. The sensational revelations in the speech soon filtered beyond the confines of the CPSU to the outside world, and had a devastating impact on the fraternal communist parties in Eastern Europe as well as in the wider international communist movement. As Archie Brown notes 'Khrushchev's revelations came close to sweeping communists from power in more than one country and, in their aftermath, threatened his own position' (Brown, 2009, p. 243). But as Figes notes, the speech, although delivered by Khrushchev, had been compiled by the top collective leadership and was designed to 'restore belief in the party and return Leninism to power by presenting Stalinism as an aberration from October's socialist ideals' (Figes, 2014, p. 351). To the rest of the communist world Khrushchev's revelations and criticisms came out of the blue, as a massive jolt, creating turbulence right across the world of international communism. Fraternal ruling communist party leaders were placed in a serious bind, a dilemma with no obvious remedy. Should they immediately follow the lead of Khrushchev and criticize Stalinist regressions from the true path, with all the dangers that could possibly herald for internal stability? Should they simply try and ignore the speech and hope for clarity and detailed instructions to come later from Moscow? Or should they try and take a stance against Khrushchev's revisionism, given that any criticism of the leader of the communist world could undermine their legitimacy? Or should they rather take the opportunity offered and go beyond the criticism of Stalin's cult and crimes and seek to radically reform the communist system itself?

There were advocates for all of the above options: sycophants rushing to repeat verbatim what the Soviet leader had said; the cowed and frightened waiting for instructions; those opposed to de-Stalinization either out of fear for their own legitimacy and positions, or out of true belief; and radical reformers who wished to grasp the moment and gain independence from Kremlin controls. As Brown notes, within the USSR itself there were Stalinists who 'believed that Khrushchev had gratuitously undermined the credibility, unity and strength of the international Communist movement' (Brown, 2006, p. 245). Their concerns were well founded, based on the repercussions of the speech in the wider socialist commonwealth. But the important thing to note is that this one speech revealed just how tenuous the so-called international communist movement was, for even at its heart, in the socialist commonwealth, the nation was clearly the main reference point for the individual leaders of the communist bloc. The consequences of Khrushchev's denunciation of Stalin would continue to reverberate through the communist world (including among western communist parties: see Chapter 4) for many years to come.

Different countries reacted in a variety of ways to the speech, some maintaining orthodoxy with communism as handed down from the CPSU, others venturing to revise communism more to account for their own national characteristics, and then those who were subject to pressures from both orthodox and revisionist responses to Khrushchev's denunciation of Stalin. Some of the members of the world socialist system as noted had already fallen out with the Soviet leadership over both ideological and national differences. The biggest split in the international communist world was that between the USSR and the People's Republic of China following Stalin's death. This split had a much greater impact on international communism, for the Chinese Communist Party (CCP) under the leadership of Mao Zedong, challenged the CPSU's right to the leading role in the movement from an ideological standpoint.

There had been differences between these two largest of the ruling communist parties ever since (and indeed even before) the CCP took power in China in October 1949. One major point of contention was over Mao's divergent approach to socialist economics, as he moved further away from classical Stalinism culminating in the disastrous "Great Leap Forward" in 1958, in which masses of peasants in the countryside were supposed to bring about industrialization through numerous small-scale enterprises. In place of modern mechanized methods, human capital employing basic technologies would overcome the specific nature of Chinese backwardness. Hence, Mao was forsaking Stalinist methods of collectivization, making use of what he considered to be the advantage inherent in the social organization of rural China by marshalling the Chinese peasantry, the only resource that China had in abundance, into communes. As a consequence of the Great Leap Forward agricultural production dropped precipitately leading to one of the worst famines in human history, in which an estimated thirty million people perished. One recent estimate based upon research from newly available CCP archives suggests that 'at least 45 million people died unnecessarily between 1958 and 1962' (Dikotter, 2011, p. xii). Mao had long been resentful about his previous treatment from the Soviet CPSU leadership. For example, Stalin had earlier supported the nationalist

Chiang Kaishek, advising Mao and the communists to forge a united front with the nationalist Guomindang. Stalin had more faith in the nationalists than he did in the communists to gain power from the imperialist occupiers of China.

Mao considered himself to be not just the leader of the Chinese Revolution, but also an ideological leader in the wider communist world. Yet Mao was obsessed with total power, and the ideological debates between the USSR and China reflected more Mao's own personal ambitions than they did any real fundamental ideological differences. This is not to deny that there were deep ideological differences between the CPSU and the CCP, but rather to say that ideology was manipulated by Mao as part of his goal of maintaining his own power. Presenting himself and the Chinese Revolution as a beacon for the rest of the Third World was also more a reflection of Mao's domestic position and legitimacy, China's confrontation with the USSR, and a mixture of national geopolitical interests. The split however should not be seen as having been inevitable. One could argue that the split was really a loss for both sides as the West and capitalism came out victorious, reflecting a massive victory for international capitalism over international communism (see Chen, 2001). Most scholars focus on a mix of factors to explain the split between the two communist giants, including ideational and geopolitical forces, and the roles of key individuals, in particular Stalin, Khrushchev, and Mao. One important text, whilst noting the multiple causes of the rift nevertheless stresses the importance of differing ideologies (Luthi, 2008).

But in the end there can be little doubt that Mao himself was largely responsible for the rift with the Soviet Union. Indeed his part was so central that one observer suggests we should refer not to the "Sino-Soviet split," but to the "Mao-Soviet split" (Levine, 2010, p. 132; see also Chang and Halliday, 2005). Mao was indeed, similar to Stalin, a brutal and driven personality who would tolerate no dissent or any opposition from within the ranks of the CCP leadership.

Although some western policy makers had always recognized the potential for divisions to erupt between the USSR and the People's Republic of China (PRC), based on historical antagonisms, old simmering territorial disputes, the balance of power, and the absence of trust—most analysts did not at the time predict a rift. It was only with the border clashes of 1969 that the seriousness of the split became clearly evident to the rest of the world. Not only were the two communist powers far from representing a unified ideological bloc, they came very close to actually going to war with one another. As noted, the United States under Nixon's leadership took advantage of the rift to forge an effective balance of power with China against the USSR. The split in the international communist world was serious, but should not be exaggerated. As noted, the world socialist system was never a single cohesive grouping, but was almost from the beginning an instrument of the Soviet national security state, in large part held together after 1945 during the Cold War by Soviet military power. After the Sino-Soviet split only North Korea sided with Beijing. Enver Hoxha, the communist leader in Albania also supported the CCP, but he had already broken with Moscow and saw the split as an opportunity to gain economic aid from China. As will be demonstrated in the next chapter, the split did have an impact further afield as both the USSR and the PRC competed for influence in the Third World, offering different non-capitalist models of development. However, for the main components of the world socialist system the split did not have a major ideological impact. Its main impact was on the wider geopolitics of the Cold War.

In a top secret report on the work and priorities of KGB foreign operations in 1984, the year before Gorbachev came to power, the head of the KGB, Vladimir Kryuchkov, made it clear that China was seen as a major adversary and priority should be accorded to the gathering of intelligence from Beijing. Kryuchkov stated that the best agents in the organization should be recruited for this purpose (Andrew and Gordievsky, p. 12). The three stumbling blocks to repairing relations, from the Chinese side, were the Soviet war in Afghanistan, Soviet support for the Vietnamese occupation of Cambodia, and the unresolved bilateral territorial disputes between the two communist giants. It is instructive to note that none of these issues really reflected ideological differences. They were all to do with classic state interests relating to perceptions of the balance of power. Although the dispute between the two communist giants was often articulated in ideological terms, the reality was much more to do with traditional notions of the national interest.

The USSR and International Communism in the Late Soviet Period

When the Cominform was abolished in 1956, the USSR was left without a specific instrument for maintaining its influence directly over the international communist movement. Soviet control over the communist states in Eastern Europe was effectively maintained through the CMEA and the WTO. Ensuring ideological adherence to Soviet communism was now embedded directly in the CPSU apparatus, as well as in parts of the state structure. It was really impossible to separate out completely state and party organizations and interests. By definition, as noted in Chapter 2, the party and the state were effectively one and the same thing. By the post-Stalin era, institutions of both the party and the state were employed to maintain control over the international communist movement, with the continuing objective of serving Soviet interests.

The KGB's stated mission was to serve the party, and not the state. The First Chief Directorate of the KGB dealt with foreign intelligence, and its organizational structure was based on departments dealing with different geographical regions of the world, although there was one department that was responsible for "Liaison with Socialist Countries." The KGB controlled large sums of foreign currency that it filtered to "fraternal parties" through its own channels. A special "International Fund for Aid to Leftist Workers' Organizations" was established by the Central Committee of the CPSU, and the KGB would disperse some of these funds—$14 million in 1972 and 1973, and then from 1973 to 1977 $15 million annually, and other various sums until the end of détente. All communist parties of the Warsaw Pact (apart from Romania's) contributed each year around half a million dollars to the fund. The major beneficiaries of the fund were the Italian, French, and American communist parties (Volkogonov, 1998, p. 341).

However, it was the International Department of the Central Committee of the CPSU that became the leading organization dealing with non-ruling communist parties and with the wider international communist movement. It was through these institutions that the CPSU sought to ensure compliance with Soviet directives in the rest of the communist bloc. The International Department also had responsibility for the one-time influential communist periodical the *World Marxist Review* (in Russian it was entitled *Problemy mira i sotsializma* or *Problems of Peace and Socialism*). When it was established in 1958 the journal was designed as a mouthpiece for the ruling communist parties, but it quickly became an organ for mostly non-ruling communist parties. With headquarters in Prague, the majority of the editors were Russian nationals, and it was published in some forty-one different languages (Chinese, after the Sino-Soviet split, was not one of them). Both the KGB and The International Department had representatives in Soviet embassies abroad. There was then a tight nexus between these institutions designed to ensure conformity in the wider communist world to strictures handed down from the CPSU.

By the late 1970s it was evident that the revolutionary momentum in the USSR had dissipated, as the leadership of the CPSU ossified into an ageing collective leadership that was chiefly concerned with stability and order. Brezhnev's path to the apex of the CPSU system was typical of his generation. At the end of the Russian Civil War Brezhnev worked in an oil mill. He later became a metalworker, receiving training at the Kursk Technical School, and headed a metallurgical institute in Kamensk before proceeding on his party work in the 1930s, as Stalin's purges made room for a new generation of working class recruits to gain rapid promotion through the party's ranks. Brezhnev was one of the beneficiaries. As with his predecessor, Nikita Khrushchev, he lacked a university education, although unlike Khrushchev he was a mediocre conformist whilst pursuing his own party career. His speeches were sleep inducing and his written expression pedestrian, riddled with grammatical errors. Brezhnev, a man with no original ideas sought simply not to disrupt the status quo. Under Brezhnev, although Stalin was not fully rehabilitated, there was a cautious and less violent reincorporation of centralized discipline following Khrushchev's removal from office in 1964. The regime tightened censorship and due to his fear that any reform could undermine the system Brezhnev relied upon "extensive growth" (putting ever more natural and human resources into production) rather than "intensive growth" (increasing production through new technologies). Resource allocation was based upon the residual principle: whatever was left over after total expenditures were outlaid went to social welfare. This was a recipe for economic disaster, and revealed a bureaucratic regime lacking in initiative, let alone having any radical revolutionary fervour remaining in the pursuit of the original Bolshevik goals. Maintenance of the national security state and the military industrial complex had become the priority.

One of the great survivors of the Soviet system was Boris Ponomaryev, who was head of the International Department from 1955 until 1986. During his long tenure Ponomaryev— who was promoted to the Politburo as candidate member in

1972—remained a dedicated true believer in the Marxist-Leninist cause. Another survivor, and true believer, was Mikhail Suslov who as chief ideologist in the CPSU (and full Politburo member) was the general overseer of the International Department in the Party Secretariat. Going back as far as 1939 he was First Secretary of the Stavropol regional committee, a post Gorbachev would later take as he began his climb up the party ladder. Yet the Marxist-Leninist ideology these old CPSU apparatchiks represented and defended had become little more than a bureaucratic conservatism designed to preserve the slightly moderated and reformed Stalinist system. Insofar as this gerontocracy had any commitment to international communism it was to ensure that the Soviet communist bloc was held together, more for the interests of Soviet national security than for any real commitment to the wider communist cause. The USSR had moved a long way from the original revolutionaries' principled internationalism, and many of the old Bolsheviks would have been turning in their graves if they had witnessed the sclerotic, corrupt, and stagnant nature of the system that had developed by the 1980s, especially given the huge sacrifices that had been made in the earlier decades.

When he became General Secretary of the CPSU following Brezhnev's death in November 1982, Yuri Andropov, who had been in charge of the KGB for the previous fifteen years, took seriously the USSR's role as leader of the international communist movement. During his time at the helm of the KGB Andropov had instigated regular meetings between the security services of the other members of the socialist bloc in the struggle against "imperialist ideological sabotage." In addition to Moscow, meetings took place in Havana, Budapest, and Sofia and were 'as much an opportunity for Moscow to give direction to "fraternal organs" as to co-ordinate activities and exchange experience' (Volkogonov, 1998, p. 341). In 1956 Andropov was Soviet ambassador to Hungary, and he played an important part in putting down the uprising there in November of that year, helping facilitate the arrest of Prime Minister Imre Nagy and Defence Minister Pal Maleter. Andropov also persuaded Janos Kadar to pursue a loyal pro-Soviet stance and to agree to head a Hungarian government put together in the Kremlin (Volkogonov, 1998, p. 334). Also serving in the Soviet embassy in Hungary at the time of the Soviet intervention was Vladimir Kryuchkov. When Chernenko died in 1985 Kryuckhov supported Gorbachev to succeed him as General

Secretary of the CPSU. At the time he was head of the Foreign Intelligence Directorate of the KGB. Gorbachev appointed him head of the KGB in 1988. Three years later Kryuchkov was one of the instigators of the coup against Gorbachev.

The main events that now brought the world's communists together were the CPSU Congresses in Moscow. At the 26th Party Congress in 1981, for example, in addition to the delegates from the ruling communist parties (minus Albania and China) there were also some sixty-nine non-ruling communist parties represented. At the end, as the Soviet communist system was about to expire, in those last few years of stagnation under an ossified ageing gerontocracy some fraternal communists from abroad still paid homage to the USSR, travelling to Moscow for instructions, for rest and recreation and, as Volkogonov notes, most of all for money (p. 390). For the ruling communist elite of the Soviet bloc visits to Moscow were more often for direct instructions from the Kremlin.

Gorbachev has been portrayed in the West as a radical reformer who brought Soviet Communism to an end. Yet during the Soviet military intervention in Czechoslovakia to put down the Prague Spring in 1968, whilst serving as First Secretary of the Stavropol communist party apparatus, Gorbachev has acknowledged that he 'took part directly in an attempt to contain rising criticism in regard to Czechoslovak events', and hence in effect to prevent any discussion as to the matter of its correctness (Gorbachev and Mlynar, 2002, p. 43). In the end Gorbachev turned out to be more the doctrinaire Marxist-Leninist than was Deng, his counterpart in China, when it came to the question of market reform, privatization and de-collectivization. In the end reforming the Soviet political system created increased freedom for the East European countries to choose their own paths. As it turned out they all, without exception, would eventually choose to break free of the Soviet embrace and also to ditch Marxism-Leninism in favour of the capitalist market and political pluralism, thereby exposing once and for all the fiction of a common "socialist commonwealth" or of any remaining semblance of an international communist movement. Brezhnev's fear of contagion through the rest of the bloc if one member should be allowed to defect turned out to be justified. Once Gorbachev loosened the ties that bound the bloc together by renouncing the Brezhnev Doctrine (that he had earlier supported in the case of Czechoslovakia) the system rapidly fell apart. The communist states of Eastern Europe had finally achieved their rights to national self-determination.

Conclusion

The original conception of the communist international (Comintern) was to foster and assist socialist revolution wherever it might manifest itself. However, it very quickly became a tool of the CPSU to serve its own interests and those of the Soviet State. This was true too of its successor, the Cominform controlled by the International Department of the Central Committee of the CPSU. This is not to say that the international component of Marxism-Leninism was no more than a cover for Soviet state interests, or that the Soviet state was no longer wedded in some manner to an internationalist approach. As will be shown in the next chapter, there developed a perceived obligation on the Soviet side to provide international support to states undergoing socialist development during the Cold War that created some very difficult situations for the USSR in the Third World, and as a consequence in relations with the United States. However, the Comintern, the Cominform, and the International Department of the Central Committee, and the First Chief Directorate of the KGB, despite their stated internationalist orientation, were in effect primarily state agents to further the interests of the ruling Soviet communist party, even where this involved support for foreign communist parties and other Marxist groups. Although these institutions represented the Soviet state, their activities in the wider international communist movement, as will be shown in the next chapter, would actually undermine Soviet national interests.

Another important lesson (covered in more detail in Chapter 6) in rethinking Soviet Communism in relation to the wider international communist movement and the world socialist system, relates to the power of nationalism. Opposition to Moscow's dictates led East European communist regimes to adopt a defensive nationalism in their attempts to break free of the Soviet embrace. Within the Soviet Union Gorbachev's political reforms led not to a strengthening of a common Soviet identity, but the mobilization of the masses around national identities. Although it was clear what most of the rest of the world thought about Marxism-Leninism and the Soviet experiment—that it had been a disaster for the Russian people, the wider non-Russian citizens of the USSR, the East European communist bloc, and for international politics during the Cold War—Gorbachev to the end clung to his belief that the October Revolution had heralded a new dawn and that a softer kind of Soviet socialism could have been created. Gorbachev's reign of all the major Soviet leaders (Lenin, Stalin, Khrushchev, Brezhnev) was the shortest: just six years (equivalent to one term for the current Russian president). Yet in that time Soviet Communism and along with it the international communist movement collapsed. In part it collapsed as a direct result of the failure of the Soviet Union to foster a common post-national identity among the various components that made up the world of international communism.

4

Soviet Communism and the Third World

To reiterate once more: Lenin and the Bolsheviks instigated the October Revolution in the name of the international proletariat, but always assumed that a socialist revolution could not succeed in Russia alone, and that it was necessary for its survival there for revolutions to take place in the more advanced countries of the capitalist West. Yet the irony was that socialism did not then come to Munich or Manchester, but it did come, in 1921, to Mongolia. Following the defeat of Nazism in Germany the Third World would actually become the main theatre of contestation between the Soviet Union and the United States. Although the sources of the Cold War were in Europe and its foundations remained there until the fall of the Berlin Wall in 1989, the major arena of superpower competition in both ideological and geo-strategic terms was in the Third World (what is now referred to as the Global South). On the eve of the October Revolution European or American colonial powers had direct rule over much of the Caribbean, the Middle East, Africa and Asia, and even as war broke out once more in 1939 around one billion of the world's population were still subject to colonial rule (Bradley, 2011, p. 464). This made fertile ground for contestation between the USA and the USSR, as national liberation movements sought independence from imperial control.

The very first issue taken to the newly established UN Security Council (UNSC) was a dispute in the Third World. Towards the end of the Second World War, Soviet and British troops had occupied parts of northern Iran to keep Germany at bay, and both sides agreed to remove them after the war, by March 1946. Not only did Stalin refuse to adhere to this agreement, he sent in an additional 15,000 troops to augment the 60,000 already there (Haslam, 2011, p. 48). Stalin recognized the potency of the Azeri and Kurdish claims for national independence in the northern part of Iran. The USSR tried to establish a separate Azeri state where Soviet troops were stationed during the war, and although the local communist party was strong Stalin had greater faith in the nationalists to counter neo-imperialism than he did the communists. One key objective was to deny the West control over Iranian oil resources. Stalin did not consider that Iran itself had true revolutionary prospects, due to its socio-economic structures and the absence of a strong working class. However, in the end the USSR's demands rallied nationalists in Iran to oppose the USSR and forced Iran to foster closer ties to Washington. This issue was only resolved after British and American pressure at the UN persuaded Stalin to withdraw Soviet forces. The Third World also saw the first major military conflict of the Cold War when, with Soviet approval, North Korea invaded South Korea in 1950, drawing in both China and the United States. The world also came closest to nuclear Armageddon in the Third World, in the Caribbean during the Cuban missile crisis of October 1962. The Middle East too was an arena fraught with dangers, linked to the Arab-Israeli conflict. And some have argued that the end of the Cold War was in large part due to the Soviet intervention and long war in Afghanistan, another Third World arena.

In relation to fostering world socialism the KGB's responsibilities in the Cold War period came to focus more on the non-communist left, leaving the International Department of the Central Committee of the CPSU to look after Soviet relations with foreign communist movements and liberation movements in the Third World, whilst the Central Committee Department of Liaison with Communist and Workers' Parties had the specific task of dealing with the ruling communist parties in the socialist commonwealth. Much has been written about the role of the CIA during the Cold War (and beyond) in US policies and practices in the Third World. Less has been said about the role of the KGB, partly due to the far less transparent nature of the Soviet communist system. Yet, as important as the CIA's role was in US Third World policy—and few would question that it played a large one—the KGB's influence in Soviet Third World policy and practice was perhaps greater still. Secret documents that have come to light since the end of the Cold War show that 'For a quarter of a century, the KGB, unlike the CIA, believed that the Third World was the arena in which it could win the Cold War' (Andrew and Mitrokhin, 2005, p. xxvi). Yet in the end it was the arena in which the Soviet Union would eventually lose the Cold War.

Lenin, the Bolsheviks, and the Third World

The Bolsheviks did not entirely ignore the Third World in the early years after the Revolution. Indeed, a Congress of the People's of the East was convened in Baku in 1920, the purpose of which was to encourage anti-imperialist revolutions in colonies controlled by the West. A small group of local communists, assisted by Soviet soldiers, gained power in Ulan Bator in 1921, henceforth turning Mongolia into a sort of testing ground for Soviet communist policy in the Third World (Westad, 2007, p. 51). One of the principal contributions Lenin made to Marxist theory was effectively to globalize it, to bring in the non-European world that was almost entirely ignored by Marx, whose main focus was on the mature capitalist states in Europe. Lenin would also veer from the economic determinism of Marxism, transforming what was a theory of the mature capitalist state in Western Europe into a theory of global imperialism, where revolution would come first to the weaker links of the imperialist chain. The laws of economics for classical Marxists, through predictable stages of development, would eventually result in victory for socialism. For Lenin the revolution could be made through a small vanguard of committed revolutionaries with the will necessary to carry it out, even in a less modernized country. In one of the most often quoted of his lines Marx wrote: 'It is not the consciousness of men that determines their existence, but their social existence that determines their consciousness' (Marx, 1859). The state of socialist development could only be reached when industrialism and capitalism had produced a solid, mass working class base.

There are those, such as Steven Smith (1983) and Sheila Fitzpatrick (2008) who have made the case that the Russian Revolution was a workers' revolution, but this cannot really stand up to scrutiny for what should be clear reasons. Russia at the beginning of the twentieth century was, as Trotsky (1964, p. 43) pointed out backward, and as Lenin (1923, p. 288) still had to acknowledge in his final writings it was a country with a tiny proletariat that lacked a mature class-consciousness (what he referred to as a working class lacking education and culture). In the end it was Lenin who had the will to lead a revolution in the name of the working class in an empire full of peasants. Bukharin had argued that it was necessary, due to the social make-up of the population, to move gradually and to 'ride into socialism on a peasant's nag' (quoted in Haynes, 1985, p. 116). The vast majority of the population of the Russian empire lived in the countryside, often in abject poverty, ignorant, and illiterate. Stalin would foreswear Bukharin's path and engage in a campaign to 'smash the Kulaks' (that is, the wealthier peasants) in a rapid drive to modernize the Soviet economy and hence build in its wake the working class that was largely absent in 1917. The forced collectivization of agricultural production was part of this modernizing project. The Russian experience from the outset was perhaps always more relevant to the conditions pertaining in the less developed world.

What came to be labelled Marxism-Leninism therefore can be viewed not so much as an adaptation of Marxism, as a departure from it. A comparison can be made here with Al Qaeda and its claim to operate according to the strictures of Islam, when in fact it too acts as a "vanguard" claiming to represent the Muslims of the world whilst acting directly counter to the strict teachings of the Koran. It perhaps was appropriate that in its third edition the *Great Soviet Encyclopedia* (1969) dropped the separate entry for Marxism that it had in the earlier editions, and carried now only the entry "Marxism-Leninism"; and a Dictionary of Scientific Communism would also have no separate heading for Marx or Marxism, but it did have a long section on Marxism-Leninism (*Nauchnii kommunizm. Slovar*, 1980).

John H. Kautsky (grandson of the leading Marxist who sparred with Lenin, Karl Kautsky) argues that one must distinguish between Marxism and Leninism, rather than seeing Marxism-Leninism as a single ideology. It is simply not credible, he argues, to claim that the leaders of German and Austrian social democracy and leaders of revolutionary movements in Ethiopia and Angola were motivated by the same ideology (Kautsky, 2002, p. xix). Kautsky argues: 'What little Marxism there was in Russia died with Menshevism and the triumph of Leninism long ago' (p. 2) Here, we see Leninism as a non-Marxist ideology, even if initially inspired by Marx's works. Marx was concerned with industrialism, Lenin with underdevelopment. Marx's focus was on the working classes in developed European states; Lenin held a strong belief in the revolutionary potential of intellectuals supported by peasants in the periphery of the global imperial system; whereas Marx saw the revolution coming about due to the contradictions within developed capitalism led by the working class, Lenin's revolution would come first in non-developed countries through a political party of a new type led by a small group of intellectuals in the name of a working class that was more aspirational than it was reality. The objective for Lenin in undertaking the Russian Revolution was modernization and development, the establishment of a modern industrial state that would become a dictatorship of the proletariat. However, although one can argue that Leninism was successful (albeit at huge human cost) in forcing modernization on the Russian-Soviet Empire, the system that was created would eventually be unable to sustain itself once an advanced industrial infrastructure had been built. And the workers were never to gain control of the state as the ruling communist party ended up creating a type of system in which power was concentrated in the hands of a small bureaucratic elite.

The Russian Revolution itself was partly justified in terms of national liberation, as Lenin promised the subject peoples of the Tsarist Empire that if they supported the Bolsheviks then they would gain their natural right to national independence. It was also recognized that Russia was on the periphery of the global imperial system. Hence, from the very outset, the dual forces of nationalism and underdevelopment were recognized by the Russian revolutionaries as key factors pertaining to the future prospects for radical revolutionary challenges to the contemporary ("highest") stage of capitalism. That stage, as Lenin described it was "imperialism," defined as monopoly capitalism. Soviet Communism from the very beginning had as a central component of its ideology, and the goals it wished to achieve, developments in what would become known in the second half of the twentieth century as the "Third World." The Third World here is defined as those underdeveloped countries controlled (politically and/or economically) by western capitalist states, from Latin America through Africa and the Middle East to Asia. One can classify Russia itself at the turn of the twentieth century as part of the Third World, due to the fact that the bulk of development at that time was financed by western loans or investments, and because Russia was largely dependent on exports of natural resources. And even then, before the First World War, all of Russia's big power stations were under foreign control, as too were 90 percent of Russia's mining industries (Hill, 1972, p. 23). Where there was heavy industry, it was mostly foreign-owned.

In the context of a world defined in economic and class terms the Third World would become the key arena in the Cold War struggle between the USA and the USSR in both the ideological dimension and in the geostrategic arena (the latter aspect is covered in more detail in Chapter 7). As noted in the previous chapter states undergoing a process of socialist orientation in the Third World were seen as comprising a key component in the "world revolutionary process." These states emerged, often through terrorism and guerrilla warfare conducted by movements of national liberation seeking to gain freedom from colonial control. And this provided Soviet Communism with the best prospects for widening its influence, or at least it was viewed this way in Moscow, especially among leading elements in the KGB and the International Department. Given that the CPSU's legitimacy was based upon adherence to Leninism and the idea of world socialism and revolution, Soviet leaders found it difficult to discriminate between anti-colonial movements on the basis of purely strategic interest, leading them to support some movements that actually undermined the Soviet national interest. At the least it was difficult for the USSR to refuse assistance to national liberation movements in the Third World if the leadership wished to be seen as being in step with its own ideological strictures.

Soviet Communism and the Anti-Colonial Movement

One of the most significant developments in global politics in the second half of the twentieth century was the demise of the European overseas colonial empires. Although there were important structural factors that would explain this phenomenon, linked to the weakening of the European powers during the two world wars, following the Bolshevik Revolution in 1917 there was also an ideational component. The Second World War had a double impact on the Third World. First it undermined imperial power in material terms, as Britain and France and Germany suffered severe losses in the relative global balance of power. And second, colonialism lost any legitimacy it ever enjoyed, as it had now become morally indefensible. As this final stage of imperialism unfolded, the Cold War between the two superpowers coincidentally became the dominant force in global politics. The balance of power after 1945 gave way to a bipolar system in which two superpowers vied for influence. The Third World was bound to become a major theatre of contestation. Clearly, the rapid development of new states provided opportunities for the big powers to expand their influence. Between 1957 and 1962 twenty-five new states were created. As noted in the Introduction, both of the extra-European superpowers had since the beginning of the twentieth century been advocates of the rights of nations to self-determination. However, Soviet communism offered the most attractive model for many new national indigenous intellectuals in pursuit of liberation from colonial rule. Although not as extensive as those of the Europeans, the USA itself had an empire (which included the Philippines, Micronesia, the Marshall Islands and Panama). It also had influence in Latin America, which it maintained regularly through military interventions (justified by the "Monroe Doctrine" established by US President James Monroe in 1823 that gave notice to outside powers that the Western hemisphere was an American sphere of influence). American interests in the African continent were also coloured historically by a sense of shame: as they had been almost entirely linked to the Slave trade.

Soviet Communism offered emerging Third World national elites a regime type and an ideological system that was sold as being more compatible for their countries than the Western capitalist and democratic systems. There was a natural affinity between Soviet Marxism-Leninism and Third World national liberation. As Kautsky has put it: 'Leninism appeals to alienated individuals in underdeveloped countries and promises to bring them to power and to realize the rapid industrialization of their backward societies' (2002, p. 3). Leninism was more suited to the Third World due to its emphasis on revolutionary modernization and anti-imperialism, and the key role apportioned to individual intellectual leaders. Lenin's conception of the single-ruling party was clearly attractive to many of the leaders in the Third World, from Mao Zedong in China; Mengistu Haile Mariam in Ethiopia; Fidel Castro in Cuba; Pol Pot in Cambodia; Ho Chi Minh in

Vietnam; and many others in various parts of Africa, Asia, and Latin America. Yet each of the key individuals, who played such important roles in their respective country's revolutions, began their campaigns in nationalist colours, seeking greater independence from either direct or indirect western controls. For Moscow the expectation was that the struggles for liberation in the Third World would shift from a national/anti-colonial stance to a communist/anti-capitalist one. But it was not only radicals in pursuit of a socialist alternative in their countries that would be influenced by the Soviet one-party totalitarian model: so too were dictators such as Saddam Hussein in Iraq and Muammar al-Gaddafi in Libya. Saddam and Gaddafi would both receive advice on secret police methods from Soviet and East German advisers. Yet the regimes in Iraq and Libya were far from being communist.

In Southeast Asia the French and the British (followed by the Americans) were faced with national liberation revolutions that would eventually take a radical socialist turn. In Northern Africa the French were confronted with national liberation movements that similarly took on socialist overtones; and then the Portuguese fought against nationalists in southern Africa who also turned to radical leftist politics. Hence, for example, we had Vietnam, Algeria, and Angola, three very different parts of the Third World, fighting for independence from their colonial masters, and all moving quickly along some kind of socialist oriented path. Whilst the USSR would seek to take selective advantage of this situation, it was at the same time in a sense compelled to assist in anti-imperial revolutions due to ideological norms. And then there was the question of competing for influence in the Third World with the other large communist power, China.

As noted in the previous chapter the establishment of the People's Friendship University (Patrice Lumumba) in 1960 was designed to provide ideological training and to influence the thousands of African and Asian students who studied there. Akin to a Marxist-Leninist Madrasa, the University was designed to create a global network of pro-Soviet elites throughout the Third World. Students shared accommodation, meals, classes, and even engaged in work brigades along with their fellow Soviet, mainly Russian, students. It is not surprising therefore that many important friendships were formed that would lead later to important political contacts. The extent to which this worked was evidenced by the important positions that some former foreign students attained in their home countries. Also, many of the foreign male students ended up marrying local Russian women, hence eventually creating a substantial Soviet diaspora in some Third World countries.

Classical, or traditional Marxism naturally did appeal to leftists in the advanced capitalist states, but *Leninism* was the radical revolutionary ideology that inspired leaders fighting against colonial rule in the underdeveloped world. Soviet Communism in essence, whatever its origins, can be more accurately viewed as a revolutionary ideology of modernization and development along non-capitalist lines most relevant to the underdeveloped Third World. As the next chapter will show, a variety of radical socialist alternatives would develop in Western Europe that would veer further away from the Soviet Leninist model. The blanket term "Euro-Communism" would gain wide currency, thus distinguishing the European communist parties from the CPSU and Soviet Communism. Leninism would have far more influence in the Third World than it would in the developed capitalist states.

The Comintern was initially the main instrument through which the Soviet regime supported rebellions against colonialism in the Third World, rebellions that were seen as both an initial stage towards possible socialist development and a means to weaken the global reach of the major capitalist powers. In the United States, President Woodrow Wilson, an outspoken champion of nations having the right to self-determination, stated in his joint session to the US Congress in February 1918 that ending imperialism was not just a high-sounding phrase, it was 'an imperative principle of action' (cited in Talbot, 2008, p. 152). Whilst Wilson was the architect of the ill-fated League of Nations, the Comintern sponsored the League Against Imperialism (LAI). The LAI held its inaugural conference in Brussels in 1927 and shared the same purpose as Wilson—to end colonialism, but not in the name of the nation but in the name of the international proletariat.

The Soviet Communist Party and government apparatus divided the anti-colonial countries along geographical lines, reflected in the development of a number of research and policy institutes of the Soviet Academy of Sciences (party-controlled "think tanks"): the Oriental Institute (established in 1930); the African Institute (established in 1959); and the Latin American Institute (established in 1961). Much of Soviet thinking on the Third World emanated from scholars attached to these institutes.

The Oriental Institute covered countries in Asia and the Middle East (which included North Africa). The following sections will go on to briefly assess each of these areas separately before then making an overall evaluation of Soviet Communism's influence in the Third World.

Africa

In Africa, South Africa was the greatest hope for class warfare from a traditional Marxist perspective, as it was the most developed and industrialized country on the continent. The first Chairman of the Communist Party of South Africa (CPSA), Bill Andrews, was a member of the Comintern's Executive Committee. A pro-communist member of the African National Congress (ANC) with links to Moscow was also appointed head of the South African section of the LAI. Nelson Mandela always denied belonging to the CPSA, but after his death in 2013 the CPSA proudly announced that Mandela had been a member of the party's Central Committee in 1960 and remained so when he was later imprisoned. Mandela also helped to impose the CPSA's strategy of violent armed struggle on what was then an otherwise reluctant ANC leadership, and he acted as the leader of the ANC's armed wing (Smith, 2014, p. 17). Although it should be noted that Mandela always disputed the common claim that the ANC shared similar goals to the CPSA, stating in his defence to the South African court after being arrested in 1962 that although the ANC had been in close cooperation with the CPSA: 'The ideological creed of the ANC is, and always has been, the creed of African Nationalism … the ANC has never … advocated a revolutionary change in the economic structure of the country, nor … ever condemned capitalism' (Mandela, 1995, p. 503). Once more, the pull of nationalism was greater than any sense of class solidarity, despite Mandela's membership of the Communist Party.

During this earlier period many African and American blacks studied in either the Lenin or the Stalin schools in the Soviet Union (see Chapter 3). They did so for the most part in secret, having been giving false identities (Andrew and Mitrokhin, p. 423). However, it was not in South Africa that communism (or a "socialist orientation") would emerge victorious, but in the less developed parts of the African continent, especially in the "frontline states" standing in opposition to the neighbouring apartheid regime in

Pretoria. The frontline states included Angola, Botswana, Lesotho, Mozambique, Swaziland, Tanzania and (after its independence in 1980) Zimbabwe. Of these, Angola, Mozambique, Tanzania, and Zimbabwe were all courted by the USSR and were considered by leading scholars in the Africa Institute at some stage of their development to be states of socialist orientation. The Soviet Union was the largest supplier of arms to the ANC during its struggle against the minority white regime in South Africa, and it gained a positive reputation for this among the frontline states. Of the thirteen Treaties of Friendship and Cooperation (TFC) that the USSR signed with Third World states between 1971 and 1984 six were with African states (see Table 4.1). States that were bilateral partners of the USSR in these treaties were considered to be the core Third World countries in Moscow's ideological and geo-strategic competition with the United States (on Soviet relations with its closest Third World allies see Light, 1993).

In addition to these core countries other countries of socialist orientation were considered important elements in the wider world socialist system. These states included at various times Algeria, Grenada, Laos, Libya, Nicaragua, North Korea, Tanzania, and Zimbabwe.

Table 4.1   Soviet treaties of friendship and cooperation with Third World countries

Country	Date	Duration
Egypt	May 1971 (abrogated March 1976)	15 years
India	August 1971	20
Iraq	April 1972	15
Somalia	July 1974 (abrogated November 1977)	20
Angola	October 1976	20
Mozambique	March 1977	20
Vietnam	November 1978	25
Ethiopia	November 1978	20
Afghanistan	December 1978	20
South Yemen	October 1979	20
Syria	October 1980	20
Congo	May 1981	20
North Yemen	October 1984	20

Angola and Ethiopia

The military coup in Lisbon that overthrew the Portuguese regime in April 1974 quickly led to the unravelling of Portugal's colonies in Southern Africa, with various independence movements vying to fill the political vacuum, leading to civil war in both Angola and Mozambique. The Angolan civil war drew in the superpowers, South Africa, and China, as well as other neighbouring African states. China was concerned that a victory for the Soviet and Cuban-backed Popular Movement for the Liberation of Angola (MPLA) would undermine Chinese influence in the Third World as a model of socialist development, and hence the CCP provided support to the National Front for the Liberation of Angola (FNLA). The US also gave support to the FNLA as well as the National Union for the Total Liberation of Angola (UNITA). In the end, thanks to the significant direct military participation of Cuban troops the MPLA, under the leadership of Soviet-backed Antonio Aghostino Neto, claimed victory. Although the USSR played a major role in facilitating the MPLA victory, Neto was actually much closer to the Cuban regime, having good personal relationships with both Ernesto "Che" Guevera and Fidel Castro. Castro's commitment to the MPLA was based on ideological foundations, whereas for Brezhnev the greater concern was the global geostrategic competition with the United States and China (see Shearman, 1987, chapter 5). Castro had a North-South conception of the world, as opposed to the USSR's dominant East-West focus. Hence Moscow and Havana came to the issue of the Third World from different starting points. The US and China were also at this time cooperating in providing training to the FNLA.

In the Horn of Africa the USSR ended up being faced with a dilemma, as two client states of socialist orientation, Ethiopia and Somalia, both recipients of Soviet economic and military aid in the mid-1970s ended up in a war with one another, forcing Moscow to take sides. When in the summer of 1977 Somalia invaded Ethiopia over ethnic, tribal, and territorial issues using arms supplied by Moscow the Soviet Union airlifted military equipment and transported Cuban soldiers to Ethiopia to help the Mengistu regime counter the attack. Soviet military advisers were also provided. Ethiopia, unlike other parts of Africa, had managed to fight off European colonization, long being ruled itself by an emperor (Haile Selassie between 1930 and 1974). After Selassie was overthrown one of the leaders of the communist Derg movement, Mengistu Haile Mariam, emerged as dictatorial leader of Ethiopia, instigating a "Red Terror" during which many thousands lost their lives (between 1977 and 1978). Mengistu fled into exile in Zimbabwe in 1991, wanted on charges of genocide by an Ethiopian court. Unlike many other Third World revolutionary leaders Mengistu had not received any education in the USSR. As an officer in the Ethiopian army he did some training in Maryland, in the United States, where he experienced racism, which helped to radicalize him and foster strong anti-American sentiments. Where the Soviet Union provided military support, in the cases for example of Angola and Ethiopia it did so either under secret agreements it had reached or under the rubric of the TFCs it had concluded with those states, for these agreements and treaties had clauses calling for cooperation in the military realm in the event of hostilities from a third party.

Although Soviet policy towards the Third World always had a strong ideological component, under Brezhnev strategic factors became increasingly important in the geopolitical competition not just with the United States, but also with China. The orthodox Leninist view considered that states of socialist orientation had created the conditions necessary for socialist development: a vanguard revolutionary party, development of a strong state, land reform, central planning, and an anti-imperialist foreign policy (see for example, Brutents, 1976; Kosukhin, 1980; Koval, Semenov and Shul'govksi, 1974). Yet it was becoming clear in the 1970s, at the time of the USSR's strongest commitment to Third World socialist regimes, and as a consequence of the intimate knowledge derived from first-hand practical experience in assisting them, that socialism was not viable in these poor, underdeveloped states. This was especially the case in Africa and Southwest Asia. They were not only lacking an industrial infrastructure and strong working class base, they were also riven with tribal, religious, and ethnic conflicts.

One should note that despite the significant aid that the USSR gave to African client states, many Soviet officials and citizens who were actively engaged in the continent showed strong signs of racism against African blacks. Many of the students at the Lenin School and at Patrice Lumumba University in Moscow also experienced high levels of discrimination and racial abuse. Whilst undertaking his studies on Marxism-Leninism in the Soviet capital in 1933, Jomo Kenyatta, future revolutionary leader of Kenya, complained in an official letter addressed to the head of the Comintern of black African students being referred to as "monkeys." He also wrote of 'the derogatory portrayal of Negroes in the cultural institutions of the Soviet Union' (quoted in Andrew and Mitrokhin, 2005, p. 424). Despite official pronouncements of class solidarity and sympathy for the downtrodden masses of the African continent indications were that many Soviet citizens and communist leaders were as racist in their views as the apartheid regime in Pretoria they sought to overthrow. This is more evidence that sentiments other than class solidarity were commonly manifest among the Soviet people, despite decades of socialization, propaganda, and ideological training. Racism would emerge as an ugly and strong force in post-Soviet Russia (see Larys and Mares, 2011; Matthews and Nemstova, 2011; Worger, 2012).

North Africa and the Middle East

Soviet influence in the Middle East began with military aid to Egypt. Gamal Abdel Nasser, aged thirty-six years, took power in Cairo in 1954 ending British colonial rule, and putting Egypt on an anti-western course. The USSR saw opportunities and by the next year, through Czech intermediaries, Moscow began supplying Egypt with military equipment. Nasser demonstrated his commitment to an anti-western stance in July 1956 when he nationalized the Suez Canal, control of which by the West was seen in the wider Arab world as a symbol of imperialist exploitation. The subsequent attempt, in October 1956, by joint forces from Britain and France, in league with Israel, to retake control of the canal served to bring the USSR and Egypt closer together. Nasser undertook a three-week tour of the Soviet Union in 1958, where he was given a hero's welcome. When he returned to Egypt, in a speech to a huge crowd Nasser stated that the USSR was 'a friendly country with no ulterior motive [and] held the Arab nation in great esteem' (quoted in Andrew and Mitrokhin, 2005, p. 149). Khrushchev honoured Nasser with the award of Hero of the Soviet Union. One of his comrades in the Soviet leadership would complain that Khrushchev was honouring a leader who 'drove Communists into concentration camps' (Andrew and Mitrokhin, 2005, p. 142). Whereas the KGB continued to forge links with indigenous communist parties in the Middle East, the Soviet Communist Party leadership was maintaining formal relations with governments that had either banned communist parties or at the least were suppressing their ability to engage in open politics.

After initially viewing the Baath regime that took power in Syria in 1963 with hostility, within a few months the anti-Western stance that Damascus took, along with its nationalization of key industries, led the CPSU International Department and KGB to see possibilities for gaining influence. Although the Baath regime banned the Syrian Communist Party the Soviet Union nevertheless began to supply Syria with arms and military advisers, and by 1964 was providing education in Moscow to the young adult children of the new Syrian elite. After the Six Day War in 1967, in which Israel took control of the Golan Heights from Syria, Damascus relied increasingly on Soviet military supplies. The Syrian regime was unstable during the first few years of Baath rule, as the party was split into factions. When Hafez al-Assad eventually took power Moscow began to supply Syria with more top-line military equipment (including surface-to-air missiles, and later more advanced SS-21 weapons systems). When the troubles began in Syria during the Arab Spring in 2011, it was estimated that there were some 30,000 Russian citizens who had been long-term residents there, mostly the wives of Syria's elite, a factor which would help, in part, explain Putin's stance on the issue (*New York Times*, July 1, 2012). The TFC that the USSR concluded with Iraq, which strengthened defence ties between the two countries, was followed by agreements for the USSR to refine Iraq's oil, to build a refinery at Mosul, and help construct a nuclear reactor. The goals here, as Iraqi communists were hounded and imprisoned, were economic and strategic, rather than ideological.

Whereas some leaders in Africa, Latin America, the Caribbean, and Southeast Asia became popular communist leaders (for example, Neto, Castro, Guevara, Mao, Ho, Allende, Arbenz, and Ortega), communists in the Middle East were generally ostracized, and the charismatic leaders and dictators in the region in their anti-Western policies took on a more openly nationalistic orientation. Arab nationalists, despite their ties with Moscow and reliance on Soviet arms ended up taking an anti-communist course. Yet the official stance in Moscow was that the Arab-Israeli dispute was a part of the global struggle pitting neo-imperialism against communism with Israel a surrogate acting in the interests of the United States. Hence the policy of supplying arms to Iraq, Syria, and (until the October war of 1973) to Egypt was justified in these stretched ideological terms. As communists were hounded in many countries, forcing them underground and in some cases defeating them entirely, ethnicity and/or religion became the chief mobilizing forces in opposing dictatorial regimes. One of the legacies of Soviet-US competition and interference in the Third World was the rise of radical Islamism that emerged at the end of the Cold War.

In relation to the global Cold War struggle with the United States in the Third World, Egypt had been the USSR's first and the most significant gain. The loss of Egypt occurred due to a variety of factors, including leadership change following Nasser's death in 1970, as his successor, Anwar al-Sadat, was part of a group in the Egyptian leadership opposed to the pro-Soviet faction. As former Soviet foreign minister Andrei Gromyko recalled in his memoirs, the Soviets had always been suspicious of Sadat, for his political history included terrorist activities, membership of the Muslim Brotherhood (although he would later be assassinated by this group), rabid anti-communism, and sympathy for Hitler and his racist ideology (Gromyko, 1989, p. 348). But more pertinent was Sadat's engagement with American officials that would lead eventually to his visit to Jerusalem in October 1977 and to the Camp David peace agreement with Israel fostered by the US under President Jimmy Carter. Also, unlike in Syria, Soviet advisers in Egypt remained aloof from the indigenous population and were not warmly received. There was little social interaction between the Soviet expatriates and the locals, and marriage between Russians and Egyptians was 'virtually unknown' (Andrew and Mitrokhin, 2005, p. 153). Then there was the greater material power and diplomatic influence that the United States had in the wider Middle East and especially relating to Israel, demonstrated in the wake of the October War in 1973. Leadership change, cultural differences, and power calculations eventually undermined Soviet influence in what had been considered the jewel in the crown of Soviet Third World influence, leading Egypt effectively to switch sides, with the US becoming its greatest source of aid.

Asia

Where communist regimes came to power independently rather than being imposed by Soviet tanks they were to be found mostly in Asia. From Korea, through China, Vietnam, Laos, Cambodia—and even Russia, if we count the Tsarist Empire as a Eurasian entity—then communism seemed to be largely an Asian phenomenon. In Southwest Asia too, the initial rise of a communist regime in Kabul after the overthrow of the monarchy in 1973 had little or nothing to do with Moscow. Indeed, the USSR had initially instructed the communist party in Afghanistan not to try to take advantage of the situation by seeking to grab power for itself. Although the Soviet leadership was obliged to justify its intervention in Afghanistan in 1979 in Leninist terms it was obvious to anyone who had private contacts with Soviet officials, that the single primary motive was geostrategic, as the Kremlin feared instability on the USSR's southern borders at a time when the US under President Jimmy Carter had announced the Persian Gulf region a sphere of vital American interest. As noted above, Russia in 1917 too was a backward country, not really part of the modernized and developed world centred in the West. Russia has always been (partly) in the West, but it has never really been fully a part of the West. As a Eurasian state, straddling both Europe and Asia, arguably it has been Russia's Asiatic characteristics that have determined its authoritarian regime types and made it more susceptible to Leninism.

Asia became a tense geopolitical and ideological theatre of superpower confrontation immediately after war against Germany. The Chinese Revolution in 1949 followed almost immediately by the Korean War were important turning points that dragged the world's two competing powers into Asia's orbit. The Soviet leadership initially saw the Chinese communist revolution in positive terms as Mao pursued a clear Marxist-Leninist path. However, at the outset Stalin actually had more faith in the power of nationalism, and: 'Even during the victorious Mao Zedong's visit to Moscow in 1949–1950 Stalin persisted in treating the Chinese Communists as representatives of a national revolutionary democratic government, rather than a communist one … Stalin aimed at getting a treaty that was conducive to Soviet security, rather than an alliance between two Communist-led states' (Westad, 2007, p. 65). Khrushchev focused more on the Third World after Stalin's death. His first major overseas visit was to China in 1954 followed by visits to India, Burma, and Afghanistan in 1955. When he came to power Khrushchev's priority in the Third World was to give momentum to the socialist alliance with China, (with the USSR playing the leading role). The total cost of the assistance program carried out under the Sino-Soviet Friendship Treaty, the Soviet Union's equivalent of the Marshall Plan for China was estimated to have been seven percent of the Soviet Union's national income for the period it was operative (Westad, 2007, p. 69). The goal of the Soviet Communist Party leadership was to stamp Soviet socialism on China: 'in every department of every ministry, in every large factory, in every city, army, or university there were Soviet advisers, specialists, or experts who worked with the Chinese to "modernize" their country and move their society towards socialism' (Westad, 2007, p. 69).

Yet soon into his tenure as Soviet leader Khrushchev would fall out with Mao. Mao was incensed by Khrushchev's overtures to the United States and the Soviet Union's policy of "peaceful coexistence," the idea that imperialism and communism could conduct their rivalry without leading to war. The Kremlin leadership was also appalled at the Great Leap Forward in China. In the end the USSR withdrew its technicians and advisers from China, refused to assist China in the development of atomic weapons, and the two states were involved in border skirmishes leading to a short war in 1969. The Sino-Soviet split in the 1960s (which lasted until the USSR withdrew its troops from Afghanistan in 1989) was articulated in ideological terms on both sides. Mao referred to Khrushchev as a 'Marxist revisionist' (see Chang and Halliday, 2005, p. 571), and Khrushchev thought Mao was an 'arrogant chauvinist' (Khrushchev, 1971, p. 474; see also Li, 2012). But there was a very strong geo-strategic logic to the Sino-Soviet conflict. It is instructive to recall that the only time during the Cold War that the USSR would actually engage in direct military hostilities with another power was not against a Western capitalist state, but an Asian communist state: against China over disputed territory in 1969.

The year before the communists took power in China the World Federation of Democratic Youth (a Soviet-communist front organization) had convened a "student conference" on Southeast Asia, held in Calcutta. Soon after the Calcutta Conference the region's communist parties (those in Burma, Malaya, Indonesia and the Philippines in particular) dropped their broad united-front strategy for one of revolutionary armed revolt (see Ang Cheng Guan, 2012, p. 11). The Viet Minh sent a delegate to this conference and it was immediately afterwards that Vietnam's guerilla struggle against colonialism switched from being simply nationalist in orientation, to including an anti-capitalist ideological component. The British colonial masters in Malaya perceived the armed revolt there in 1948 against its power as part of a communist conspiracy inspired and controlled by the CPSU in Moscow. Despite the opening of many relevant archives in Moscow and elsewhere there has been subsequently no evidence to support a Soviet conspiracy, although the USSR as part of its general foreign policy supported states seeking liberation from colonial rule.

One leading Soviet authority on the Third World working in the Oriental Institute argued that the revolutions taking place in Vietnam and other parts of Asia proved decisively that history was marching towards socialism (Kim, 1982). Following the Sino-Soviet split the Chinese and Russian communist leaders competed for influence in various parts of the Third World, but nowhere perhaps was this more intense than it was in Southeast Asia. Chinese President Liu Shoqi and Premier Zhou Enlai visited twenty countries in the Third World between them in just one year, in 1963, and one outcome was Chinese funding for the construction of a railway linking Zambia to the Tanzanian coast (Westad, 2007, p. 163).

During the Sino-Soviet conflict Mao accused Soviet leaders of being "fascist renegades" out to restore the capitalist market, and Khrushchev specifically of betraying Marxism-Leninism. However, by the time of Mao's death in 1976 already the most significant areas of disagreement between the two ruling communist parties were concerned far more with concrete conceptions of the national interest than they were with any fundamental ideological differences. China saw the Soviet Union as a new hegemonic power seeking domination in Eurasia. China's reconciliation with Tito's Yugoslavia following the Soviet intervention in Czechoslovakia in 1968, its warmer relations with the USA under Richard Nixon in the early 1970s, and its Friendship Treaty with Japan in 1978, were all aimed at blocking what was considered the Soviet threat to the national security of the Chinese state. This threat was seen clearly in material terms, not in ideological ones. And this fear was related to what was perceived as representing Soviet gains in the Third World, especially in Southeast and Southwest Asia.

China was particularly incensed by two developments it considered as potentially direct threats to its security and national interests. The first development was Vietnam's entry into the CMEA in 1978, and the signing in the same year of a Treaty of Friendship and Cooperation with the Soviet Union. The second development was the Soviet military intervention in Afghanistan in 1979, the year after Moscow had concluded a TFC with Kabul. The post-Mao Chinese leadership made dealing with these issues, including the removal of large deployments of Soviet troops in Mongolia and disputed territorial issues, a precondition for improving relations with Moscow. In the end, due in large part to the failure of Soviet policies in the Third World, Gorbachev would agree to each of these conditions and Sino-Soviet relations would improve—just as the USSR was about to expire.

During the Vietnam War (what the Vietnamese refer to as the American War) the USSR and China both sought to gain influence, but in the end, due in part to historical rivalries between the Vietnamese and Chinese, Vietnam turned to the USSR, even eventually joining the "socialist commonwealth of nations" as a member of the CMEA. Ho Chi Minh became convinced of the need to employ violent revolution to overthrow French imperial rule after reading Lenin's *Theses on the National and Colonial Question* (Priestland, 2009, p. 236). Having studied Marxism-Leninism in Moscow, Ho came to accept unquestionably its basic tenets, but its major appeal to him was as a mobilizing force for Vietnam's independence from colonial control. The United States became embroiled in the war in Southeast Asia due to a fear of "dominoes" falling into the Soviet/Chinese communist orbit. The USA misunderstood the indigenous forces that gave rise to conflict in the first place (nationalism and anti-colonial movements, not communism) and failed to recognize (until it became plainly obvious when they started fighting each other) the serious rifts between the two communist giants, the USSR and China. The Chinese leadership sought to persuade the US of the geopolitical dangers of Soviet power encroaching into Southeast Asia, as Deng, for example, 'continually berated his American interlocutors for insufficient hostility to Moscow, warning them that Vietnam wasn't just "another Cuba": it was planning to conquer

Thailand, and open the gates of Southeast Asia to the Red Army' (Anderson, 2012, p. 21).

One of the key political figures in Asia in the second half of the twentieth century, Lee Kuan Yew, former Prime Minister of Singapore, recalled in his memoirs that the Association of Southeast Asian Nations (ASEAN) was formed in 1967 as the war in Vietnam was spreading into Cambodia. The entire region was confronted with communist insurgencies and Lee noted that the main stimulus for the establishment of ASEAN was that 'We had a common enemy—the communist threat in guerrilla insurgencies, backed by North Vietnam, China, and the Soviet Union. We needed stability and growth to counter and deny the communists the social and economic conditions for revolution' (Lee, 2011, pp. 329–330). In 1954 the USSR purchased Burma's entire rice crop when it was unable to sell it elsewhere (Longworth, 2006, p. 269). Although ASEAN declared its objectives to be economic, social and cultural, in reality the countries of the region were joining together for political objectives to help ensure stability and security. The fall of Saigon in 1975 provided a further stimulus for integration, and then Vietnam's occupation of Cambodia put a very severe test on the organization.

At the trial of ex-Khmer Rouge leaders in November 2011, the defendants stated that the rise of a national communist movement in Cambodia was in part a reaction to American bombing during the war the USA was fighting against the Vietcong. Hung Sen, the great Cambodian survivor (former member of the Khmer Rouge, and still in 2015 the Prime Minister of Cambodia) once said that if it was not for the US bombing of his country he would have gone on to be an airline pilot, rather than a revolutionary. Khieu Samphan at his trial at the special tribunal for crimes against humanity in Cambodia said in his court testimony: 'You seem to forget that between January 1970 and August 1973, that is the period of two and a half years—the United States carpeted the small Kampuchean territory with bombs' (*International Herald Tribune*, November 24, 2011, p. 4). The Third defendant in the trial, through his lawyer, issued a statement that called for Henry Kissinger to be put on trial for 'war crimes' as he was the main architect of the bombing campaign on Cambodia.

The Khmer Rouge were a radical communist movement with roots in the Vietnam War. The group was responsible for the death, through killing, starvation, disease, or forced labour of perhaps

1.7 million out of a total population of 8 million. Although it was inspired by Marxism-Leninism, the USSR had no relations with this group, rather supporting the Vietnamese invasion and occupation of Cambodia in 1979. The Chinese Communists supported the Khmer Rouge, and so effectively did the United States after the Vietnamese invasion by supplying aid to those fighting the occupation. It is really not sensible and certainly not convincing to argue that the actions of these outside forces could be explained in purely ideological terms, as opposed to motives relating to material and geostrategic conceptions of the national interest.

Latin America

Recognized as being in America's "sphere of influence," the USSR was careful not to draw US wrath by directly intervening in Latin American affairs. However, with the election of Jacobo Arbenz, a 38-year-old radical, as President of Guatemala in 1950 a clear opportunity arose for Moscow, as the communist party was legalized and proposed land reforms threatened US companies. The economy in Guatemala was dominated by United Fruit Company, an American multinational corporation. As would be the case with Egypt, Khrushchev arranged for the sales of military equipment to be supplied through Czech intermediaries. When this was discovered by the United States it gave further impetus to President Eisenhower to assist in the coup that overthrew the Arbenz regime in 1954, placing an American puppet in power. The shipment of arms was supposed to be kept secret, but the CIA soon discovered them whilst they were still in transit. The military hardware was denounced by the USA as part of a "communist conspiracy." House Speaker John McCormack said the cargo was like 'an atomic bomb' planted in the 'rear of our backyard' (quoted in Fursenko and Naftali, 2006, p. 61). Clearly this was considered intolerable in Washington and there was ultimately little that the USSR could do apart from protest in front of the UN of illegal US interference in the domestic affairs of a sovereign state. This was a lesson for Khrushchev: later American threats to another small Caribbean state would in fact result in an attempt to place real atomic weapons some eight years later, on the island of Cuba.

Although Cuba eventually developed a Leninist system, and more recently President Chavez in Venezuela embarked upon a path modelled to an extent on revolutionary Cuba, both Castro and Chavez at the outset were nationalists, also seeking to revive the sense of solidarity among Latin Americans that had been fostered by the likes of Simon Bolivar and Jose Marti. Both Castro and Chavez were national patriots with a wider vision of Latin American solidarity. For survival in the early years of the Cuban Revolution Castro was compelled, in the face of US hostility, to turn to the USSR for assistance. When he led the revolution in 1959 Castro was not even a member of the Cuban communist party, although Cuba would go on to develop a Leninist-type system with Soviet assistance following US antagonism to the new regime in Havana. In a televised address in 2009 Chavez encouraged Venezuelan citizens to read Trotsky, stating that he supported Trotsky's idea of 'permanent revolution' (Chavez, 2010). Trotsky's theory of permanent revolution had then come to be associated with a prescription for revolution in the Third World. It has been said that Che Guevara always carried a copy of Trotsky's *Revolution Betrayed* in his backpack (*Socialist World*, September 27, 2009). Castro (2008, p. 181) stated that he had never read Trotsky and never discussed Trotsky with Guevara. Rather he was a 'devout Leninist.'

But it was only after gaining Soviet backing for the Cuban Revolution that Castro announced that he was a Marxist-Leninist. Just before Guevara was killed in Bolivia Castro stated that he had himself read Isaac Deutscher's trilogy on Trotsky, coming away from these volumes believing more strongly that there 'could be no real revolution until there is a world revolution'. He argued that it was not possible for Cuba to build socialism in 'splendid isolation', and therefore support for guerrillas in other Latin American countries was considered to be an obligation. As noted in the case of Angola, rather than acting as a Soviet surrogate, Cuba was very much an independent and ideologically committed supporter of national liberation revolutions in other Third World arenas (see Shearman, 1993). This commitment from Castro would come to upset the Soviet leadership for whom the imperative had become not so much support for global revolution, as it was to ensure the USSR's national security, which Castro's radicalism threatened to undermine by antagonizing the United States. Castro said in return that 'Unfortunately the imperialists seem to be the only true internationalists left' (Reid-Henry, 2009, p. 370). Whatever Castro's true thoughts about Trotsky at that time, he could not profess to be a follower of Trotsky if he wished to continue receiving Soviet assistance. Détente between the superpowers in the 1970s was partly stimulated by the scare in Cuba during the missile crisis in October 1962, but it was partly Cuban and Soviet support for Third World socialist-oriented regimes in the 1970s that would end up causing the death of détente by the end of that decade.

It was common for foes of the USSR to label Cubans as Soviet 'surrogates'. This was a term used, for example, by Francis Fukuyama then a low level official in the Policy Planning Staff of the US Department of State in the Reagan Administration dealing with Third World issues (Fukuyama, 1986). In fact the Cubans were willing executioners of their own chosen policies, often only gaining Soviet assistance for radicals in other parts of the Third World following strong advocacy and persuasion on their part. They were certainly never stooges (or surrogates) for policies made in Moscow. For example, in the one case that actually brought on a direct US military invasion, in Grenada in 1993, the Soviet communist party had been very reluctant to provide any encouragement whatsoever to the self-professed Marxist-Leninist group, the New Jewel Movement (NJM), in its stated goals of a socialist path for Grenada. It was only though Cuban lobbying on behalf of the NJM that the Soviet Union was persuaded to give the small amount of support that it did (Shearman, 1985). Although the USSR had always been enthusiastic supporters of Third World states engaging in a socialist-oriented path, it was realistic about the prospects and possibilities in each specific case, and in this particular case, we knew already before the collapse of communism, due to the large number of NJM party documents that the American troops discovered during their invasion, that the Soviet leadership and especially the International Department, was very sceptical about assisting the NJM.

The fate of Salvador Allende, who was overthrown in a US-backed coup in Chile in 1973 is well known; less well known is the fact that communists won elections in Chile as part of a Popular Front government much earlier, in 1938. It was the civil war that wracked the old colonial power, Spain, in 1936, that helped the communists gain increased legitimacy and support in many Latin American countries at this time. Allende enjoyed the legitimacy of being elected leader through democratic elections and hence had a mandate to undertake radical leftist policies. Yet despite clear US antagonism towards Allende leading up to the eventual military coup, the USSR was circumspect in its limited economic transactions, with aid conditional on Chilean purchases of Soviet products (Shearman, 1986, p. 345). A leading Soviet specialist on international relations said in relation to the coup against Allende 'The tragedy of Chile is an imperious reminder that *revolutions must be able to defend themselves*' (Pavlenko, 1983, p. 133). By the early 1980s there was no way that the Soviet leadership was going to contemplate defending the latest socialist regime from local or US threats, hence when Reagan invaded Grenada to overthrow the NJM in 1983 the Kremlin did nothing.

By this stage it was evident, to those especially in the regional research institutions of the Academy of Sciences, among younger members of the KGB, and of the International Department of the CPSU, that poor, backward, weak states without any infrastructure or a strong working class were far from being ripe for socialist development. The treasure trove of secret NJM documents that were discovered by invading American troops in Grenada demonstrated a number of important truths: that the NJM were indeed self-professed Leninists who sought to model themselves on the Soviet Union; that Fidel Castro was their most powerful patron and supporter, who acted as an advocate for their cause in Moscow; but that now Soviet officials were becoming increasingly disenchanted with immature Third World revolutionaries employing Marxist-Leninist ideology to justify policies and to construct regimes that were totally unsuited to their circumstances.

Mention should be made of the Non-Aligned Movement (NAM). As its name implies, the Non-Aligned Movement represented a group of states that sought to maintain neutrality in the bipolar conflict between the USSR and the USA (see Lawrence, 2013). It was founded in Indonesia in 1955, and the eventual idea was to foster a positive sense of neutrality, rather than a passive one, a sense of neutrality that championed freedom from the influence of the great powers. In practice, however, the movement had little influence, and it did not always uphold its own basic principles—for example, both Cuba and Vietnam as members of the NAM nevertheless provided military bases for the USSR, whilst the Philippines and Saudi Arabia and Iran were effectively aligned with the US. Although in its original goals a movement condemning the bloc system, at times it acted more as forum for Cold War politics, as Cuba, for example, used the NAM summits to berate 'US imperialism'. Third world leaders such as Sukarno in Indonesia, Nasser in Egypt, and Nehru in India used the NAM to give agency and voice to Third World interests and to secure their interests within the difficult structural constraints of the Cold War. This was a logical policy to pursue, given the fact that the two superpowers' geostrategic, military, and ideological conflicts became global. Yet as will be further charted later in this book, their objectives were compromised by the structure of bipolarity, with the Cold War conflict causing crises and conflict in much of Asia and Africa, including bloody wars in Southeast and Southwest Asia in which the superpowers themselves participated. The aspirations of the early architects of Non-Alignment foundered on the logic of bipolarity and the conflict between Soviet Communism and Western Capitalism.

Soviet Communism and the Experience of National Liberation in the Third World

To return to the question of Soviet Communism's ideological influence in the Third World one can perhaps agree with Kautsky (2002, p. 27) when he writes that Lenin represented 'one of the first ideologists of revolutionary modernizing movements in underdeveloped countries and as the leader of such a movement and its revolution in underdeveloped Russia.' Soviet Communism's influence in the Third World was then an inspiration for revolutionaries fighting for national liberation and development, and the USSR provided material aid, both military and economic, to select Third World clients. This aid was provided on the basis of the dual logic of a geostrategic competition with the United States in terms of the balance of power, and an ideological conflict as both sides sought to remake the Third World in their own image.

The appeal of the Soviet Communist model was due to its opposition to colonialism, its ideological stance in favour of national liberation, its developmental model in the economy, and politically its conception of the vanguard party. As Hobsbawm points out despite the collapse of Soviet Communism 'it is important to remember that the major and lasting impact of the regimes inspired by the October revolution was as a powerful accelerator of the modernization of backward agrarian countries' (Hobsbawm, 1994, p. 9). Hence, Soviet Communism was at one and the same time an example of how to escape from the shackles of western imperialism—an ideology of revolution—and a model for development. Lenin provided the ideology of revolution with his conception of the vanguard party and Stalin went on to provide the mechanisms, through forced industrialization, nationalization of the economy, and collective farming. Whereas in the West Soviet Communism was more strictly an ideology of revolution, for the Third World it was more importantly an ideology of modernization (see Fitzpatrick, 2008, p. 26).

The form that Marxism took under Lenin and Stalin can be seen more as an anti-imperialist and pro-national liberation ideology than one that counters capitalism as defined by Marx, hence its appeals to radical groups in the underdeveloped Third World. Although, as covered in the next chapter, western Marxist parties for the most part supported the USSR during the Cold War there were always serious tensions between them, and Soviet Marxist-Leninist ideology did not represent an attractive model to copy in the already industrialized world. Non-industrialized countries found Leninism appealing as a practical guide for liberation and modernization. However this did not end up equating with loyalty to Moscow or to strict conformity to Soviet communist ideology.

The Third World played an enormously important role in Soviet ideology and, especially from the 1970s, in Soviet foreign policy. Leading thinkers on non-alignment and the national liberation movement argued that these phenomena represented new forces in the anti-imperial struggle, although their original underlying characteristics were neither proletarian nor bourgeois (Brutents, 1977, p. 9). Yet there was an inherent contradiction in this understanding of the terms. For non-alignment and national liberation were defined as being primarily anti-imperialist, and therefore in Soviet parlance favouring a non-capitalist path of development. It was not even considered possible for the Third World to opt out of the great contest between capitalism and socialism, hence the very idea of being neutral or not in alignment with one or other of the two blocs was itself counter-revolutionary. The ideological conflict between the two blocs was seen in global terms, and there was no room in this perception for neutrality or non-alignment as an intermediate status between them. The assumption also was that as there could be no national forms of capitalism, de-linked from the global imperial capitalist system, so too there could not be any real form of national socialism. National liberation was seen not as an end in itself, but rather as a process leading naturally (objectively) to a socialist orientation and hence becoming a component of the world socialist system.

Despite the aid provided to client states in Africa, Asia, and Latin America, the USSR never really gained any great rewards, either in strategic terms or in terms of access to the rich natural resources with which some of these countries were endowed. In Africa for example, although they were all poor, many of the countries there had a rich abundance of natural resources. Angola had substantial oil deposits and was rich in diamonds, yet these continued to be exploited by the United States even as Soviet assistance helped Cuban troops defend the revolution. In effect Soviet economic assistance was enabling Cuban troops to defend Angola's oil for the benefit of US corporations. And Cuba too was costing the Soviet Union substantial sums it could ill afford, as it sold oil at well below market prices and bought Cuban sugar at well above the market rate. It was estimated that this in effect was costing the USSR around one million dollars each day (Shearman, 1987). The regimes in Algeria and Libya also, although having at some stages close relations with the USSR, never gave up control over their oil and natural gas resources. Vietnam too was an economic burden on the Soviet Union, and Moscow's aid to Hanoi was not matched by political influence. As the Soviet correspondent for *Izvestia* in the Vietnamese capital put it in an article in 1968, whereas the USSR accounted for approximately 80 percent of total aid to Vietnam, the share of political influence for Moscow was between 3 and 8 percent (quoted in Andrew and Mitrokhin, 2005, p. 265). Having always recognized the power of national identity, seeking to take advantage of it in the end paid very poor dividends for Soviet Communism, as the national liberation anti-colonial movements, even where they did result in ruling communist parties, did not lead to tight integration into a Soviet-led wider communist commonwealth.

It should be pointed out here that other post-colonial countries that avoided the radical socialist oriented path did much better in economic terms. The Asian Tigers, for example, provided a more attractive alternative to Soviet-sponsored socialism. These Newly Industrialized Countries (NICs) demonstrated that it was possible to modernize and enjoy impressive economic growth using a capitalist economic model whilst not being dependent on the western capitalist states for capital. Countries such as Hong Kong,

Taiwan, Singapore, and South Korea saw rapid and continuous economic growth from the 1960s through to the 1980s, undermining the attractiveness of the Soviet path of development. This was especially the case when compared with the relative economic stagnation of other states in Southeast Asia such as Vietnam and Laos that followed the Soviet model.

Another notable feature of the period of Third World socialism during the Cold War is that an ostensibly shared Leninist (or Marxist-Leninist) ideology did not prevent organized violence breaking out between socialist states. Wars and military hostilities took place, for example, between the USSR and China in 1969, Vietnam and China in 1979, Vietnam and Cambodia in 1978, Ethiopia and Somalia in 1977, and Ethiopian Marxists versus Eritrean Marxists (the latter having received support from Cuba and South Yemen). Although the USSR and China shared the fundamentals of a Marxist-Leninist approach to world politics and initially forged an alliance that comprised a massive international communist bloc throughout Eurasia, in the end the two communist states were closer to going to a major war with one another than either did with the United States. In the end Soviet Communism's influence in the Third World was limited and could not be maintained. Egypt defected back to the West after the Middle East war of 1973, and in the wider Middle East many of the USSR's client states also had conflicting interests with one another (for example Syria and Iraq) and also Moscow was left, after the defection of Egypt, with restricted relations with only the main "rejectionist" states in the Arab world—that is, those states who rejected any moves towards making peace with Israel. The USSR ended up being isolated for the most part in Africa, the Middle East, Asia, and Latin America, at least when it came to the important issues and the most significant players.

Conclusion

When finally the Cold War came to an end, so too did Soviet aid to the 3rd World. The USSR pulled out of Afghanistan and cut aid to its former socialist allies Cuba and Vietnam. Even at the end of the communist era, the Soviet Union, although having successfully and rapidly modernized after the Bolshevik Revolution (again, at massive human cost) remained effectively a type of Third World economy as it continued to be an exporter of natural resources, and had not been able to compete with the advanced capitalist states in manufactured goods. Leninism did provide a model for many in the Third World, but it was not one that resulted in strict adherence to Soviet dictates. Soviet Communism then was an important factor in inspiring Third World anti-colonial elites and Soviet power was useful in assisting many Third World leaders to gain power. However the Cold War competition in the Third World would eventually be part of the reason for the Soviet demise.

Anti-Western, anti-colonial sentiments and alternatives to liberal market capitalism continued to live on in the Third World after the end of Soviet Communism. This is shown, for example, with continued leftist radicalism throughout Latin America. Chavez in Venezuela was the one most often referred to in this light. Daniel Ortega, the socialist radical supported by Moscow in the early 1980s, in 2013 was the elected President of Nicaragua. And the Castro brothers still ruled Cuba in 2014. However, the global competition for influence in the Third World now pits the USA against China, as the Third World remains an important arena for great power competition for reasons relating to resources and geopolitics. Post-Soviet Russia has a much smaller influence than it did during the Cold War, when it offered an ideological and economic model for newly independent states. China now offers perhaps the most attractive non-capitalist path, a hybrid type of non-western state capitalism for future development as it has moved away from a rigid Marxist-Leninist economic model. In 2014 China had over one million of its citizens in Africa. The first three non-Soviet communist states were in Asia: Mongolia, China, and North Korea. They were also contiguous to the former Soviet Union. Two of them (China and North Korea) continue to be controlled by a single ruling communist party. One, China, has engaged in radical economic reform that has led to decades of miraculous growth. At the same time China learned the lessons unwittingly provided by Gorbachev in the USSR—that political reform in a large Leninist empire leads to collapse. North Korea remains a dangerous Stalinist backwater with nuclear weapons. Mongolia is today a Third World state that has jettisoned Leninism in favour of democracy and the market and is now growing exponentially on the back of rapid development of its natural resources. Mongolia is now once more an arena of great power competition for influence. Vietnam and Laos also continue to be ruled by one-party communist regimes, but like the Asian tigers and the NICS of the 1970s, and more recently China they are also now opening up their economies, making these states too, ripe for penetration by the large powerful capitalist states. In all of this Russia is a player, but is being left behind by China in the ideological and strategic struggle with the former USSR. In this sense Communism with Chinese characteristics has emerged the ultimate victor over Soviet Communism (or communism with Russian characteristics). I take up this issue again in Chapter 6. In the next chapter I will turn to examine the impact Soviet Communism had in the West.

5

Soviet Communism and the West

When examining the role that Soviet Communism had in the West it is necessary first to define the "West." This is not as straight-forward as it might at first seem. West signifies a geographical orientation. Yet in terms of geography Russia itself is part of the West—well, at least part of it is part of the West, for it straddles across nine time zones from Europe through the Ural Mountains to Pacific Asia (hence the idea of Russia as a special Eurasian entity). Although the bulk of Russian territory is east of the Urals, the bulk of its population has always been to the west, in the European part. In a continual expansion of the empire/state Russians sought to impose their own (western) customs and traditions and culture on newly incorporated territories, whether in the Far East, Central Asia, or the Caucasus. For not only is Russia physically part of the West, it is at a very deep level also part of the West in cultural terms. From Alexander Pushkin to Boris Pasternak to the present, Russian literary figures have been part of a wider western canon, which is true of the arts more generally. Orthodox religion in Russia, although often used with the prefix "eastern," derives from western Christianity. The first step Russia took in adopting the religion of the Eastern Roman Empire was in Kieven Rus' at the end of the tenth century. The Russian Orthodox Church would come to see itself as the rightful successor to Constantinople, with Moscow as the "Third Rome." During the course of the nineteenth century and the earlier part of the twentieth century, political ide-ologies replaced religious doctrines as sources of individual moral-ity and group affiliation, especially in the West.

151

The Western Roots of Soviet Communism

Marxism, a class-based ideology, was not just a challenge to religion's dominance, it threatened to destroy it—the most systematic attempt to do so occurring in Russia after the October Revolution, in the name of a western ideology and a western utopian project. It is important then to note too that the ideology of communism was itself derived from the West: Marxism was a quintessentially western ideology, born in the West, its main empirical referents (naturally given that it was a critique of capitalism) were western states, and its intended practical application was designed for the West. Marxism was considered to be a scientific analytical approach and hence can be seen as coming out of the western Enlightenment. Marx himself was influenced by a line of classical western philosophers, running from Thomas Hobbes (1588–1679), Rene Descartes (1596–1650), John Locke (1632–1704), and the "Utopian Socialists" Robert Owen, Charles Fourier and Claude Henri de Saint-Simon of the nineteenth century, and the revolutionaries and anarchists such as Pierre-Joseph Proudhon (1809–1865), Louis Blanc (1811–1882), and Mikhail Bakunin (1814–1876). Bakunin was of course a Russian anarchist leader (who would eventually engage in bitter polemics with Marx), but he was a westernized anarchist who studied philosophy in Berlin and translated Hegel into Russian. Other important influences were Adam Smith (1723–1790), David Ricardo (1772–1823) and Charles Darwin (1809–1882). It was Hegel who had the greatest influence on Marx, with his conception of the dialectic, and the three stages of dynamic development (thesis, antithesis, and synthesis). Marx adapted these ideas in his formulation of a historical materialist approach to the study of political economy, his critical analysis of the state as actor, and his idea of perennial class conflict based upon one's relationship to the means of production.

Therefore, going back to the roots of early Marxism we can easily identify Europe as the founding home. Marx and Engels, Lenin and Trotsky all identified with, were members of, and were influenced by developments in the West. The early debates within the communist world concerned the most appropriate path to pursue for reaching the common goal of socialism. Much of Lenin's earliest writings engaged with European socialist groups, with the German Social Democratic Party (SDP) being the inspiration for much of what Lenin invokes in his book *What Is To Be Done?* The SPD had a massive influence on international socialist parties, trade unions, and worker groups. When it was first established in 1875 the SPD provided an institutional affiliation for both revolutionary groups and reformists. Despite attempts to suppress the party under legislation enacted by Chancellor Otto von Bismarck, the SPD continued to thrive, and in the German town of Erfurt in 1891 the party adopted the famous "Erfurt Program" in which socialism was now to be achieved only through democratic means, following a parliamentary path.

Karl Kautsky, editor of the SPD's theoretical journal *Die Neue Zeit*, was seen at the time as a natural successor to Marx and Engels (Townshend, 2007, p. 48). Lenin would eventually take issue with Kautsky (the renegade), and much of Lenin's writings were responses to or polemics against the ideas expressed by this other great Marxist thinker, the 'most distinguished' Marxist of his generation (Lih, 2011, p. 14). In 1918, exactly one year after the October Revolution, Lenin wrote a pamphlet entitled 'The Proletarian Revolution and the Renegade Kautsky', in which he unleashed a scathing attack on what he argued was Kautsky's deviation from Marxism. He especially took issue with the distinction Kautsky made between the "dictatorial methods" used by the Bolsheviks and the "democratic methods" of the Mensheviks (Lenin, 1918). In his pamphlet Lenin justified disbanding the Constituent Assembly in January 1918 in part on the grounds that a republic of Soviets represented a higher level of democracy than a bourgeois parliament. Lenin was essentially justifying his conception of a proletarian dictatorship. Kautsky and other critics at the time were justified in their fears that this would give rise to a single ruling *party* dictatorship over the people (see Kautsky, 1934). The disagreements between Lenin and Kautsky were a forerunner of the later deep divisions within the communist movement, the rise of Euro-Communism, and the split of many western communist parties from the Soviet line.

Kautsky, in Lenin's view, committed a number of acts that were irreconcilable with a proper Marxist approach. For example, Kautsky initially remained neutral on the question of German participation in the war in 1914; continued to support the democratic, bourgeois, parliamentary road to socialism; opposed the Bolshevik Revolution; rejected Lenin's conception of Russia as the weakest link in the chain of global imperialism; was critical of disbanding the Russian Constituent Assembly in January 1918 by the Bolsheviks; and he rejected Lenin's idea of "proletarian dictatorship," which he argued could at best create a state capitalist system, and not a socialist one.

The Initial Impact of the October Revolution in the West

Although Soviet Communism had its origins in the West, it took on specific national characteristics, influenced by Russian political culture, historical traditions, socio-economic circumstances, and the influences of powerful personalities such as Lenin, and in particular Stalin following Lenin's death in 1924. The Cold War that developed between East and West after 1945 was effectively a competition that reflected the realities of the international balance of power, exacerbated by two competing political and socio-economic systems. But both of these competing systems emanated from western experiences and western political philosophy. The Cold War was a struggle then between two different western conceptions of how society should be ordered. Yet we are saddled with the term East-West to refer to this Cold War conflict, hence the West in the rest of this chapter will pertain mainly to the USA and states in Western Europe, as an examination is made on the impact that Soviet Communism as an ideological threat had on these countries. The Cold War as a geostrategic competition in terms of the balance of material power will be covered in Chapter 7. And although we termed this an East-West competition, in fact it was global and one in which the South played a critical role, as discussed in the previous chapter.

Soviet communism had a pervasive influence in the West, with the October Revolution being a polarizing event. 100,000 British and American troops landed at Murmansk, Vladivostok, and Odessa, to fight against the communists following the Revolution. One thousand of these would lose their lives. Yet others, communists and a variety of leftist groups in the West saw October as having great promise to liberate the world from the inequities of the capitalist system. Whilst western intervention was occurring, workers groups in the West were expressing their support for the Bolsheviks. The Revolution immediately created a spark that would ignite instability and deep divisions within western countries. Although it did not lead to successful socialist revolutions, the effects were nevertheless profound and would last for the entire century.

It was noted in Chapter 1 how, after the Bolshevik Revolution and Russia's Civil War the leading Bolsheviks grappled with the problem of trying to build a communist society in what was essentially a backward, and arguably in this respect a non-western country—non-western at least in terms of being economically underdeveloped and politically conflicted about its identity. The West of course was central in the early Bolshevik mindset, for the capitalist states in the West, being far more developed (in the sense of capitalist economic production and social relations), were expected at first to instigate socialist revolution, but then after October 1917 to be pushed towards revolution following the Russian example. There was at least some foundation for this hope among the Russian revolutionaries, as Germany, with its strong working class had demonstrated its radical potential in a series of strikes. In 1917 there were over five hundred strikes in Germany involving 1.5 million workers (Priestland, 2009, p. 106). During the First World War there were also many strikes in the UK, especially in Glasgow, in what was termed, for good reason, "Red Clydeside" between 1910 and the late 1920s. This militancy in Scotland was given further impetus by opposition to Britain going to war in 1914. There were also massive strikes in other parts of Europe, particularly in the Austro-Hungarian Empire in early 1918. Yet even in the West, communist revolutionary potential was strongest in the less urbanized, less well-developed parts of Europe, such as Hungary, which was still essentially an agrarian society in the first part of the twentieth century.

It has been shown how Stalin gained ultimate dictatorial power as he pushed the idea of building socialism in one country. Stalin's main focus was on building socialism in Russia and, whilst not entirely ignoring the outside world, he did not make any moves in the underdeveloped world, despite what Khrushchev would soon recognize after Stalin's death as the greater opportunities both for gaining Soviet geo-political influence and for encouraging the development of a non-capitalist path modelled on the Soviet experience. However, as good Marxists, still the Soviet leadership considered that the West offered the greatest hopes for an expansion of communism, given the higher levels of economic development there and, in some cases, large indigenous communist parties.

The Mass Appeal in the West of Soviet Communism

The USSR's alternative, non-capitalist path of development, had a great appeal to large numbers of radical leftists in the West, some of whom actually uprooted themselves with their families to migrate to the promised land. For example, Mary M. Leder, at fifteen years of age, accompanied her working class parents in 1931, in search of a new Jewish, socialist homeland, to Birobidzhan, a corner of the Russian Far East. They had been living in California. Leder recalls thinking, as she set sail for Siberia that they were heading for a socialist collective 'where it was said there was no unemployment and the workers ruled the world' (Leder, 2001, p. 56). Birobidzhan was an area that Stalin had designated for the relocation of Jews from both inside and outside the USSR. As a young teenager Leder was already a member of the communist youth group at her high school in Monica, California (one of 25 members). Leder's parents were Jews who had escaped the pogroms in Russia during the late Tsarist period. Her father was a socialist, a tradesman who considered the Bolshevik Revolution to have been the coming of the workers' paradise, and Stalin's USSR offered hope to a poor, unemployed Jewish immigrant to the United States.

Leder's parents quickly became disillusioned with Stalin's Russia and returned to the USA. However, Mary had taken out Soviet citizenship and as a consequence was not permitted an exit visa to travel to the US. She still supported the communist cause and wished to remain in the USSR, now a resident of Moscow. Her innocence and ignorance, remarkable for a committed communist living in the Soviet capital and studying Marxism-Leninism, can be gleaned from the fact that when she read about the killing of Kirov in December 1934, she had never even heard of him. She was active in the Young Communist League and remained a committed communist and Stalinist even as people around her were being arrested in the purges. What she knew about collectivization of agriculture came from official pronouncements that she did not question, and she understood that 'The Kulak was the class enemy who had to be destroyed' (Leder, 2001, p. 62). She even worked for a period as an informant for the secret police, believing at first that the work she was doing was important and necessary to protect the gains of October. She remained faithful to the communist cause until after the war against Nazi Germany, when her own application to join the CPSU was turned down, in the face of what she now was coming to understand was anti-Semitism, reflected in Stalin's campaign at the time against 'rootless cosmopolitans'.

At one stage she gave Russian lessons to the son of the Italian communist party leader, Palmiro Togliatti at the Lux Hotel in Moscow. Mary was fortunate, in the end getting an exit visa to return to the USA in 1965. Her story, as she tells it in her auto-biography, is also one of the most insightful accounts of everyday life in Stalin's Russia. It demonstrates just how determined some foreign communists were to help build socialism in the USSR, and escape what they perceived to be the inequities of capitalism. Whereas the educated Western elites for the most part cheered Soviet communism from the distant terraces, never venturing inside the stadium, many workers uprooted themselves to build what they hoped would be better lives for themselves. In the event many of them became disillusioned, whilst others became victims of Stalin's purges and terror. One of the most infamous of the show trials of the Stalin period involved British engineers who were accused of sabotaging the Soviet electrical industry (the "Metro-Vickers trial"). Metrolpolitan-Vickers (formerly Westinghouse) was a British company dealing with heavy electrical works. Six of its employees were put on trial and found guilty of espionage and 'wrecking' when some problems were found with some of the turbines they had constructed. They were eventually freed and allowed to return to the UK. However, their fate demonstrated the risks involved for westerners working in the USSR in the Stalin era. And given the extent of the suffering in the cause of communism it is difficult, especially at this distance in time, to understand how people could continue to be true believers. One answer to this puzzle is suggested by Hochshild who writes that it 'was precisely because people were suffering so much that they were willing to delude themselves and to deny the obvious. Without the denial, all the terrible suffering would have seemed purposeless' (Hochshild, 2003, p. 59).

At the same time that Mary Leder was in Moscow studying Marxism-Leninism, the very same year that Kirov was assassinated in Leningrad giving rise to Stalin's great purges, two British academics were putting the finishing touches to their book *Soviet Communism: A New Civilization* (Webb and Webb, 1937) based on primary research and personal experience of the USSR.

Sidney and Beatrice Webb (who along with two fellow members of the Fabian Society had earlier helped to establish the London School of Economics, in 1895) were British socialists who held a favourable opinion of Soviet Communism, and their book was designed in part to spread the word. Writing in her diary in April 1932, before their visit to the USSR, Sidney Webb wrote that her wish was that Russian communism would succeed, but it was a 'wish that tends to distort one's judgments' (Webb, 2008, p. 375). There were many other supporters of the Soviet regime in the West, and although they were aware of the excesses of Stalin, including the purges and the gulag, nevertheless they managed to convince themselves that the excesses were excusable, and could ultimately be forgiven (if not forgotten) in justifying the wider cause of achieving communism. As is commonly (and possibly mistakenly) attributed to Stalin: to make an omelet, it is necessary to break eggs.

Their shared Marxist political ideology led those on the left to justify Soviet crimes and to protect and defend Soviet Communism in pursuit of the longer-term good (Applebaum, 2004, p. 58). Intellectual supporters of Soviet Communism had a mix of motives for their stance. Robert Conquest referred to a certain kind of intellectual as a 'true idea addict' (Conquest, 2001, p. 8). Raphael Samuel recalls that faced with public hostility members of the British Communist Party felt continually under siege hence 'we maintained the simulacrum of a complete society, insulated from alien influences, belligerent towards outsiders protective to those within' (Samuel, 2006, p. 45). Samuel stated simply that 'The Soviet Union was, of course, our promised land' (Samuel, 2006, p. 48). Unlike workers who voyaged to the promised land, most western intellectuals actually never went near the USSR, and hence never experienced life under Soviet Communism at first hand. There was indeed much wishful thinking.

Among the many factors as to why western intellectuals and academics were either pro-Soviet or remained uncritical of the Soviet system was a tendency for some individuals to follow fashion. Then there was the conceit of a sense of "radical chic," to be a contrarian and a dissident thinker. A leading public intellectual, prolific writer and journalist, the late Christopher Hitchens, one-time disciple of the communist project (as a Trotskyist), subsequently siding with the American neo-conservatives over the war in Iraq in 2003, perhaps slots into this category. Hitchens can be seen as a non-conformist who seemed to feel most comfortable in an oppositional stance to the dominant thinking of the day. Hitchens clearly liked to shock, writing books on Henry Kissinger as a war criminal (2001), Mother Theresa as a phony (1995), and Bill Clinton as a cheating, callous, narcissistic, self-pitying, wife-cheating, pseudo-intellectual (1999). Hitchens, in his memoirs *Hitch 22,* recalls his time as a member of the Trotskyist International Socialists when he was an undergraduate student at Oxford, and how his group felt, 'yoked to the great steam engine of history ... the conviction [that one's political stance is right] is a very intoxicating one' (Hitchens, 2010, p. 98). As noted in Chapter 3, many of those who were active and influential neo-conservatives on the right in the George W. Bush administration were earlier active members of Trotskyist groups, with one commentator referring to 'Trotsky's ghost' lurking in the White House (Heer, 2003). Patrick Buchanan, a leading paleo-conservative, referred to the neo-conservative establishment in the United States as the 'neo-Comintern' (Buchanan, 2011, p. 95), comparing the neoconservatives' mission of spreading democracy with Lenin's Comintern in 1919 and its goal of exporting communism. The neo-cons were calling, like the Trotskyist groups to which they had once belonged, for a type of "permanent revolution," only rather than pushing aggressively to develop socialism, now we had the export of liberal democracy. Whereas the original Comintern after the October Revolution was the instrument to foster socialist revolution, the main agency for the spread of democracy for the neo-conservatives was the National Endowment for Democracy. It is important to point out that Trotskyists were of course critical of Stalin; but loyal to the original Bolshevik goals.

One of Conquest's great friends, the novelist Kingsley Amis, was a member of the Communist Party of Great Britain, and expressed his loyalty to Moscow during his undergraduate days at Oxford, from the time the USSR was invaded by Hitler's troops until Khrushchev sent Soviet troops into Hungary in 1956. Neil Powell suggests that for Amis the Communist Party had two particular attractions: 'It was an infuriating snub to his parents' middling liberalism ... and at Oxford it was a way of mixing with girls' (Powell, 2008, p. 35). This is not to trivialize what actually were important political and ideological factors that led some of the West's intellectuals and public figures, artists and writers, to embrace Communism and the Soviet cause.

But it should be noted that many of the intellectual supporters of Soviet Communism in the West were either ignorant or callously unconcerned about the terrible costs people in the USSR paid in the pursuit of a communist society that they themselves would have found it difficult if not impossible to live under.

In trying to make sense of those western intellectuals who supported Soviet Communism Raymond Aron dissected what he called the 'three myths' of radical thought: the Left, the Revolution, and the Proletariat (Aron, 2005, p. 323). Each one, Aron claimed, was seen in ideological terms rather than being practical or illuminating concepts. He demonstrates how noble ideas can lead to tyranny and writes of a 'secular religion'. His principal targets were French intellectuals such as Jean-Paul Sartre and Maurice Merleau-Ponty. He saw ideology as offering intellectuals hope against reality: 'the longing for a purpose for communion with the people, for something controlled by an idea and a will. The feeling of belonging to the elect, the security provided by a closed system in which the whole of history as well as one's own person find their place and their meaning, the pride in joining the past to the future in present action—all this inspires and sustains the true believer, the man who is not repelled by the scholasticism, who is not disillusioned by the twists in the party line, the man who lives entirely for the cause and no longer recognizes the humanity of his fellow-creatures outside the party' (Aron, 2005, p. 323). To put this into context, this was an age of mass violence and total war and economic crises in which socialism offered a more just, if not perfect, alternative to what was viewed by many as the exploitative and militaristic nature of modern capitalism. In the 1930s, with the rise in Europe of the Far Right, especially in Italy and Germany, this marked a period when perhaps communism enjoyed its strongest influence in the West. Not only did communism, and the Soviet Union as head of the communist movement, have a strong following among intellectuals, also communists gained impressive support in trade union movements and, in some countries, at the ballot box.

This was also the period when the USSR was undergoing the traumas of Stalin's terror and purges, but leftist groups in the West, confronted with the threat from the main enemy on the far right, tended to overlook Stalin's "excesses." The Soviet Union had also fought on the right side of the Spanish Civil War, bore the brunt of the fighting against Nazi Germany, and supported independence for the colonies. After the Second World War Nazism was demonized and surviving leaders of the regime were put on public trial at Nuremburg for war crimes and crimes against humanity. Although Stalin's regime was responsible for millions of deaths during industrialization, collectivization, and war, no such stigma was attached to Soviet Communism. There was a tendency on the radical left to try and rationalize the mass repressions under Stalin's rule as understandable reactive measures to genuine opposition and anarchy (Harrison, 2005). Soviet opposition to German Nazism raised the prestige of the Soviet Union and 'did more than anything to drum up sympathy for the Soviet Union' (Service, 2007, p. 208). Of course, it should be noted that whilst many on the left tried to rationalize the repressions under Stalin, many others did indeed abandon the communist cause. Others holding to communist views, as noted, criticized Stalinism for deviating from the true path.

Cambridge University during this period contained a group of young students with sympathies towards communism and the USSR, who on graduation would engage in espionage activities against the West in the name of Soviet Communism. Donald Maclean, the son of a British cabinet minister, was recruited as a Soviet agent whilst serving as Third Secretary in the British embassy in Paris in the 1930s. In 1944, then working in the British embassy in Washington, Maclean passed key documents on nuclear planning to his Soviet handlers. He defected to the USSR in 1951, having been tipped off by Kim Philby that he was under suspicion from MI5. He took Soviet citizenship and worked for the Soviet Ministry of Foreign Affairs. He died in Moscow in 1983. Guy Burgess, who was educated at Eton before going up to Cambridge, was recruited as a spy for the USSR in 1934. Burgess served at one stage as Personal Assistant to the British Minister of State for Foreign Affairs, until eventually becoming First Secretary in the British embassy in Washington. He defected to Moscow along with Maclean in 1951. Philby, educated at Westminster School and then Cambridge would eventually become head of the Soviet desk at M16, when in actual fact he was a double agent working for the Soviet Union. Philby was even considered at one stage as a potential Director General of MI6. Philby would eventually follow Burgess and Maclean to Moscow, ten years after their own defections. Philby went on to train Soviet KGB operatives in Moscow (see Philby, 1968; Macintyre, 2014; and Milne, 2014).

He must surely be the only person to be awarded both the Order of the British Empire (1946) and Hero of the Soviet Union (post-humously, following his death in 1988), the USSR's highest award for services to Soviet Communism. A photograph of Philby also appeared on a Soviet postage stamp after his death.

Anthony Blunt, who would eventually be revealed as the "fourth man" was one-time Surveyor of the Queen's Pictures and was knighted for his performance in this role. Blunt's espionage activities were publicly revealed in 1979 by Prime Minister Margaret Thatcher and he subsequently had his state honours revoked. He died in 1983. The fifth member of the Cambridge spy ring has been identified as John Cairncross, who also became a member of MI6 and passed over critical information to the Soviet Union, including what might have been atomic secrets. Eric Hobsbawm, although never a spy, was also drawn to Marxism whilst at Cambridge and was a contemporary of and friends with Burgess, Maclean, and Philby. A.N. Wilson claims that even 'Long after the collapse of the Soviet Union, and the death of Mao Tse-Tung in China, the most brutal forms of communism found their defenders in the university lecture halls of Britain' (Wilson, 2008, pp. 28–29). It is interesting to note that whilst intellectuals in the West were singing the praises of the Soviet Union, many intellectuals in the "Eastern bloc" were being sent to the gulag, forced into exile, or even exterminated for holding and expressing any dissident views.

The fact that there were sympathizers of the Soviet communist cause in various sections of society left it open for this to become a polarizing issue in domestic politics in western countries. The British *Daily Mail* in October 1924 published a letter just days before the British general election purporting to be from the Comintern, the impact of which was to ensure that the incumbent minority Labour government under Ramsay MacDonald would fail to gain re-election, especially given the already slim prospects of victory. The letter, dated September 15, carried the signature of Zinoviev, then head of the Comintern, and was a directive to the CPGB to mobilize revolutionary action among the working class for uprisings in English districts. The letter was an embarrassment to the government and gave added momentum to the Conservative Party's election campaign and its opposition to a recently negotiated bilateral trade agreement between the UK and the USSR. At the time the letter was thought to be authentic, despite denials from Moscow. Since then a number of investigations left the matter inconclusive, although one by the Foreign and Commonwealth Office in 1999 concluded that the letter was a forgery by a MI6 source which was then leaked to the *Daily Mail* (see Norton Taylor, 1999). The point to be made is that the letter not only had a major impact on the general election, basically determining its outcome, it further undermined the legitimacy of the CPGB as a genuine and effective opposition movement in British politics.

It should be stressed also that the appeal of Soviet Communism would be strengthened by the sufferings of the Great Depression in the West, seen by many at the time as a crisis of the capitalist system. The Great Depression both undermined faith in the western capitalist model, and increased the appeal of the alternative Soviet model of development. Indeed, it is perhaps unlikely that social welfare and public health services would have developed in the West when they did after 1945 had it not been for the attractiveness for many of the Soviet model. Western political and economic systems were modified in part due to the perceived need to counter the appeal of Soviet Communism. Hence it was not just radical leftists and Marxist intellectuals, but many too among the average voters, for whom elements of a non-capitalist system were appealing. One then needs to understand the context of the Cold War to fully appreciate the origins of welfare policies and the success of social democratic and communist parties in some western countries.

The situation in France was different from that in the UK. Following elections in France in 1936, newly elected Prime Minister Leon Blum invited members of the French Communist Party to join his new government. This was during the Comintern's anti-fascist united front strategy discussed in Chapter 3. The French communist party leader, Maurice Thorez—despite the fact that until recently he had been a disciplined supporter of the ultra-leftist line against 'social fascists'—now found himself in support of communists joining the cabinet of a socialist government. However, through the Comintern Stalin would eventually instruct Thorez, now an enthusiastic advocate of joining the government, to refrain from doing so. Thorez reluctantly agreed to Moscow's instructions. In Spain the left-right division led to civil war. Priestland considers that 1936 was perhaps "the high point of Communist prestige in the West" (Priestland, 2009, p. 195).

The Spanish Civil War brought in many leftist volunteers from around the western world to fight against General Franco's forces following the military coup that he had led. As, in more recent times, the Jihadist appeal has drawn volunteers from across the world to fight in Afghanistan, Iraq, Syria, and other parts of the Islamic world undergoing conflict, the Spanish civil war attracted people from some fifty countries to fight with the international brigades against Franco's fascist forces, including some 4,000 volunteers from the United Kingdom, mainly communists, socialists, trade unionists, including film makers, poets and novelists. Many of these perished. Americans, mainly from the CPUSA and other leftist groups, supplied around 3,000 young volunteers to fight in Spain. The USSR under Stalin supplied hundreds of planes and tanks. Josef Broz (later Marshall Tito, communist leader of Yugoslavia) assisted the recruitment and logistics of sending volunteers to join the International Brigades in Spain from his base in Paris at that time.

Victory in the war against Germany, rather than witnessing a resurgence of liberalism among the European states, as one might reasonably have expected given the knowledge and for many the experience of the terror inflicted from both the radical right (in the form of Nazism) and the radical left (in the form of Stalinism), saw a growth in support for Soviet Communism. Even in the UK, although the Communist Party never looked in the slightest bit threatening, a more radical Labour Party won the election in 1945, despite the general sense of gratitude to Winston Churchill for being instrumental in winning the war. In France the Communist Party gained 28.6 per cent of the vote; in Italy the Communist Party garnered 19 percent of the vote and Greece was soon after the war beset with civil conflict in which the communists looked set at one stage to win. In Czechoslovakia the communists won nearly 40 percent of the vote. It should not have been so surprising that the radical left should do so well at the ballot box given that it was the Soviet Union that had won the war, the Nazi and Fascist far right had been delegitimized, and liberalism had been shown to be willing initially to engage in appeasement with Hitler's regime in Berlin. In 1942, during the war against Nazi Germany, Stalin was anointed man of the year in *Time* magazine. The role of the Red Army in defeating the Nazis was widely admired in the West. Laurence Rees quotes a British Communist Party member who had enlisted to fight against Nazi Germany, who said that if he had been asked to fight against the USSR he would have 'crossed over', because his loyalty to the Soviet communist revolution was stronger than loyalty to his country. He stated: 'We didn't see it, of course, as another country. We were the British section of the Communist International—theirs was the Russian section and they happened to be the ones who had made the revolution first and they were therefore in the leading position' (Rees, 2008, p. 45). He went on to say he would have instigated acts of violence in the UK if called upon to do so and 'The Soviet Union was the light of the world, to put it in religious terms. And one could commit many small crimes in order to achieve a greater goal ... you know, the end justifies the means' (Rees, 2008, p. 45).

The Cold War Era

Yet, no sooner had the Second World War ended than the Cold War began. Here it is worth returning briefly to the question of defining the West. Without Soviet Communism there would have been no West as it came to be understood in the second half of the twentieth century. Without the Cold War there would have been no sense of a unified West at peace with itself. In the Cold War between 1947 and 1989 the Soviet Union and its influence in the world—political, ideological, and strategic—provided a strong incentive for those same western states that had fought bloody wars against each other in the first half of the twentieth century to unite in countering what was viewed as an existential struggle against Soviet Communism in the second half. The very idea of the West became associated then with contestation with the USSR. Hence, in rethinking the international politics of the twentieth century it is necessary to recall just how important Soviet Communism was, not simply as a security threat defined in traditional military terms, but as a threat to the traditional foundations of politics and society.

British intervention in the Greek Civil War, CIA aid to the opponents of communism in Italy, the Marshall Plan and the Truman Doctrine of Containment all helped to ensure that the communists were defeated in Western Europe. Soviet tanks and repression ensured that loyal communists took power in Eastern Europe. Yet it was not only the Soviet side that went to extremes based on the fear of being ideologically contaminated by the other. In the United States too there were anti-communist witch-hunts, symbolized in the excesses of McCarthyism in the 1950s. There were good reasons for Western governments to be concerned about a "fifth column" of communist "fellow travellers" (as noted above, for example, with the Cambridge Five) but the loyalty-security reviews and public hearings of the House Committee on Un-American Activities went too far, undermining the very freedoms they were supposedly designed to protect. Indeed, they tended to foster not so much anti-Soviet sentiments among intellectuals but rather concern at the undermining of democracy at home. In a way perhaps McCarthyism did for anti-communism what American treatment of prisoners at Abu Graib during the war in Iraq did for democracy promotion: it undermined the foundations of American democracy whilst simultaneously risking the rallying of more recruits to the very cause against which the campaign was directed.

Many in the West, and not just communists, were also impressed with the speed with which the USSR was rebuilt after the devastating war against Nazism, and the impressive Soviet achievements in science and technology, the most noticeable being the development of the Atom bomb and then, spectacularly, having the first craft to orbit the earth (Sputnik in 1957) and then later the first man into space (Gagarin in 1961). The biggest impact these developments had was to mobilize the Kennedy administration in Washington, as the self-appointed defender of the western world, to ensure that the USA would maintain military superiority and also win the space race by placing the first man on the moon (see Cadbury, 2006). The space race more than the arms race was seen as critical in the political and ideological push for world dominance.

Soviet communism had a major impact too in Australia, part of the wider cultural West situated far to the east in the Asia Pacific. As with the experience in other western states there were fellow travellers among the intellectual elites in Australia too, those with influence who provided a positive picture of life in the USSR. For example, the leading Australian historian of his day, Manning Clark, following a three-week visit to the USSR in 1958 wrote the book *Meeting Soviet Man* (1960), which portrayed life in the Soviet Union in a generally positive light. As with the book by Beatrice and Sidney Webb in the UK, Clark's book was attacked as representing nothing more than Soviet propaganda. Clark's father had been an Anglican priest and it was particularly galling for many that in *Meeting Soviet Man* comparisons were made between Lenin and Jesus. Clarke was not a communist, although he was of the left. He would later take part in anti-Soviet demonstrations regarding the persecution of dissidents. Yet the controversy surrounding Manning's visit and his subsequent book reflected the inherent fears within the Australian political and cultural elites of the power of Soviet Communism to threaten domestic stability. Similar to McCarthyism in the United States, although not with such systematic vigour, fear of communist subversion in Canberra fed conspiracy theories of communist plots. In 1951 Prime Minister Robert Menzies held a referendum proposing an amendment to the Australian Constitution that would have enabled him to pass legislation dissolving the Communist Party of Australia (CPA). The referendum was defeated. As in the UK and the USA, the CPA (founded in October, 1920) had never posed a real electoral challenge to the traditional left, represented in Australia by the Labour Party. One of the founders of the CPA in Sydney in October 1920 was Adela Pankhurst, daughter of Emily Pankhurst, the British suffragette.

As in other parts of the West the Australian left experienced a serious rift due to counter-posing views of Soviet Communism and what role the CPSU should play in the international communist movement. Following the controversy over the referendum on the CPA the rift became so serious that it split the Labor Party, resulting in the formation of the mainly Catholic-led Democratic Labor Party in 1955, which helped to prevent Labor gaining power again in Canberra until the election of Gough Whitlam's government in 1972. As with the CPGB, although having some influence among trade unions, the CPA experienced declining membership in the 1960s. Following the Soviet invasion of Czechoslovakia in 1968 the party split with a minority pro-Soviet core creating a new Socialist Party of Australia. In the 1970s the smaller CPA continued to lose influence and membership despite joining the Euro-communist bandwagon of that time, until it was eventually dissolved in the same year that the USSR expired, in 1991. The Socialist Party of Australia renamed itself the Communist Party of Australia in 1996. In 2009 it registered itself with the Australian Electoral Commission (AEC) as the Communist Alliance. Although it continued to exist in 2012 the CPA was no longer a registered political party after failing to register with the AEC, perhaps because at that stage it had less than the required 550 minimum members to qualify (*The Australian*, May 31, 2012).

In the end revolutionary communists were unable to gain power in Western countries, and communist parties for the most part sought to gain influence and power by operating through the party systems and institutions of democratic society. However, even here they were not very successful. For example, in the UK the best electoral performance for the CPGB was in the general election of 1945 when two candidates were elected to the House of Commons—Willy Gallacher in West Fife, and Phil Piratin in Mile End, London. Yet in this best ever result the party gained only 0.4% of the total national vote. Communism was always really only a minor irritant to the established order in the United States. Indeed it was difficult to be a communist during the Cold War, almost like being a radical Islamist during the "global war on terrorism." In the United States in the 1970s student activists against the Vietnam War, the civil rights movement in the South, and the peace movement against both US neo-imperialism and the nuclear bomb all converged to create what was termed the American "New Left," a movement that challenged the orthodox "old left" of the established and previously ineffective political parties. The CPUSA had never really built up a following or an effective organization to challenge the status quo, due in part to the persecution of party members in the McCarthy "witch hunts," in part to internal fighting, and in greater part to the legitimacy of the US liberal capitalist system as the world became divided into two opposing blocs with the advent of the Cold War. The communists failed almost completely to have any influence on the American political scene. In the 1970s membership of the CPUSA was never more than 12,000 strong. The US also had no strong leftist movement to challenge the dominant consensus. Socialism is a negative concept in the USA, to say nothing of communism. Fox News and other media outlets in the USA have labelled Barak Obama a socialist (a ridiculous claim) in an attempt to discredit him in the eyes of the wider population. Not only did some European countries have strong indigenous communist and socialist parties, they have shared power in coalition governments.

Euro-Communism

The term "Euro-Communism" only came into currency in the mid 1970s and was most often associated with the three big

Mediterranean communist parties in France, Italy, and Spain. These three parties in particular were influenced by events in the international communist world dealt with in other chapters in this volume (the Sino-Soviet split; the Prague Spring; and the relative erosion of Soviet hegemony in the communist world on both sides of the iron curtain). Khrushchev's denunciation of Stalin at the 20th Party Congress, as noted, also had a major impact on the international communist world. Santiago Carrillo, head of the Spanish Communist Party, recalled how his party felt insulted and cheated as it was expected simply to follow like sheep the Soviet Communist Party lead. Recalling also the way that the European communist parties were supposed to follow the Soviet line in the split with Tito in 1948 Carrillo wrote: 'we felt that we had been so cruelly deceived and so vilely manipulated that this completed the demolition of what remained of the mystical and almost religious element in our attitude towards the Communist Party of the Soviet Union' (Carrillo, 1978, p. 112). Other influences included the US withdraw from Vietnam, the radicalization of politics in the late 1960s and the rise and challenge of the New Left, all against the backdrop of increasing economic integration in Western Europe. Whilst these new developments were underway the big communist parties in the western half of Europe appeared to be standing still, seemingly stuck in the past, unable to offer prescriptions and policies enhance the prospects of building socialism. The obsolescence of the traditional approach gave rise to new ideas that would set these Euro-Communist parties apart from and often in opposition to the Soviet Communist Party, as they developed social and political pluralism, rejecting traditional Leninist conceptions of the role of the party (as the vanguard of the working class).

The Italian Communist Party leader Palmiro Togliatti employed the term 'polycentrism' to describe this new approach, which reflected the requirement to appreciate national and local factors, rather than having ideology and policy determined in Moscow. Polycentrism can be contrasted with Lenin's conception of "democratic centralism" discussed in Chapter 3. Each individual communist party should be free to develop policy on the basis of their own national traditions free from any strictures from a communist "central." The easing of tensions in the Cold War with East-West détente in the 1970s also lessened the perceived requirement for a disciplined approach to follow the Soviet Communist

Party line. There was also a new political space emerging for the Left to fill, following the erosion of the Right's influence in Spain (with the end of the Franco era), France (the end of the Gaullist era), Italy (the relative demise of the Christian Democrats) and Portugal (with the overthrow of the Salazar regime). Although "developed socialism" might be an appropriate revolutionary outcome for the USSR it was no longer seen, insofar as it had ever been so, as a model appropriate for others in the West to follow.

Part of this also related to the emergence of new generations. October 1917 was distant history for those born after 1945 and hence there was no lingering sense of loyalty to the Soviet system. In addition, no longer was the Far Right a realistic threat to the political order, and into the 1970s increasing affluence and the advent of the "post-material" society gave more time and scope for leftist alternatives to emerge. At a time when a younger generation of leftist radicals in western Europe were seeking new avenues for progress along socialist lines, the CPSU was hierarchical in structure, disciplined in organization, rigid in its ideology, secretive in its practices, cautious in its policies, and stagnant in its thinking. Clearly this was unappealing to the new generation of young radicals. Under Brezhnev's stewardship the USSR had become conservative. Cuba's independent Third World activism under Castro's communist regime in the 1970s and 1980s, noted in the previous chapter, had often frustrated the rulers in the Kremlin who saw this as undermining not only their own leading position in the world communist movement, but also threatening to undermine East-West détente. Castro looked upon support for national liberation revolutions in the Third World as part of his internationalist duty as a socialist, and the USSR's reluctance to always support guerrillas in Latin America led him to conclude, as noted in Chapter 4, that the capitalist imperialists were the only true internationalists. For young revolutionaries in the West Castro and Che Guevara represented more of an inspiration than the conservative, bureaucratic, and repressive Soviet leadership. No one in the West wore T-shirts with Brezhnev emblazoned on them. In the West Soviet Communism simply lost the limited appeal it once had, although it continued to have wide appeal in parts of the Third World.

Euro-Communism then marked a departure from Leninist party norms as the Mediterranean communist parties advocated the democratic and parliamentary path to socialism, expanding their support base by seeking the votes of other social and economic groups than those simply of the traditional working class (for example, apart from the more obvious trade unions: women's and environmental movements). Although it deviated from Leninism, Euro-Communism derived directly from older Marxist traditions going back to Kautsky. However, in the context of this study the important factor to consider is the extent to which Euro-Communism marked a break with the USSR. As noted in previous chapters there had been earlier disputes over alternatives to Soviet Communism (from Tito, Mao, and Dubcek). Hence, there had already been serious rifts within the communist world marked by opposition to the Soviet brand of Leninist communist ideology. But each of these alternatives was either from within the system (Trotskyism), from within the wider "socialist commonwealth" (Titoism; "socialism with a human face"), or from the Third World (Maoism). Euro-Communism then was the latest attempt, now coming from the West, to differentiate local communist ideology to that of the USSR. By this time the USSR had designated its own concept to define the stage it had reached on the road to communism: "already existing socialism" or, more simply, "developed socialism." However, unlike Trotskyists and Maoists, the Euro-Communists did not challenge the CPSU to be seen as the true guardians of the original Bolshevik tradition. They did not see the need any longer to locate their ideological stances and policy prescriptions in accordance with the Leninist tradition and the October Revolution or the subsequent development of existing socialism in the USSR.

Increasing numbers of Euro-Communists came to view that maintaining solidarity with the USSR on every issue was having a negative impact domestically, for the perception amongst voters who might otherwise have leftist sympathies was that the communist parties would remodel their societies in the Soviet image should they gain power. And the image was not a positive one. Holding strict allegiance to the CPSU limited the appeal of the West European communist parties, as electors could not be certain that the goal was not to impose a similar system as that pertaining in the USSR. For most people by the 1970s the Soviet system was looking tired, stagnant and unappealing, with an ageing conservative gerontocracy ruling over a crippled dysfunctional system.

The main features of Euro-Communism can be listed as the following:

- Polycentrism (independence from Moscow)
- Different paths to socialism
- National specificity
- Critique of the Soviet experience
- Pluralism, democracy
- Condemnation of abuses of human rights

Given that communism remained until the end of the USSR an "international movement," the critiques of Soviet society from among previously loyal communist parties in the West threatened to impact also in the USSR itself. Although Khrushchev revealed many of the crimes of Stalin and rehabilitated many innocent victims of Stalin's terror, the CPSU leadership had never been able to come around to rehabilitating the main Bolshevik victims of Stalinism. Two names in particular come to mind here: Trotsky and Bukharin, each representing an alternative model of socialism to that developed by Stalin under the rubric of "socialism in one country." To give Bukharin his good name back would have been not simply to rehabilitate the person, but also to rehabilitate the ideas he represented, and this was always (until the late Gorbachev period) considered to be too risky (see Cohen, 1980). The Italian Communist Party leader, Berlinguer, was approached by Bukharin's son with a personal appeal to secure Bukharin's rehabilitation, and the party's newspaper, *L'Unita* called in 1978 for justice to be done for all of the 'eminent representative(s)' who fell victim in the trials of the 1930s (cited in Menashe, 1980, p. 301). Euro-Communism can be viewed as a separate path of communist development, although providing an alternative to Soviet Communism that nevertheless used what were considered to be the best parts of the CPSU's heritage. The development of Euro-Communism is only understandable with reference to its origins as a response to developments in Soviet Communism.

Euro-Communism's objective to provide an alternative to the two other leftist traditions of social democracy and Soviet-style communism—a new third way between the two—in the end did not endure. There was an inherent contradiction in its underlying attempt to create an alternative post-national or pan-European ideology when in fact at its core it was fundamentally based on assumptions concerning the importance of national peculiarities. As Rick Simon has put it, Euro-Communism's 'coherence, such as it was, derived from a temporary coincidence in the evolution of national parties, much as an eclipse produces a transitory alignment of celestial bodies whose trajectories are radically different' (Simon, 2007, p. 81). It should be pointed out too that Euro-Communism was not a phenomenon restricted to Europe, for in Asia the Communist Party of Japan, in Latin America the Mexican Communist Party, and in Oceania the Communist Party of Australia all shared some of the ideas of Euro-Communism. Yet each of these communist parties across different continents and cultures expressed and reflected not so much internationalist as national tendencies (on this see Mandel, 1979/1980). In the 1980s the various communist parties began to drop their previously stated allegiance to Leninism and repudiated the idea of the "dictatorship of the proletariat." Hence, it was not simply a denunciation of Stalinism that was manifest in Euro-Communism, but a rejection of the very foundations of the Leninist system.

In the end most communist parties would reject the revolutionary road to socialism, and would ultimately (for the most part) advocate a parliamentary path through the democratic (bourgeois) pluralist system. Reformism and gradualism and cooperation with other progressive forces were now seen as the way forward. If communism could be achieved through democratic parliamentary means, through the ballot box, then the notion of proletarian dictatorship did not fit. It was not only the established right wing parties that were now criticizing Soviet Communist intolerance of dissent, and the practices of incarcerating dissidents in mental asylums or sending them into internal or external exile, for now the communist parties in the West too, in the early 1980s, were voicing their opposition to Soviet 'human rights abuses'. It should be noted here that although the Euro-Communist parties abandoned their commitment to proletarian dictatorship and expressed support for parliamentary democracy, democratic procedures did not extend to leadership selection procedures in their own party organizations. Centralization remained (or what Lenin termed 'democratic centralism') in which the higher organs of the party employ a method of self-selection in which the Politburo selects delegates at each level of the party and state system to ensure they themselves are always re-elected. Democratic Centralism was also critically a means of disciplining party members into conformity with the commands of the central party apparatus, and preventing the formation of any "loyal opposition" within the party's ranks. The leadership was then able to impose its own will on the wider party membership. But then this should not be surprising given the human tendency to cling to power once gained, true of any political system (see de Mesquita and Smith, 2011). Nevertheless, in the 1980s the western communist parties were splitting from the Soviet Union, being no longer willing to subscribe to CPSU instructions.

New Political Thinking and the Common European Home

It was of course not only new generations of leftists in the West who recognized that Soviet Communism had atrophied and become dysfunctional, for so too did many in the CPSU apparatus itself come to realize that without reform the system could no longer survive. At the plenum of the Central Committee of the CPSU in January 1987 Gorbachev stated that the 'theoretical concepts of socialism remained to a large extent at the level of the 1930s and 1940s, when the tasks being tackled by society were entirely different' (Gorbachev, 1987, p. 116). The Soviet leader then went on to outline clearly why this had been the case, stating that debates and creative ideas had been disallowed as 'authoritarian evaluations and opinions became unquestionable truths, that could only be commented on … as dogmas left no room for an objective scientific analysis' (p. 116). It is often noted that Gorbachev and many of those he brought into the Soviet leadership in the late 1980s were so-called "men of the sixties" (*shestidesiatniki*), referring to individuals whose formative experiences were Khrushchev's "thaw" and the more liberal period between Stalin's death and the advent of Brezhnev's era of stagnation. Yet these men of the sixties were never advocating a radical or fundamental change of the system. As Gorbachev himself stated in conversation with Zdenek Mlynar, although at that time he held hope for some 'change in the direction of greater openness … the thought that we were travelling on the wrong road, that it was necessary to change the whole system of economic and political relations down to their foundations—there was no such concept' (Gorbachev and Mlynar, 2002, p. 27).

Gorbachev's priority on taking power was to stimulate the economy (the key Russian term was *uskorenie* meaning acceleration) through a variety of means, including measures to increase the efficiency and accountability of industrial managers. His original emphasis was on personnel changes and providing incentives for increased production. The failure of superficial measures to accelerate the economy led to more significant reforms under the rubric of *perestroika* (restructuring) and *glasnost* (openness) and eventually *demokratizatsia* (democratization). These attempts at reforming the system would very quickly lead to systemic crisis and ultimately the dismantling of the USSR. One other aspect of Gorbachev's reformism was in the area of foreign relations and Soviet Russia's place in the world. The interesting point here is Gorbachev's view that the USSR was part of the West. This was articulated in terms of Russia as part of what Gorbachev referred to as a "Common European Home." Gorbachev first used this term during his first overseas visit as General Secretary, during a press conference in Paris, when the concept simply came to his mind. As he acknowledges in his memoirs: 'The idea of Europe as our common home had been a spontaneous thought, but the symbolic image eventually acquired an existence of its own' (Gorbachev, 1995, p. 428). Yet after careful reflection Gorbachev came to the realization that Europeans East and West had 'common roots' and were part of a 'fundamentally indivisible European civilization' (Gorbachev, 1995, p. 428) eventually leading him to an awareness of the 'artificiality' of the political blocs and the 'archaic' nature of the iron curtain. As will be shown in Chapter 7, Gorbachev's reformulation of Soviet ideology relating to foreign policy, in particular his conception of common human values, would eventually lead to what some would criticize as a weakening of the Soviet Union's power and influence in the international system, particularly in Eastern Europe, and what others would applaud as measures leading to the end of the Cold War. When the USSR fell in 1991 post-Soviet Russia under Gorbachev's successor Boris Yeltsin continued to push for Russia's integration into a wider West. However, as Roy Medvedev would put it, the widespread belief in post-Soviet Russia by the late 1990s was that Yeltsin and Gorbachev brought hunger and humiliation to Russia (Medvedev, 2009). Further attempts to integrate with the West under Vladimir Putin's leadership would also fail.

Conclusion

With the October Revolution the Bolsheviks effectively instituted
a radical break with traditional social democracy and socialism,
creating a new Marxist hegemony in the name now of Marxism-
Leninism. Marxism-Leninism as it developed in the USSR had
its adherents in the West, but this was not widespread and was
only among a small number of committed revolutionaries, some
communist parties, trade unionists, and intellectuals. Soviet
Communism had very little impact on or appeal to that group
in the West that it claimed to represent, the bulk of the working
class. It was rather, as analysed in the previous chapter, the masses
in some underdeveloped countries in Asia and Africa and Latin
America where Soviet Communism had its greatest direct impact.
In the West the Soviet Communist model became one to avoid,
not one to emulate. Communist parties in the West sought to gain
their objectives through parliamentary means and reformism, not
revolutionary means. There developed in the course of the second
half of the twentieth century what might accurately be described
as a western form of Marxism, taking its cue from Kautsky and
Bernstein in rejecting democratic centralism and the dictatorship
of the proletariat, collectivization and centralized one-party state
control, in favour of a reformist, democratic, parliamentary path
to obtain socialist objectives. At the same time that Soviet tanks
were putting down the reformist movement of the Prague Spring,
communist parties in Western Europe were themselves moving
towards what was termed "reform communism." This ultimately
led to the logical outcome of the western communist parties supporting dissident reformist movements within the Soviet communist bloc, such as Charter 77 in Czechoslovakia and Solidarity
in Poland. It was the institution of martial law in Poland to put
down the Solidarity workers' organization that led the Italian
Communist Party to formally break with the CPSU.

In the final analysis, what eventually would win out in the
USSR was not the appeal of Euro-Communism, but the appeal
of Euro-Capitalism. It was not the ideals of social democracy
that Soviet citizens found attractive so much as the idea that they
could go shopping for the consumer goods that had long been
denied them. It was not the high culture of the dissident movements in the communist bloc that would prove to be the principal influence on the wider public, but the mass, popular culture

of music and fashion and the freedoms of expression associated with these that eventually won out. And when freedoms were eventually permitted in the Soviet bloc the masses were mobilized around the banner of national identity, as will be shown in the next chapter.

Given the pluralist nature of the western democracies, opportunities existed for the articulation of issues and policy preferences that by definition were not permitted in the totalitarian systems of Eastern Europe. Hence, many activists in social movements in the West, many with radical leftist tendencies, put pressure on the local communist parties to incorporate these issues in their political programs. Feminist and environmentalist groups, for example, were frustrated by the absence of any serious consideration of their concerns within the hierarchies of the indigenous communist and socialist parties, and hence began to organize themselves into separate political factions within existing parties, or even establishing their own parties. This not only put pressure on the communist parties to adapt and take these issues more seriously, it also further undermined the reputation of the CPSU among radical groups in the West, for Soviet Communism was increasingly perceived as conservative, patriarchal, and no longer offering an attractive alternative to global capitalism. Many feminists also did not see the world simply through the conceptual lenses of class conflict, but rather through hierarchical structures of gender relations and how these were reflected in both domestic politics and in the global international political economy (a landmark study here was Enloe, 1989, 2014). Whilst it was the case that women in the USSR were well represented in the institutions of state, this was only on a proportional system allocated through the ruling CPSU, and did not reflect real power for women. The higher up the state and party hierarchy one went, the fewer women were represented, until at the very top women were noticeable by their almost complete absence. One thinks of the Red Square parades with the Soviet leaders, all elderly gray men in dark suits, taking the salute standing above Lenin's mausoleum.

Communism was a western ideology that originated in the West and appealed to many intellectuals and workers in western countries. Yet communism never took hold in the West (as the West came to be defined in the Cold War). Where it did take hold it was imposed upon people in the East against their will. Everywhere that communist regimes arose they did so against the will of the majority of citizens in that country, with very few exceptions (for example, Yugoslavia). And those intellectuals in the West who did sympathize with the Soviet communist regime were not for the most part inclined to live their dream by moving to the USSR. Also the West came late to recognizing and understanding the serious nature of the divisions in the communist world, in part based upon the overriding pull of national identities and traditional notions of the national interest bound up with territory. The boundaries of the territorial state in the end proved much more resilient than any pull of class solidarity. It was not a matter of East versus West in ideological terms that ultimately mattered—although the ideological component of the conflict was a contributing factor of the conflict—it was traditional notions of the national interest defined in terms of power.

During the reformist period under Gorbachev in the late 1980s, the West became actively involved with the Soviet transformation. During the period of intense internal rivalry in the Soviet leadership, by 1987 western political leaders had clearly taken sides with the liberal reformers and Gorbachev himself. Gorbachev had become heavily dependent on western loans and each of the main western capitalist states had their own specific agendas for giving support to Gorbachev and the more liberal reformers. The British wished for a more open, democratic and transparent system; the Germans for a reduction in tensions especially relating to the question of East Germany; the French were thinking in terms of a French-led pan-European détente; and the Americans were hoping for an end to the Cold War confrontation (see Trenin, 2007). At the end of the day each state in the West was primarily concerned with its own national interest, and not any wider common interest linked to any threat of Soviet communism as ideology.

Summarizing the influence of Western Marxist theories in changing the world Glaser and Walker conclude emphatically that it must be judged a failure: 'It has inspired no social upheavals of the kind Marx would have recognized, and few of its leading figures bothered to involve themselves in the struggles of the working class' (Glaser and Walker, 2007, p. 115). It is worth bearing in mind that even during the revolutionary student movement of 1968 and the radicalization of the workers across Europe the Communist Parties remained on the sidelines and had no real or effective influence on events. In part this must have been due to the taint of the product emanating from the Soviet experience. In the UK there were radicals on the left who had some wider influence, but they acted largely within the established social democratic side of the political spectrum or in the trade unions.

In the end the actual practice of Soviet Communism was revealed to even the most die-hard fellow traveller for what it was: a repressive authoritarian (or totalitarian) system that was clearly a poor fit for the West.

6

Soviet Communism and the National Question

Previous chapters have each demonstrated in different ways the powerful influence that national identities and nationalism have had in the Soviet Communist experience. This chapter will deal with the national question in detail. Ernest Gellner pointed out that from a Marxist perspective 'History is the history of *class* struggle. It is not, or only superficially, the history of *national* struggles' (Gellner, 1994, p. 6). Marxists saw nationalism as an instrument used by the bourgeois to divide and rule the international proletariat. Afflicted with nationalism the workers in each country would not recognize their natural and proper allegiance to their fellow workers overseas. The workers would be subjected to false consciousness. The Soviet Communist Party leadership in its public discourse, of necessity, employed the language of Marxism-Leninism and class conflict. However, although the twentieth century was in many ways defined by ideological contestation between Soviet Communism and International Liberalism, the key factor in some of the major events of the century was the role of nationalism. The idea that it was liberalism that eventually triumphed over communism is a simplistic take on the dynamics that would eventually lead to the end of the Cold War and the demise of Soviet Communism. Michael Madelbaum's claim that liberalism 'triumphed decisively' over Soviet Communism due to the victory of liberal values needs qualification (Mandelbaum, 2002, p. 49; see also Fukuyama, 1992).

The Power of Nationalism and National Identity

Although the Soviet social, economic, and political system had not been able to compete with the West, and although it is the case that civil movements in the USSR and the Eastern bloc were calling for liberal reforms, the chief dynamic that explains the crisis of communism was linked to culture and the politics of identity. As Samuel Huntington put it: 'Identity ... is like sin: however much we may oppose it, we cannot escape it' (Huntington, 2004, p. 21). Yet it was ethnic national identity, not liberalism that eventually triumphed over Soviet Communism. The end of Soviet Communism marked not the end of history, but rather the renewed resurgence of ethnic nationalism. A large number of ethnic conflicts broke out following the end of the Cold War in such disparate parts of the world as the Balkans, Sub-Saharan Africa, Northern Africa, the Middle East, Southeast and Southwest Asia, China, and parts of the former Soviet Union. Europe too has seen the rise of far right nationalism and immigration is a salient issue in elections in western countries, including the USA. In the end it was not liberal ideology that brought the system down, but identity politics relating to culture and in particular the idea of the nation. It has not been civilizational identities that have been the key threats to international and regional security, but local identities.

In the late nineteenth century western imperialism stimulated anti-capitalist national liberation movements. In the early twenty-first century opposition to what some see as western neo-imperialism has bred a new anti-western form of fundamentalism based on religion and nationalism in the form of fundamentalist Islam. Russian Marxist revolutionaries at the turn of the twentieth century, many of them living abroad, saw themselves as internationalists, foreswearing national identities or any sense of loyalty to their country, free from any sense of patriotism. Rather they saw themselves as part of a wider post-national or transnational community that was also opposed to imperialism. Only this was anti-imperialism in the name of the international proletariat. The slogan, taken from Marx and Engel's *Communist Manifesto* was 'Workers of All Lands Unite.' Although they did not spend much energy on the subject in their writings, Marx and Engels acknowledged that nationalism was a potent force that could be mobilized by the bourgeois rulers to dampen working class solidarity and class-consciousness. As Bhukharin put it, in very simple terms in his famous communist primer: 'The workers of all lands are brothers of one class, and they are the enemies of the capitalists of all lands' (Bukharin, 1966, p. 194). Yet even in those bodies established to represent the international proletariat, nationalist sentiments were strongly held. For example, the published minutes of the General Council of the First International (1864–1866) reveal that on the few occasions when Russia was on the agenda, each time it was in relation to Russian suppression of the Poles (The General Council of the First International, 1964). The Bolsheviks inherited ideas on the nature of the nationalities from the Tsarist authorities as well as from their understandings of Marxism. In Central Asia, for example, the Bolsheviks considered that they were conducting a sort of "civilizing mission" to help the "natives" overcome nomadism and Islam (see Ali Igmen, 2012). Empire builders of the past, from Alexander the Great to Queen Victoria, recognized the need to learn about the cultures of 'their subjects if they were to rule over them with any authority' (Rashid, 2008, p. XLVIII).

Nationalism is more than ideology or a form of politics, it is also related to culture and identity, and is 'ubiquitous, pervasive, and complex' (see Smith, 1991, p. 143). It has proven to be the most potent force for mobilizing the largest number of people, across time and space, at different levels of development and within different political systems. As one noted scholar on nationalism pointed out, many countries have tombs to the "unknown soldier," but there are no tombs to the "unknown Marxist" (Anderson, 1983, pp. 9–10). The victory over German Nazism, Italian Fascism, and Japanese Imperialism did not mark the end of the national idea. The idea of the nation state is something that has strong appeal still to those nations without a state, such as the Palestinians and Kurds (and among almost half of the Scots, as revealed in the referendum on Scottish independence in 21 September 2014).

Of all collective identities which humans share, national identity is the most fundamental. One of the leading scholars of nationalism and the politics of national identity has demonstrated in his writings that of all shared identities nationalism has the greatest potential for political mobilization of the masses (Smith, 1991, p. 143; see also Bloom, 1990). To give the obligatory reference to Benedict Anderson (1983), the national community is an 'imagined community.' Yet it is no less real for having been initially imagined. An imagined community is not then an *imaginary* community, but one through which individuals perceive themselves as belonging to a wider collective membership—it has real meaning in peoples' lives.

Each nation creates myths and symbols relating to shared experiences, and then develops historical memories that serve together to create a sense of belonging to a separate community distinguished from others. The Bolsheviks constructed the Soviet state according to the powerful logic of national identities, with each of the major nations of the former empire given its own territorial boundaries and permitted to develop both political and cultural institutions to preserve and enhance its own language and culture. Thus the two key components central to most definitions of national identity—language and territory—were institutionalized at the foundation of the Soviet state. Lenin had stated in his treatise on the national question that as the most important means of human intercourse the 'unity and unimpeded development of language are the most important conditions ... for a free and broad grouping of the population in all its various classes' (Lenin, 1947, p. 8). He was talking about the development of the national idea linked to capitalism, but this would come to apply also to the USSR.

Although there is a tendency in political and popular discourse to use them interchangeably, the two terms "nation" and "state" are distinct. A nation can be defined as a 'named human population sharing an historic territory, common myths and historical memories, a mass, public culture, a common economy and common legal rights and duties for all its members' (Smith, 1991, p. 13). From this definition it is clear that the nation should be distinguished from the state. The nation is a historical concept founded upon cultural identity shared by a specific community, whereas the state is a political unit comprising public institutions representing (and or ruling over) the population of a specific bounded territory. The two concepts are though closely interlinked, because since the beginning of the modern era the nation has come to form the main principle for legitimizing the political institutionalization of the state, in the form of the nation-state. The fact that few states are neatly comprised of a single homogenous nation does not detract from the fact that the nation-state provides the boundaries within which political argument and contestation takes place. The institutions of the state provide the basis for political loyalty in the form of citizenship. The idea of the nation promotes an emotional relationship through which citizens gain a sense of identity. Hence, in forging this national identity there exists a symbiotic relationship between nation and state, with domestic political groups within the state mobilizing national identity for their own instrumental goals. In the Soviet case, attempts to foster a common class identity based upon proletarian internationalism and the new "Soviet man" failed in the end to transcend the pull of the national idea, and the conception of the nation-state. To demonstrate the significance of the national question throughout the Soviet era we should turn back to the beginning, and the ways in which Soviet Communism dealt with the "national question."

Lenin and the National Question

The USSR was established at a time when the main organizing principle of international relations was linked to the right of national self-determination. This confronted the Bolsheviks with serious challenges, and would continue to have profound consequences for the future development of Soviet Communism until the very end. As the previous chapters make clear, nationalism, national identities, and conceptions of the national interest, always usurped the power of class as a determinant in the most significant developments relating to the USSR's place in the wider world. At the outset it was necessary for Lenin to try and manipulate the nationalist sentiments of the minority peoples of the Tsarist Empire to construct a new multinational entity that could ultimately be transformed into a *post*-national one. Hence, to consolidate power after 1917 in the name of the working class, the communists found it incumbent to construct what became the 'first modern state to place the national principle as the base of its federal structure' (Pipes, 1964, p. 11). Lenin pandered to nationalist sentiment as a tactic in his longer-term strategic internationalist revolutionary goal, but in so doing he set in place an institutional structure that would eventually be used to undermine this objective.

Many of the Bolsheviks who took power after 1917 had long been divorced from the Russian masses, by being in prison, in exile, in hiding, or simply in a different cultural world. And those masses, in whose name the Bolsheviks had instituted revolution, were comprised mainly not of workers, but of peasants. Many if not most of the workers in the big industrial enterprises too were themselves recent migrants from farms in the Russian countryside. The Bolsheviks always had a secret fear that Russian nationalism was a stronger force than labour solidarity. The Tsarist Empire faced challenges from various quarters at the beginning of the twentieth century, many of these coming from national minorities. For example, in 1902 national liberation movements sprang up in Armenia, Finland, and in Ukraine. The divisions among the Bolsheviks on the question of the national minorities in the years leading up to the revolution were often intense, with party members in Ukraine holding the strongest views in support of decentralization based on ethnic nationality.

By the 1970 census there were 23 nationalities in the USSR with a population exceeding one million, and thirteen of those exceeded two million. To put this into some perspective, in 2014 of the 193 member states of the UN, forty of them had a population in excess of one million. In just one state, the USSR, there were roughly half as many nations as those represented in the United Nations with a population over a million at that time. Soviet Communism in the USSR was a truly remarkable experiment in social engineering, seeking to integrate a complex mix of cultures and religions and nations into a single post-national entity. A union between Muslims and Orthodox and Catholic Christians, and Buddhists, was always going to be a challenge. In an age of nationalism, a voluntary union incorporating peoples with their own specific histories, living in some cases ten time zones away from one another, with no shared language, was difficult to conceive. A kaleidoscope of peoples and cultures with such radically different levels of political, social, and economic development makes the European Union in comparison look more like a single coherent family, in spite of the numerous languages that are spoken. Another interesting factor is that some of the subject peoples of the Soviet state did not have a written form of their own language before the Revolution in 1917. The Bolsheviks therefore provided them with this key instrument for fostering a sense of a distinct and separate national identity.

Lenin had always recognized the power of the national idea, noting that a 'precise formulation' of the problem of the national question could not be avoided by Marxists (Lenin, 1947, p. 8). The matter had been dealt with not only in the Russian Bolshevik Party Program of 1903, but also in the earlier resolution of the London International Congress of 1896. Although Bukharin was typical among the Bolsheviks in offering a Marxist explanation for the causes of national prejudices and enmity between nations, he traced what he termed 'intertribal enmity' back to the pre-capitalist period of human history. However, under capitalism the working classes had been hoodwinked into accepting a status quo that kept them in poverty and subject to capitalist exploitation. It was necessary after 1917 therefore to foster among the workers and peasants of the world a sense of their belonging to a common class in opposition to international capital. It was necessary for the workers to unite, forgetting their national differences, 'in one worldwide league for the struggle with the capitalists. Forgetting all the national differences that tend to hinder union, they must unite in one great army to carry on a joint war against capitalism' (Bukharin, 1966, p. 194). Bukharin also recognized that there was an apparent contradiction between the stated Bolshevik objective of a unified proletarian world and the call for independent nation states. He went on to argue that the Bolsheviks should initially champion nation states and 'to countenance the temporary separation of one nation from another' (Bukharin, p. 198). Hence it was simply a pragmatic policy that was designed in the end to override the national idea, for the Bolsheviks never seriously contemplated enabling the national minorities of the defeated Tsarist Empire to gain actual independence, even as they encouraged national minorities among other empires to fight for their independence.

It was the Great War that brought Lenin to the view that a revolution in the name of the proletariat could bring the workers of the world together united against the bourgeoisie, and to turn the war of nation against nation into a class war. Lenin set out these ideas in his *April Theses*, published in *Pravda* on April 7, 1917 following his return to Petrograd just a few days before (Lenin, 1917). But loyalty to the nation proved to be resilient. During the war the Tsar changed the Germanic name of the Russian capital, St. Petersburg, to the Russian name of Petrograd. During the same period the English Royal family changed its name from the German-sounding Saxe-Coburg Gotha, to the more English sounding Windsor. The royal houses of Europe recognized during these times the power of the national idea. It was not so much the spectre of communism that they faced, as it was the spectre of nationalism.

Stalin and the National Question

Stalin's first role in government after the October Revolution was as commissar (i.e., minister) of nationalities, as he initially came to Lenin's attention for his writing on the national question in the Russian Empire. In his famous thesis on the national question Stalin qualified the right of nations to self-determination by stressing that there was also 'the right of the working class to consolidate its power, and to this latter right the right of self-determination is subordinate. There are occasions when the right of self-determination conflicts with the other, the higher right—the right of a working class that has assumed power to consolidate its power'. Stalin made it clear that class identity and class politics superseded those of the nation. He went on to state bluntly that if such conflicts occur between nation and class, that 'the right to self-determination cannot and must not serve as an obstacle to the exercise by the working class of its right to dictatorship' (Stalin, 1936, p.110). The official depiction of this relationship was said to be a federal state that was national in form, but socialist in content.

In 1936 Stalin would claim that in the sphere of nationality relations a new multi-national socialist state had developed with equality and no exploitation, based upon genuine feelings of mutual friendship between the different nationalities that make up the USSR. Stalin himself was well aware of the power of the national idea, as he himself, as a member of a national minority in the Russian Empire, first flirted with nationalism. In his youth Stalin was a Georgian nationalist who wrote poetry in his native tongue. Stalin may have studied in a religious order and composed poetry in his native Georgian language, but he also took a hard line against the Georgian communist party for seeking autonomy for the Georgian nation after the Bolshevik Revolution. It is an interesting aside to note how many authoritarian nationalists came from a different ethnic group to that which they led: Stalin was a Georgian, Hitler was an Austrian, Napoleon was Corsican, Alexander the Great was Macedonian, and Milosevic was Montenegrin.

However, as the Commissar for Nationalities, Stalin set about preventing practical autonomy for the various nations of the new post-imperial state, despite their ostensible constitutional rights to national liberation. Stalin's priority was to ensure that the national minorities would not revolt, but remained under Moscow's (Russia's) control. Although the Russian Civil War was clearly an internal war pitting supporters of the old regime against revolutionaries fighting in the name of socialism, both the Whites and the Reds sought to rally national support to their own side by demonstrating that they were the true supporters of the Russian nation. Bolsheviks were prone during the Civil War to what was termed "Red Russian patriotism." Before he died in 1924, Lenin was horrified to discover that apparently one of the Bolsheviks most infected with Russian Red patriotism was none other than the commissar for nationalities himself. Lenin dictated a letter in December 1922 in which he criticized Stalin for 'Great Russian chauvinism' (Tucker, 1977, p. 104). Tucker noted also that after the split of the RDLP into factions Stalin actually considered the Bolsheviks to be the Russian faction and the Mensheviks the Jewish one. One should note also that just before he died Stalin was planning a purge on the basis of an alleged plot to kill him and other leading communist figures by a group of medical doctors, who all happened to be Jewish. The role of Jewish figures in the history of Soviet communism (indeed in most communist parties in the West too) is fascinating, and a separate subject in its own right. When the Communists took power briefly in Hungary in 1919, 32 of the 45 members of the communist leadership were Jewish, and in 1930, 35% of the membership of the Polish communist party were Jewish, whilst during this same period roughly half of the membership of the US Communist Party were Jews (Brown, 2009, pp. 80, 130, 132; see also Lane, 1968; and Judt, 2007, pp. 181–166). One factor explaining the high proportion of Jews as communists is that they did not have a nation state to which they could hold allegiance, hence they were perhaps more naturally prone to internationalism.

In his report, "On the Draft Constitution of the U.S.S.R." to the Extraordinary Eighth Congress of Soviets of the USSR on Nov 25, 1936, Stalin stated that developments in the USSR with the end of NEP, the liquidation of the kulaks, and the establishment of collective farms, 'means that the exploitation of man by man has been abolished, eliminated, while the socialist ownership of the implements and means of production has been established as the unshakable foundation of our Soviet society.' Stalin went on to say that with this new socialist economy there was no unemployment, no poverty, and all citizens could enjoy a prosperous and cultured life. Hence the class structure for all exploiting classes had been eliminated. Now Soviet society was comprised, he said, of the 'working class', the 'peasantry', and the 'intelligentsia'. The Soviet working class therefore should no longer be called the 'proletariat', because the Soviet workers had been emancipated and hence transformed into an entirely new class that controlled the means of production along with all the people. Soviet peasants were now said to be officially emancipated from their exploiters, and hence represented a new class based not on private, but on collective property. And the new Soviet intelligentsia was not from the old aristocracy or the bourgeoisie, but from the working class and the peasantry, therefore no longer serving a wealthy capitalist stratum, but now serving 'the people'. Hence, in official proclamations the USSR no longer had class contradictions, and the national question was said to be resolved.

The endorsement of "socialism in one country" resulted in a new focus in the media and in official ideology on the dangers not so much of global capitalism and the international bourgeoisie, but rather the German or British or French or American venal exploiter. During a period, in the 1930s, when Fascism and Nazism was on the rise in Europe, Soviet authorities were warning of the dangers of foreign enemies who were seeking to undermine the Soviet communist system. The dangers of Nazism, clearly the most significant threat at the time, were largely ignored. The appeal then was to national pride, Already, by the late 1920s, Stalin was promoting a new representation of Soviet society based upon national identity in which the 'active internationalism of the civil war and moderately pragmatic cosmopolitanism of the NEP ... waned. In their place appeared ethnocentrism and Soviet exceptionalism and ... public expressions of xenophobia and isolationism' (Brooks, 2000, p. 38). It was at this time, in its developmental stages, that anti-foreign rhetoric was used to crush internal dissent. It also created a sense of an existential threat to the homeland, and was used as a mobilizing instrument to foster a Soviet collective identity. These external threats were then employed as a device to achieve internal, domestic goals: legitimating communist rule and creating a cohesive Soviet identity, albeit one with Russia at the core. There was a genuine fear also that ideas emanating from outside could infect Soviet citizens, and hence challenge the purity and rightness of Marxist-Leninist ideology, upon which rested the CPSU's title to rule.

There was then ample evidence that Stalin appreciated that national sentiments and forces were potentially far more potent than class affiliations. This would become clear in a number of separate domestic and foreign policies that Stalin would later pursue. Before and during the Second World War Stalin had good reason to be fearful of disloyalty and treason from within, given the fact that some national minorities had sought to gain autonomy or even independence from Moscow. Stalin trusted no one and his bloody purges inflicted death and suffering on massive numbers of innocent victims. Between 1937 and 1938 around 250,000 Soviet citizens were shot on 'essentially ethnic grounds' (Snyder, 2011, p. 89). During the high period of Stalin's purges it has been estimated that one-third of those executed were members of ethnic minorities (Roberts, 2008, p. 19). There can be no justification for such murderous policies; but it is I believe necessary to understand the paranoid fear that Stalin had of national minorities destabilizing centralized authority in Moscow. During the Second World War Stalin sought to mobilize the Soviet population around a new conception of Soviet patriotism, mixed with socialism, something that followed naturally from his earlier conception of socialism in one country.

Following the Nazi-Soviet Pact and the invasion of Poland, Soviet troops executed or deported numerous ethnic Poles, and in one infamous incident in 1949 in Katyn, they massacred some 20,000 Polish officers. There was also the tragedy for the peoples of the Northern Caucasus, as Stalin implemented in 1944 a policy of ethnic cleansing, forcibly deporting Chechens and other nationalities in the region to the outer perimeters of the Soviet empire, chiefly to Kazakhstan. This was a much more systematic and brutal treatment of the minority nations than had occurred under the Tsars. Over 700,000 non-Russian Soviet citizens were uprooted from their homes in the Caucasus, for the most part Muslim in faith, and sent in cattle trucks and airless freight trains to Central Asia. Many thousands died during transportation. It is estimated that 30 percent of the entire Chechen population were killed as a direct consequence of the deportations (Wood, 2007, p. 38). This ethnic cleansing became a defining event for the

Chechen people, comprising an important component and symbol of their national identity, and fostering hatred of the Russian people, whilst creating a mobilizing dynamic for gaining their own territorial independence. This would lead to the two wars of independence against Russia following the collapse of the Soviet Union.

John Gray notes that 'The Stalinist regime murdered many more people than the Nazis. Entire peoples such as the Volga Germans and the Crimean Tatars were subject to deportations that were genocidal in their effects' (Gray, 2008 p. 53). Stalin's attacks on the nationalities occurred in waves, with Ukrainians, Poles, Koreans, Iranians and other minority nationalities living in the USSR being subject at different times to purges, labour camps, or forced deportations to Central Asia. The first total forced deportation that Stalin undertook was in 1937 when 175,000 Koreans were sent from the Soviet Far East to Kazakhstan and Uzbekistan (Naimark, 2010, p. 87). The Bolsheviks lost the war against the Poles between 1919 and 1920, but after the signing of the Molotov-Ribbentrop Pact and Soviet intervention into eastern Poland Stalin had his revenge. The *Osadniks*, those former Polish partisans who fought against communist Russia and settled on the border with Ukraine, having been given land by the Polish authorities, were singled out by Stalin and packed off to Siberian labour camps. It has been estimated some 320,000 Poles between 1939 and 1940 suffered this fate (see memo.ru, 2010).

Stalin's fear of disloyalty among the non-Russian populations of the border areas of the USSR during the war was far from unwarranted paranoia. The United States interned many ethnic Japanese residents in the US during the war for fear that they would be disloyal and act as a fifth column for Japanese imperialism, and more than 60 percent of those held US citizenship (see Truman Library, 1942–1948). It was not just the Soviet state that engaged in ethnic cleansing during this period. The holocaust against the Jews, the worst genocide in history, resulted in 5.7 million deaths. In Croatia some 592,000 Serbs, Muslims and Jews were killed by the *Ustashe* regime. The end of the war in 1945 actually exacerbated ethnic cleansing and the deportations of populations on the basis of ethnicity. As Keith Lowe notes: 'Between 1945 and 1947 tens of millions of men, women and children were expelled from their countries in some of the biggest acts of ethnic cleansing the world has ever seen' (Lowe, 2013, p. xvi).

Ukrainians massacred Poles, Bulgarians massacred Greeks, and Hungarians massacred Serbs (Lowe, 2013, p. 21). Several million Germans were driven out of East Prussia, Silesia, and Pomerania by the Soviet Red Army, with those parts of eastern Germany handed over to Poland.

It is also worth recalling that Stalin supported, along with the USA, the establishment of the state of Israel on previously British-occupied territory in Palestine, for he considered this a positive step in undermining the power of the British Empire. When war broke out between Israel and the Arabs soon after the establishment of Israel, in 1948, Stalin supported the Zionists seeing this nationalist movement as a force undermining both British colonialism and Arab feudalism (Halliday, 2010, p. 117). Had Lenin survived he might have pursued different policies from those of Stalin—but like Lenin, Stalin based his policies on pragmatic calculations, taking into consideration the power of nationalism and the balance of power. Stalin, however reluctantly, understood the power of nationalism only too well, and even the idea of a united socialist Germany inspired fear rather than aspiration.

The National Question from Khrushchev to Brezhnev

Stalin's eventual successor in the Kremlin, Nikita Khrushchev, whose wife was Ukrainian, also understood the dangers posed by nationalism to the Soviet multinational state. Coming himself from a peasant background he was particularly concerned about the power of religion, fearing that religious freedoms could undermine the cohesiveness of the 'Soviet family of nations', as religion was linked strongly to national sentiments, thereby undermining class solidarity. In the context of the USSR religions were associated with different nations, not the Soviet state. Stalin's use of religious motifs in the war against Nazi Germany was not comprehensive, but was largely designed to mobilize Russians, the dominant nationality, to fight for their nation. Clearly Stalin saw this as a much more effective rallying cry than that of proletarian internationalism, or even that of Soviet Communism. Stalin had even permitted the reopening of Russian Orthodox churches that had previously been forcibly closed down, and allowed the construction of new ones. Baptisms and church burial services among Orthodox Christians also became more common in the late Stalin years. As Catherine Merridale notes, despite the mass suffering in the Soviet Union during the Stalin years, with literally millions dying in warfare, through famine, or the purges—with the absence of church services there was no allowance or framework provided for mourning (Merridale, 2000, p. 8). Those who lost loved ones, especially ones killed in the camps or in the purges, were forced to keep their pain hidden. Stalin's earlier attack on religion transformed cemeteries into parks, and new educational campaigns were instituted to instruct in Marxism-Leninism and to foster atheism.

Stalin's reversed course was significant, and it was based on a pragmatic acknowledgement of the need for people to have spiritual guidance and comfort from the church, something that could not be supplied in times of emergency, such as the struggle against Nazism, by Soviet Communism and the Soviet state. It is instructive to note that both Gorbachev and Yeltsin, who were born within a month of one another in 1931, had been baptized in their local village Orthodox churches. They were both born in small rural settlements far from Moscow, Gorbachev near the Caucasus, Yeltsin east of the Urals. Both Lenin and Brezhnev had also been baptized (for this revelation on Brezhnev see *Interfax*, 2006). Stalin was baptized and began training in a seminary. Putin relates how as a one-month old baby in 1950 he was taken by his mother to a central Orthodox church in Leningrad to be baptized, unbeknownst to his father, who was a communist in good standing (Putin, 2013). Putin himself is a professed religious observer.

Khrushchev's renewed assault on religion was in part linked to the domestic power struggle following Stalin's death, and to his de-Stalinization campaign. His attack on the church, which would involve a fresh purge of the church hierarchy, increased taxes, anti-religious propaganda, and the closing of churches and monasteries was justified as a return to the more radical Leninist anti-religious and internationalist approach of the earlier revolutionary period (Taubman, 2003, p. 512). Khrushchev argued that he was freeing the Soviet people from those relics of the past that had hindered development, and that this was necessary to undermine the most potent relic of all, that of nationalism. As a young boy growing up in the tiny village of Kalinovka, Khrushchev was taught to read through the scriptures, and had to pray in front of Orthodox icons in the local Church in which he too was baptized. He recalls in his memoirs how one of his schoolteachers, a Bolshevik revolutionary named Lydia Shevchenko, instilled in him his first political consciousness, saving him from what he saw to be the insidious effects of religious belief (Khrushchev, 1971, p. 22). When he was Moscow Party Chief in the early 1930s Khrushchev had already instigated a major attack on religion. It was Khrushchev who supervised the blowing up of Moscow's most famous and revered Orthodox Church, with much of the marble from the ruins used in the construction of the Moscow Metro, a project that Khrushchev also oversaw. After Stalin's death he returned to this attack on religion by closing down thousands of churches and mosques across the entire USSR. Having stated this it should be noted that Khrushchev would, as part of his personal bid for power after Stalin's death condemn the deportations of the people of the Caucasus as a violation of Leninist principles. In his speech to the 20th Party Congress he suggested that Ukrainians had only been saved from the same fate because there were so many of them and because there was no place left to resettle them.

With the incorporation of the three Baltic countries and Moldova into the USSR after the Second World War, the Soviet Union was divided into federal units on the basis of ethnic groups at different levels of autonomy. Those ethnic national territories that had borders with foreign states were accorded full Soviet Republican status (see Table 6.1). By the late Soviet period each Republic had come to show significant numbers of ethnic Russians. As can be seen from the Table, Russians accounted for a substantial percentage of the population in Kazakhstan and the Baltic republics, and it was in those four republics that the first stirrings of anti-Soviet (that is, anti-Russian) nationalism would manifest themselves when Gorbachev implemented reforms in the mid 1980s. Within the non-Russian republics, ethnic Russians tended to reside in the larger cities. For example, in 1989 Russians accounted for 47.3 percent of the population in Riga, the Latvian capital, 41.2 percent of the population in Tallinn, the Estonian capital, 59.1 percent of the population in Alma-Ata (Kazakhstan), and 55.8 percent in Dushanbe (Tajikistan). Many among the titular indigenous nationalities in these cities considered the Russians to be colonial overseers. Russians comprised fewer than 20 percent of the population of Kazakhstan in the mid 1920s—by 1979 this had increased to over 40 percent. Yet only one percent of the Russians living in Kazakhstan could speak

Table 6.1   The ethnic composition of the Union of Soviet Socialist
Republics (1990)

Republic	Population	Percentage of Titular Nationality Living in Republic	Three Largest Ethnic Groups (% of Republic's population)
Armenia	3,304,000	66.6	Armenians (93.3) Azeris (2.6) Kurds (1.7)
Azerbaijan	7,020,000	85.3	Azeris (82.6) Russians (5.6) Armenians (5.6)
Belorussia	10,149,000	78.7	Belorussians (77.8) Russians (13.2) Poles (4.1)
Estonia	1,556,000	93.8	Estonians (61.5) Russians (30.3) Ukrainians (3.3)
Georgia	5,396,000	95.1	Georgians (70.2) Armenians (8.1) Russians (6.3)
Kazakhstan	16,463,000	80.3	Kazakhs (39.7) Russians (37.8) Germans (5.8)
Kyrgyzstan	4,258,000	88.0	Kirgiz (52.3) Russians (21.5) Uzbeks (12.9)
Latvia	2,667,000	95.1	Latvians (52.0) Russians (34.0) Belorussians (4.5)
Lithuania	3,673,000	95.3	Lithuanians (79.6) Russians (9.4) Poles (7.0)
Moldova	4,3332,000	83.2	Moldavians (64.4) Ukrainians (13.8) Russians (12.9)
Russia	147,002,000	82.6	Russians (81.5) Tatars (3.8) Ukrainians (3.0)
Tadzhikistan	5,090,000	75.1	Tadzhiks (62.2) Uzbeks (23.5) Russians (7.6)

(*continued*)

Table 6.1   Continued

Republic	Population	Percentage of Titular Nationality Living in Republic	Three Largest Ethnic Groups (% of Republic's population)
Turkmenistan	3,512,000	92.9	Turkmen (71.9) Russians (9.5) Uzbeks (9.0)
Ukraine	51,449,000	84.7	Ukrainians (72.6) Russians (22.0) Jews (0.9)
Uzbekistan	19,808,000	84.6	Uzbeks (71.3) Russians (8.3) Tadzhiks (4.7)
USSR Total	285,689,000	N/A	Russians (50.99) Ukrainians (14.45) Uzbeks (5.84)

Source: 1989 census

Kazakh. In Estonia the Russian population accounted for 8 percent of the total population in the 1930s—by 1989 the figure had reached 30 percent. When the Soviet Union expired in December 1991 25 million Russians, comprising more than 17 percent of the entire Russian population of the USSR, found themselves living in foreign states with respect to Russia. Half of those Russians living in what now Russians officially termed the "near abroad" were born there. Still part of the Russian nation, they were now living in and subject to the laws of a foreign state. The term near abroad (in Russian: *blizhneye zarubezh'e*) emerged in 1992 and referred to the other fourteen former republics of the USSR. The term indicated how difficult it was for Russians to accept the fact that they were indeed now foreign countries. Events twenty-two years later in Crimea and eastern and southern Ukraine would bear this out.

There were some fifty nationalities in the USSR in 1989 with a population in excess of 100,000 (and many more with less than this number). As noted, twenty-three nations had over one million. Between the two censuses of 1979 and 1989 the overall population had grown from 262 million to 285 million, an increase of 9 percent. However, there were some worrying trends for the CPSU leadership as the ethnic groups showing the largest percentage increase, by far, were the Muslims of Central Asia. Whereas the Russian population had grown by 5.6 percent between 1979 and 1989, the Tajik population had grown by 45.5 percent, the Turkmen by 34 percent, the Kirgiz by 32 percent, Kazakhs by 24 percent, Azerbaijanis by 24 percent, and there were large increases among the Muslims in the Northern Caucasus (Dagestan and Chechnya). Under Brezhnev this demographic imbalance was perceived as a critical issue. Although the Bolsheviks promised the peoples of the USSR that their cultures would be preserved, in reality the Muslim populations suffered the most discrimination of any religion. Islam was lambasted as an outdated and dangerous relic of a bygone, feudal era, with no place in Soviet communist society.

The vast majority of those deported from the Caucasus and Crimea by Stalin during the Second World War were Muslims. Up until the Gorbachev period the Soviet Communist Party leadership would often refer to the Islamic communities of the USSR as "backward peoples" (Andrew and Mitrokhin, 2005, p. 370). During the Cold War, the USSR was the fifth largest Muslim country in the world in terms of population, with only India, Indonesia, Pakistan, and Bangladesh having larger Muslim populations. In 1981 Brezhnev passed discriminatory laws in an attempt to influence trends in fertility rates by providing inducements to Slav populations to have larger families. Child allowances in regions with predominantly Slav populations were increased to 50 roubles per month, whilst other regions had to be satisfied with 35 roubles. In addition, generous maternity leave with pay for mothers was introduced, but again only in certain areas (implementation of such legislation in the Central Asian republics and the Caucasus had to wait for such benefits to come into force at a much later date). I have noted how social revolutions have tended to come from the villages into to the towns. Another worrying factor for Brezhnev in 1981 was the fact that Kazakhs made up only 12 percent of the population of Alma Ata, the capital of Kazakhstan, whereas Russians comprised over 70 percent. Yet the Kazakhs made up around 93 percent of the population in most rural areas of the republic. There was a perceived strong possibility of a rural uprising of the indigenous population against the Russians, stirred up by dissatisfied members of the intelligentsia among titular nationalities in the cities, frustrated at seeing the best jobs and the plum positions going to Russians. Some saw this situation as a tinderbox waiting to go up (Shearman, 1983, 1984). Indeed, the first real signs of trouble would come in Kazakhstan in 1986 in the early Gorbachev era.

Each of the republics had its own academy of sciences, and its own national media (newspaper, television, and radio), thereby providing the instruments necessary for fostering a sense of national community. In addition, and this would be critical to how the USSR would eventually be dismantled, each of the republics had its own institutions of government (ministries, parliaments, and councils), separate communist party organizations, and even their own national branches of the KGB (in the cases of Ukraine and Belorussia, they also had separate individual membership of the United Nations). Thus the republics had the institutions for both elite and mass channels for reinforcing a sense of national identity. The only republic not to enjoy these privileges was Russia. Power in the USSR was centralized in the Kremlin, and here Russia and ethnic Russians dominated (notwithstanding the fact that Stalin was a Georgian), hence it was considered unnecessary for the Russian Soviet Federative Socialist Republic (RSFSR) to have the same privileges as the other republics.

There were clear tensions between the goal being pursued— of creating a new post-national Soviet identity—and the actual provision of the institutions that encouraged the continuation of national identities. The objective was to create a "flourishing" of nations on an equal basis (*rastvet*) whilst simultaneously drawing the nations together (*sblizhenie*) through a process of socialization (Sovietization), to create the new "Soviet person" (Shearman, 2000, p. 84). Given the Communist Party's control over the means of communication, over the educational curriculum, and other forms of socialization with an elaborate construction of symbols and myths, the leadership was in a powerful position to be able to construct a new, imagined Soviet community. The myths that developed to create this sense of identity revolved around Lenin as the great foundational leader (the cult of Lenin was enshrined in the Mausoleum after his death). In addition to this foundational myth relating to the great October Revolution and Lenin as the "founding father" of the Soviet state, a sustaining myth revolved around the idea of the collective Soviet people working together to build socialism, and an eschatological myth in which the USSR was playing the vital historical role in developing communism on a world-wide basis (see Barner-Barry and Hody, 1994). One can compare this aspect of Leninism with religious belief, and Lenin's tomb as a place of religious pilgrimage. The objective of creating these narratives and myths was to foster a sense of loyalty to the Soviet communist state. But to be effective, myths have to be believed.

In 1943 the French-inspired *Internationale* of 1871 was superseded by a new Soviet "national anthem" which referred to the 'unbreakable union of free republics, which "Great Russia" [*Velikaya Rus*] has welded forever to stand'. The previous capital, St. Petersburg—Petrograd after 1914—associated with a more western-orientated period of Russia's past was renamed Leningrad after the founder of the new Soviet state. Scores of other towns across the USSR changed their names to commemorate Lenin (e.g., we now had Leninabad, Leninogorsk, Leninsk, Leninskiy, Leninskoye Leninakan), as well as streets and squares and buildings named after Lenin. Lenin was, quite simply, ubiquitous. Leninakan, a small town in Armenia, took the brunt of the devastating earthquake that killed some 20,000 people in 1988. The town was renamed in 1990 to its old Armenian name of Gyumri.

Despite the officially stated objective of transcending national identity, the Soviet people (the *Sovietskii narod*) was essentially constructed from a form of great Russian chauvinism. Official Soviet discourse used the term *narod* rather than *natsiia* (nation) to describe Soviet citizens, but it was clear that in the shared Soviet history that the Communist Party propagated—through all state-controlled media, through school texts, and military training programmes—Russia and Russians dominated. In 1937 the Stalin Prize for Literature (of 75,000 rubles) was won by Professor A. V. Shestakov for his *A Short Course in the History of the USSR* (Shestakov, 1939). The heroes of Shestakov's history are Russians, and Russia plays the leading role in the narrative. The text became the main source for an interpretation of Soviet history and also a key influence in establishing a new Soviet identity in the USSR (see Brandenberger, 2002, p. 260). The influence of the book was profound, as it was used not only as a school text but also was widely read by adults. It was perhaps the single most influential source (and official source: Stalin was closely associated with its early production and dissemination) for fostering a new sense of patriotism with Russia at the core, from the late 1930s through to the late 1950s.

Yet the propagated myth of a cohesive Soviet people failed to create a strong collective sense of belonging to a new community. On the contrary, policies of ethnic cleansing during the war, Russification of Soviet society, and practical discrimination against ethnic minorities in the political realm undermined prospects of achieving the stated goals. Rather, the myths of the ethnic nation were much stronger and had more resonance among both elites and the masses, and their origins could be traced back over a much longer time frame than 1917. These myths proved to be much more potent. Indeed, one can argue that in the end identity with the new Soviet community existed chiefly in the minds (or at least in the rhetoric) of elites in the CPSU in Moscow (and among some western Sovietologists). Therefore one can say that the Soviet community of nations *was* an imaginary community. The territorialized and national nature of the federal Soviet system helped to create a *national* intelligentsia in the republics which eventually would utilize a narrative of their own distinct national histories, symbols, and myths which ultimately had far more power and legitimacy as a mobilizing force for politics, in what effectively became the politics of national liberation. (Shearman, 2000, p. 85). The "shared" culture of the Soviet people came to be viewed as one of imposition by a neocolonial power.

There developed under Brezhnev's leadership what appeared to be an unwritten rule whereby the First Communist Party Secretary in each of the Union Republics was a member of the titular nationality, with the Second Secretary an ethnic Russian. The Second Secretaries were in charge of the *nomenklatura* system of appointments at all other senior levels, thereby giving Moscow (Russia) effective control over the constituent parts of the federal state. Russians also predominated in the highest all-Union party and state structures. The non-Russians appointed to holding high posts were the most trusted, and often the most Russianized (see Carrere d'Encausse, 1978). If First Secretaries in the republics demonstrated any independence from Moscow's dictates then they were quickly removed. To take just one example, Khrushchev in 1954 was faced with opposition to his agricultural policies in Kazakhstan from the First Secretary, Rakhmizhan Shayakhmetov. Khrushchev determined that the opposition was not due to any differences over policy, but rather Shayakhmetov, an ethnic Kazakh, had been 'infected with the virus of nationalism'

(Khrushchev, 1974, p. 158). The Soviet leader thought that the opposition was due to a fear among Kazakhs that an expansion of agricultural cultivation in the republic would lead to an influx of ethnic Russians (which of course it did, leading to ethnic clashes in the 1980s under Gorbachev). Khrushchev replaced Shayakhmetov with a more reliable ethnic Slav. He also appointed Leonid Brezhnev, the future Soviet leader, to the post of Second Secretary in Kazakhstan.

Russian nationalist sentiments were also becoming manifest, including in some quarters of the CPSU. This was something Alexander Yakovlev brought attention to in an article published in the Soviet Writers' Weekly, *Literaturnaia Gazeta* (15 November, 1972). Yakovlev at that time was head of the CPSU Central Committee department dealing with propaganda, and a committed Marxist-Leninist. In his article he alluded to the manifestations of Russian nationalism appearing in contemporary books, journals and newspapers, warning of its dangers to the communist cause. Yakovlev had mistakenly assumed that the Kremlin leadership would take heed of his warnings, but instead he was exiled to distant Canada where he would serve as Soviet ambassador for the next ten years. It seemed as long as fundamentals of the system were not challenged, Brezhnev could tolerate, if not openly support Great Russian nationalism within the party apparatus (see O'Connor, 2008, p. 56). Fearful of non-Russian nationalism, Brezhnev nevertheless encouraged an element of Great Russian chauvinism.

Nationalism and the Wider Communist World

Khrushchev and his successors in the Kremlin were confronted not only with the possibility of nationalist threats from within the USSR, but also threats from nationalism in the wider communist world. The German question had been of major importance since 1945, with crises over Berlin in 1953 and then again from 1958 through to the construction of the Berlin Wall in 1961. Khrushchev was faced with a crisis in Hungary in 1956, with the Hungarian communist party seeking to gain national independence from the Soviet bloc, a revolt that was put down in the end by Soviet tanks. When he took power from Khrushchev, Leonid Brezhnev too was faced with the forces of national identity, again from both within the Soviet Union itself and among the satellite states in Eastern Europe.

One of the reasons that the Brezhnev Doctrine was originally instituted was to prevent the reformism of the Prague Spring from infecting the western-most republics of the USSR, as the Kremlin feared the development of nationalist challenges to the Russian centre in Moscow. Here it is important also to recall the actual origins of the Prague Spring in 1968, something too often forgotten. The reformist movement in Czechoslovakia had its origins in tensions between the dominant Czechs and the minority Slovaks, with the latter being more interested in greater authority for themselves than any commitment to socialism or democracy (see Silnitsky, 1975). Soon after the collapse of the communist system Czechoslovakia would divide into two separate states (the Czech Republic and Slovakia) based on the two dominant ethnic groups.

Each of the individual communist states, even those which had communism imposed upon them by Soviet tanks, developed communism with certain national characteristics. It was also the case that the communist leadership in each communist state focused on, and used as a foil, what they portrayed as "foreign outside forces" that threatened the stability of the system, with foreign powers said to be seeking to undermine the cohesiveness of the collective communist community. Outside forces were demonized in nationalist terms and not in terms of class. In some cases outside forces did indeed seek to undermine the system by encouraging national dissent within the communist bloc. For example, the Reagan administration recognized the pull of Polish nationalism in the Solidarity trade union movement in the early 1980s, which led also to cooperation with the Polish Pope at that time. The coalition of the willing that effectively formed between the US President, the leader of the Polish trade union movement, and the Pope, demonstrated to many that Stalin's famous dismissal of the power of the Catholic Church was premature. In reality Stalin always recognized the potential power of religion, what in contemporary parlance is called "soft power." But the important point to note here is that each communist state demonized some outside force (most often the USA and the wider West, but not always, as noted it could be another communist state) in such terms as to foster not a sense of class solidarity but a strong sense of patriotism/nationalism.

In the wider communist world, in every single communist country, without exception, nationalism was a key factor in the origins of revolution, and then in how the political systems subsequently developed, and finally how they collapsed. One cannot fully understand the differences between communist systems, the antagonisms that often developed between them, and even within them, without an appreciation of distinct cultural forces, in particular that of nationalism, and the national identities that differentiated them. The Sino-Soviet dispute, Stalin's rift with Tito, and other squabbles and conflicts within the communist world were at least in part, if not in the main, caused by nationalist tensions, the politics of identity, and the balance of power. Tito had reacted to Soviet claims that he was engaged in revisionism and "Bernsteinism" by saying 'No matter how much each of us loves the land of socialism, the USSR, he can, in no case, love his own country less' (quoted in Wilson, 1979, p. 56). The Sino-Soviet rift was officially defined in ideological, class terms, at least for public consumption as the two communist parties sought leadership in the Third World (in struggles for "national liberation"). Yet privately and in secret official documents the conflict with the Chinese was seen in national terms. For example, in a secret report from a commission established by the CPSU Politburo, chaired by the chief ideologist Mikhail Suslov, a lengthy briefing paper was produced on the 'national-psychological' characteristics of the Chinese and how these impacted on China's foreign relations (see Andrew and Gordievsky, 1993, p. 195). A number of (uncomplimentary) national characteristics were listed that were said to make it very difficult to deal effectively and in a straightforward manner with the Chinese.

The majority of states of "socialist orientation" in the Third World emerged not out of class conflict, but out of nations seeking their liberation from foreign control, or for the overthrow of regimes linked to external powers. Nationalism was a chief mobilizing factor in stimulating social revolutions. This included, for example, the revolutions across three continents, in Cuba, Vietnam, and Angola. All these states did eventually turn to socialism. However, they too all developed socialism with national characteristics. In Cuba Jose Marti and not Karl Marx was originally the main inspiration for Fidel Castro, who was first and foremost a Cuban patriot who wished to establish a more equitable relationship with the United States. In Indochina Ho Chi Minh initially called on Woodrow Wilson to live up to his own ideals and to support the right of the Vietnamese people for national determination; and in Angola the leaders of the various insurgency groups were all initially led by strong nationalists fighting for independence from Portugal. All of the great Third World revolutionary leaders were nationalists before they were communists. And as we will see, as the Cold War ended and the Soviet Union was dismantled, leaders of formerly communist states quickly took on the mantle of nationalism themselves. It would turn out to be an easy transformation for the likes of Slobodan Milosevic, a communist leader of multinational Yugoslavia, to become almost overnight a nationalist leader of an independent Serbia. Nationalism in the Balkans was responsible for the outbreak of bloody conflicts both at the beginning and at the end of the twentieth century. The assassination of Archduke Franz Ferdinand in Sarajevo on 28 June 1914 led directly to the First World War; and Sarajevo then suffered the longest siege in the history of modern warfare during the Bosnian War between April 1992 and February 1996. In both instances nationalism was a key factor leading to hostilities.

In Chapter 4 it was noted that the Comintern-sponsored League Against Imperialism had its headquarters in Europe, in Berlin (later this moved to Paris), and its objective based on Marxism-Leninism, was to foster class solidarity and socialist revolution in the Third World. An article in 1930 in the weekly organ of the Communist League of America specified clearly that the 'village inevitably follows the city' (Landau, 1930, p. 5). Yet in practice the League Against Imperialism provided a forum for Chinese, African, Indian, and Irish nationalists, who were pushing for the villages to take the leading role in countering the colonial authorities (see for example O'Malley 2003). The original title of the organization was the League Against Imperialism and For National Independence, reflecting the importance of national identity rather than class. The original stimulus for the League was the debate between Lenin and Roy at the 2nd Comintern Congress in 1920 on the best way forward to counter the colonial authorities. The small vanguard parties that led their countries to independence and undertook a non-capitalist path of development from the 1950s through the 1980s began as movements of national liberation. Hence, although their revolutions were conducted in the name of Marx they were not designed as part of a universal socialist scheme, but had very particularistic features around the idea of the nation.

Ho Chi Minh's ambition, as with Mao's in China, 'was strongly driven by nationalism' (Knight, 2007, p. 148). In Latin America the Peruvian socialist Mariategui (the continent's Gramsci) saw Marxism in national terms, in that each individual country would adopt and adapt Marxist ideology accounting for the concrete situation pertaining in any specific time and place. However, like many other Marxists in the region, Mariategui was an advocate of internationalism throughout Latin America (Munk, 2007 p. 156; see also Becker, 1993). The communist insurgency in Malaya has been described as representing an 'extreme form of nationalism, but it did offer to many people in Malaya hopes of an end to colonial subjugation and humiliation' (Cheah Boon Kheng, 2012, p. 31). Many Soviet specialists on the Third World came to recognize that, because the territorial boundaries bequeathed to countries in the former colonies by the imperial powers did not reflect ethnic or tribal lines, there were always increased risks to both internal and external stability as groups would fight over contested territory (see for example, Brutents, 1977). The previous chapter noted the national origins of Euro-communism and then how the different parties pursuing Euro-Communism did so with specific national characteristics, whether in Italy, France, or Spain, and even in Japan. If the origins of the communist regimes that were created can be found in the initial appeals of nationalism, then so too it will be shown that it was nationalism that was responsible also for the death of Soviet Communism.

Also, in every communist system, across time and space and cultures, each at some point in its development engaged in pogroms, and these included attacks on ethnic and national minorities. The mass killings in Cambodia under Pol Pot have most often been put down to the maniacal nature of Pol Pot and the Khmer Rouge, based on their class hatred towards the educated population and intellectuals. However, as one of the most in-depth studies shows, ethnicity was an important part of the mix that helps to explain the mass bloodletting (see Kiernan, 2008).

The Empire Strikes Back

In the USSR then, although class was supposed to override nationalism as the primary focus of identity, during the entire Soviet era nationalism and ethnic issues were always simmering below the surface. The "nationality problem" was, as one influential study found 'the weakest link in the chain of Soviet armor' (Inkeles and Bauer, 1968, p. 338). On the fiftieth anniversary of the Nazi-Soviet Pact, on 23 August 1989, two million citizens of the three Baltic Republics formed a single human chain, linking hands in peaceful protest across some 400 miles, from Vilnius to Riga. This was a demonstrative symbol of the power of the nation and at the same time a reflection of how far the USSR under Gorbachev's reformism had moved away from the stifling repressive totalitarian system developed under Stalin.

There was a consensus among the CPSU leadership in the mid-1980s that, faced with a stagnating economy, changes were necessary to ensure the survival of Soviet Communism and the USSR's place in the wider world. The USSR was being left behind in terms of technological developments partly due to its isolation from the globalizing forces that had been underway during the past decade. The world was becoming increasingly globalized, yet the Soviet Union and the communist bloc were almost totally left out. Globalization therefore was not global, and the USSR as a great power was being pushed to the periphery of the international political economy. Simply put, in its productive capacity it could not compete with the USA and the wider western world (Brooks and Wohlforth, 2000/2001). Gorbachev's initial priority was to accelerate the Soviet economy (*uskoreniie*) by integrating the USSR into the global economy, encouraging foreign direct investment, and by providing incentives for individuals to engage in limited and restricted private enterprise, whilst also cutting defence expenditure. When there were no immediate and positive results from these limited economic reforms Gorbachev instituted his more radical political and social reforms of *perestroika, glasnost,* and *demokratizatsia.* By August 1989 the groups that had begun to take the most advantage of these reforms were the non-Russian ethnic minorities.

Gorbachev was surely correct when he stated that most regional elites in the various Soviet republics were playing a game to strengthen their own positions vis-à-vis the centre, and not to deliberately instigate the downfall of the USSR itself (Gorbachev and Milnar, 2002, p. 74). However, this was only true at the outset, for once elites in the republics began employing a national identity dynamic to mobilize support for their cause, mass nationalist sentiments would eventually carry them further than they may have originally planned to go. A tidal wave of nationalist senti-ments pushed elites into the turbulent waters of disputes involv-ing ethnic differences. Reflecting later upon the break up of the USSR Gorbachev castigated 'the ambitions, haughtiness, and arrogance of leaders—primarily Yeltsin and Dudaev [the leader of the Chechen nationalists]' for using nationalism and religion mainly as 'a political slogan in support of a break with Russia' (Gorbachev, 2004, p. x). Gorbachev was correct about leaders' personal ambitions motivating their opportunistic nationalist mobilizations, but he did not appreciate at the time the strength of the national idea among the wider population. Even in the Spring of 1991 Gorbachev continued to believe, as he put it, that 'History decreed that a number of bigger and smaller nations became united around Russia ... assisted by the openness of the Russian nature, its readiness to work with peoples of other nation-alities' (quoted in Braithwaite, 2002, p. 151). Valery Tishkov, director of the Institute of Ethnography and Anthropology of the Russian Academy of Sciences argued after the outbreak of the Chechen war that conflict was not caused by intrinsic cultural differences between the two ethnic groups, nor by historical griev-ances of the Chechen people, but rather due to the instrumental acts of individuals in a struggle for power (Tishkov, 2004). It is indeed the case that the immediate trigger for the Chechen con-flict was linked to contemporary clashes of interests in a struggle for power, but the deep and intermediate causes were due to the historical and cultural factors that Tishkov discounts. Without these it would not have been possible to mobilize the population to engage in such a bloody war.

Political elites in troubled times do often stir up nationalist sentiments. But they do so because they can: because, as William Bloom has noted, 'The mass national public will always react against policies perceived to be a threat to national identity ... and will always react favorably to policies which protect and enhance national identity' (Bloom, 1990, pp. 79, 81). Therefore a politi-cian who can successfully mobilize a national identity dynamic stands to gain majority popular support, for it transcends politi-cal and economic factors. This was the case with the Baltic peoples who formed their human chain in 1989. The first open outbreak of ethnic conflict under Gorbachev was in December 1986 when anti-Russian rioting broke out in Alma Ata, the capi-tal of Kazakhstan, after Gorbachev appointed an ethnic Russian to the post of First Secretary. It was an indication that the masses themselves could be mobilized around the banner of nationalism without any stimulus from ambitious politicians.

In the Soviet system of internal passports it was a requirement from the age of sixteen to list one's nationality. If a teenager's parents were from different nationalities then a choice of one or the other had to be made. Second generation Russians born in Central Asia or the Baltic republics considered themselves Soviet citizens but Russian nationals and had Russian stamped on their internal passports. For them Russian and Soviet were one and the same thing, with no contradiction between them, unlike other ethnic groups in the Union. So when Uzbeks and Estonians began demanding independence from the Union, Russians were conflicted. Russians living in these republics became alarmed and were forced to re-evaluate their own status and identity. Given that the essence of Russian national identity was bound up with the territorial space of the USSR, the Russian language, the Bolshevik Revolution, and the long history of Russian Empire, threats to the integrity of the Union were certain to impact on Russians' self-identity as a nation. Russian elites took advantage of this to rally the population around a new national identity dynamic in a competition for power.

The first political party allowed registration under Gorbachev's reform, once the monopoly of the CPSU was broken with the rescinding of clause 7 of the Soviet constitution, was Zhirinovsky's ultra-nationalist Liberal Democratic Party of Russia. But it was Boris Yeltsin's struggle against Gorbachev that would tear the Soviet Union apart. Under Yeltsin's leadership, Russians in the RSFSR also made demands on the centre for more autonomy from the federal authority in Moscow. This began with demands for the same institutions that the other fourteen subjects of the federation enjoyed, and it was then through these newly created and partially democratic political institutions that Yeltsin, in his personal struggle for power against Gorbachev, ultimately managed to gain power in the Kremlin. Yeltsin found mobilizing a Russian national identity dynamic far more potent an instrument to employ in his struggle against Gorbachev than any conception of the capitalist market or liberal democracy, although these also did form part of his stated project for Russia. Yeltsin now claimed that he had always 'been pained about Russia, its history, traditions and culture', and that it would be difficult for the centre to fight against "giant Russia" if it were to assume its real position and power (quoted in Morrison, 1992, p. 143). He was of course precisely right. Once Russia began to challenge the remnants of the centre in a divided Kremlin there was no real competition. Gorbachev became increasingly powerless and isolated in the face of a resurgent Russian president with the legitimacy of having been democratically elected, mobilizing the people of the Russian republic. This was humiliatingly demonstrated to Gorbachev during US President Bush's official visit to Moscow at the end of July 1991. A private luncheon was held for Bush and his wife Barbara in the Kremlin and Gorbachev had invited Yeltsin, as President of the Russian Federation, to attend, in addition to other republican leaders and government officials. Yeltsin, however, refused to attend. Russia was pursuing its own foreign policy with the US, and hence protocol would dictate that any business would therefore be dealt with at a separate audience President Yeltsin was to have later with the American President (see Beschloss and Talbott, 1993, p. 412).

In the end Marx's depiction of national struggles being superficial turned out to be seriously wide of the mark, as the late Soviet period came to be afflicted with national confrontation. The workers, cooperating with the intelligentsia, challenged Soviet Communism, being mobilized by nationalist and patriotic sentiments. The staying power of nationalism is also evident in post-communist states, including post-Soviet Russia. Even China, still controlled by a communist party, has moved towards nationalism as a legitimizing device as the centralized leadership has instituted radical market reforms. Nationalism was the main factor that led to the unraveling of the Soviet Union. It can be said that in the end the USSR was dismantled peacefully, with very little bloodshed, due to the federal institutional structures based on the core fifteen titular nationalities, established by Stalin. The USSR was effectively a land-based empire-state, as opposed to most other European maritime empires, which spread their influence globally through overseas colonies distant from the political centre. The fact that the Soviet republics had their own constitutions provided the institutional means through which they were able to break away legitimately from the Soviet centre and gain complete sovereignty. The fact that each of them also had external borders was an important factor facilitating their independence. However, this still left problems in other parts of the post-Soviet space, with conflict and organized violence taking place, for example in Chechnya and other parts of the Northern Caucasus (Sussex, 2012). Nationalist and ethnic violence would also break out after the collapse of Soviet Communism in many of the other former republics of the USSR (for example, in Moldova, Georgia, Azerbaijan/Armenia; Tadzhikistan, and Uzbekistan) and conflict would erupt in Ukraine between the Russian-speaking western part of the country and the more western-oriented eastern part following the annexation of Crimea in March 2014. The fact that Putin's popularity in Russia skyrocketed to over 90 percent during the crisis over Ukraine is further indication of the mobilizing power of nationalism.

Another indication of the power of nationalism lies, literally, in the Kremlin: that Lenin's mummified body rests still, at the time of writing, in the Mausoleum ninety years after his death, and a quarter of a century after the end of Soviet Communism, is not due to any nostalgia for the communist past so much as it is a reflection of Russian national identity. Lenin of course is closely associated with Marxism, but his present relevance is more about Russia's sense of nationhood and Lenin (and Stalin, who rests in the Kremlin wall behind the mausoleum) has become symbolic and representative of what many see as Soviet Russia's past as a great power. It is unimaginable that Hitler's mummified body could be lying in state in Berlin's Reichstag, with Goebbels' grave lying nearby, with Germans still paying homage to them. The fact that Russia has not completely renounced its Soviet past is due to a sense among many that the Soviet Communist regime provided a global status for Russians that was lost with the USSR's demise.

Conclusion

Gorbachev in the end was not willing to use the force that would have been necessary to try to hold the Union together. Perhaps looking back at the end of Soviet Communism and the end of the Soviet state, future historians will be perplexed that it all ended with such relatively little conflict and bloodshed. With a different leader in the Kremlin things could well have turned out otherwise. Many, especially in the Russian Federation, criticize Gorbachev for giving up without a fight—but surely that is the very thing for which we should be eternally grateful, for any such fight would likely have resulted in massive bloodshed. The empirical evidence is clear: Since the end of the Second World War intra-state conflicts have been far more common than interstate wars; organized violence is much more likely between neighbours; and disputes over territory are often the trigger for war. Two thirds of all conflicts in the first part of the twenty-first century have an ethnic dimension. (see Duffy, 2006; Vasquez, 1993 and 1995). The Cold War seemed to effectively freeze ethnic conflicts. Given the history, demography, the ethnic composition and the economic conditions of the USSR it can be seen from our vantage point thinking back to the 1980s that the Soviet Union was destined to fall. Perhaps what is most remarkable though is that it did so with (relatively) small amounts of bloodshed. This was in part, ironically given its objectives, due to the federal system that Stalin built, and in part to the personality, character, and leadership of Gorbachev. However, the system also left the potential for future conflicts if minority rights in post-Soviet states were not guaranteed, or in the event of disputes between Russia and its neighbours where there still reside large numbers of ethnic Russians. Hence, as events in Ukraine have shown, we are witnessing still the belated consequences emanating from the end of the Russian/Soviet Empire.

There are those who claim that had the Union Treaty been signed and had the coup attempt against Gorbachev not taken place in August 1991 then the USSR and Soviet Communism would have survived. Asked some ten years after the collapse whether he still thought that if the Union Treaty had been successfully concluded that there would have been the possibility of evolutionary development to socialism Gorbachev answered unequivocally 'Yes, without a doubt' (Gorbachev and Milnar, 2002, p. 75). However, the evidence points the other way: the strength of the national idea and the illegitimacy of the Soviet communist empire could not have withstood the forces that had been unleashed by reform. Once the door had been opened to national mobilization, there was no closing it—or not without that fight that Gorbachev was unwilling to wage. Gorbachev's place in history as a great leader will be assured. This will not be for his economic policies, but for the way in which he came to manage decline, his instrumental role in preventing internal wars, for his role also in ending the bipolar confrontation with the United States, and for his willingness in the end to give up his own power without a final struggle.

One further thing of note is that no one predicted or anticipated that the national question would be the critical factor in undermining Soviet Communism. Walker Connor asked why it was that scholars were so slow to recognize what the masses had felt and what some political leaders had recognized regarding the psychological and emotional pull of the national idea. He suggests that it was due to the experts' discomfort with the 'irrational' side of politics and a focus on quantifiable and hence more tangible explanations for political behaviour (Connor, p. 75). However, in the case of the former Soviet Union the answer is more complex, a question I will take up again in the concluding chapter to this volume. Next I will turn to examine how the Soviet Communist experiment impacted on issues of international security.

7
Soviet Communism and International Security

On taking power in 1917 the Bolsheviks were faced from the out-set with a very insecure environment, something that would con-tinue with various levels of threat throughout the entire Soviet era. This fact would have a fundamental and lasting impact on Soviet perceptions and policies in the security domain. From a realist perspective the international system of anarchy and the security dilemma this creates inevitably led to Soviet Russia seeking security through military means and alliances. Despite the rhetoric, and as noted in previous chapters, to a certain extent the practice of seeking to spread communism overseas, the logic of international politics, always pulled the Soviet lead-ership back, using whatever means were required, to defending the "national interest" (for which read state interest) as the first priority. In the realm of international security the question most often asked was whether communism served the state, or did the state serve communism? In other words, was the Soviet leader-ship in its foreign and security policies motivated chiefly by ideo-logical, or state interests? This was never a simple question to answer, and even with access to key archival materials since the Soviet Union expired there is still no consensus on this matter. However, the wrong question was being posed. The question is not really one of an *either/or* kind, but rather: to what degree in any particular instance did ideology *and* state interests count? The evidence shows that both ideational and material interests were at work.

The Formative Years: The Origins of the National Security State

After taking power all revolutionary regimes are faced with the realities of the international system. As a consequence they will initially follow a twin-track policy in foreign and security policy, one within the formal diplomatic apparatus of the state, the other using a second string, often working in secrecy, representing the revolutionary aspirations of the regime. In addition to the foreign ministry, diplomatic missions, the trade and defence ministries and other institutions of the Soviet state, the Bolsheviks also established the Comintern to pursue wider internationalist communist goals. However, even here, as demonstrated in other parts of this book, each of the various incarnations of the communist international was eventually employed by Moscow as an instrument to serve Soviet state interests, rather than the cause of international communism. Yet all great powers have used, in addition to traditional diplomacy, secret intelligence services and clandestine operations. Stalin famously remarked that a diplomat was someone sent abroad to lie for his country. He also stated that 'A sincere diplomat is like dry water or wooden iron' (Plokhy, 2010, p. 181). During the founding conference to establish the United Nations in San Francisco (April–June 1945), there were some 850 delegates, including 37 foreign ministers and five prime ministers. It is instructive to note that the United States bugged the communications of forty-three of the forty-five original delegations to the conference (Urquhart, 2004, p. 9). Although Edward Snowden's more recent revelations of the extent of US surveillance on a global scale were shocking, they should not be so surprising. It is somewhat ironic that in 1950, the US State Department official who chaired the San Francisco Conference, Alger Hiss, would later be accused of spying for the Soviet Union (see Shelton, 2012; Weinstein, 1978; White, 2004).

I noted in earlier chapters the important causal role that wars played both in the Russian Revolution and in the nature of the regime that emerged following the Civil War of 1918–1921. The early Soviet regime was forged amid the most bloody mass organized violence that the world had hitherto experienced. A hardened communist leadership emerged that had witnessed and participated in the worst horrors of warfare, giving rise to a militarized culture and a strong sense of insecurity, with a heightened fear of internal and external enemies. Practically all of the leading

Bolsheviks of the 1940s had served as young men with the Red Army some twenty years earlier, as military commanders or political commissars during the Civil War (there were no women in leadership positions). Such service was also seen as a key instrument for gaining social advancement (Daniels, 2007, p. 124). But it also had the effect of creating a hardened and suspicious political class, and helped to foster centralized control over the economy and the political system. As a consequence, the Bolsheviks demonstrated strong *realist* tendencies in the conduct of foreign and security policy.

Lenin was an ideologue wedded to the Marxist cause, yet he was himself also a pragmatist, and adapted policies in accordance with changing circumstances. This was demonstrated in the domestic realm with the establishment of the New Economic Policy in 1921, and with Lenin's stance on the nationalities question. In the international sphere Lenin's willingness to compromise was demonstrated by the agreement at Brest-Litovsk to end the war with Germany, for this involved losing large tracts of Russian territory, including Ukraine, Poland, Finland, the Baltic countries and part of the Caucasus bordering Turkey. In the summer of 1918 Russia's territory had shrunk to its pre-Romanov level, being roughly the size of the Grand Duchy of Moscow in the fifteenth century. In the East, the Japanese controlled Vladivostok; French forces were in Odessa; and Turks were intervening in the Caucasus. On February 28, 1918, at a meeting of the Bolshevik Central Committee, a group led by Bukharin (the "Left Communists") mustered four dissenting votes against the decision to accept the peace terms dictated by Germany. Four others, including Trotsky, abstained on the basis of the formula "no war, no peace." Lenin mustered five votes in favour, providing the narrowest of victories. The victory resulted from a split in the left vote, and the outcome was a mark of the early differences within communist ranks on foreign policy priorities, but in the end it also marked how the Bolsheviks came to prioritize the survival of the state. As Robert Daniels put it, this immediately 'relegated revolution to the secondary, instrumental role that it continued to play throughout the life of the Soviet regime' (Daniels, 2007 p. 109).

Security issues were paramount from the outset, forcing the young revolutionaries to focus on ways of ensuring the security of the Soviet territorial state as they were in the very process of constructing its institutions. In addition to threats from internal and external anti Bolshevik forces, in 1921 there was a leftist uprising among Bolshevik sailors of the Russian Baltic Fleet in Kronstadt. It is unsurprising then that the priority of the new regime was to build a strong military machine, and to focus on traditional notions of state security.

As Melvin Leffler notes, Lenin was impelled to sign the treaty with Germany in 1918 to gain the time necessary to develop the military means that would be required to defend against expected multiple opponents, who were then already threatening from each direction (Leffler, 1994, p. 4). Stalin would later refer to 'capitalist encirclement,' but it was an immediate reality already in 1917. For Lenin, the agreement with Germany was a necessary compromise, a matter of basic survival. Responding to an attack from the Socialist Revolutionary Party about Brest-Litovsk Lenin argued that failure to make the agreement would have been akin to refusing to give up money to a bandit who would otherwise shoot you. Hence, giving up your wallet for your life is excusable: 'It would be difficult to find a sane man who would declare such a compromise to be "inadmissible on principle," or who would call the compromiser an accomplice of the bandits' (Lenin, 1920, p. 511). Lenin was unwilling to countenance the assured destruction of the fledgling revolutionary regime that continuation of the war with Germany would surely have brought about. Lenin justified the agreement with Germany to delegates at the Seventh Party Congress in Petrograd, in March 1918, by arguing that the peace talks with the Germans had 'turned the imperialist war into civil war.' (Volkogonov, 1994, p. 31). Lenin maintained that now there was an alternative to capitalism, as long as capitalism and socialism exist there could be no peace, 'a funeral dirge will be sung either over the Soviet Republic or over world capitalism' (Lenin, 1935, p. 297). Lenin was justifying in ideological terms a policy he pursued out of material considerations relating to state interests.

Lenin was again confronted with the dilemma of having to engage in traditional realpolitik diplomacy when the Great Powers met at the Genoa conference in 1922 to discuss issues that had been left unresolved from the Versailles Treaty. The key issue was how to resolve relations with Russia and Germany and other states in the eastern half of Europe. Many Bolsheviks were reluctant to send delegates to this great power assembly of imperial states, but Lenin's insistence prevailed once more. Lenin was concerned that Russia would be isolated and sidelined to the periphery of the international system if Germany was to be reintegrated into the western-dominated capitalist economies. Lenin was also hoping for western loans to assist Russia's economic development. The subsequent separate agreement Russia made with Germany at Rapollo was further evidence of Lenin's pragmatic realism when it came to national security issues. The Rapollo Treaty was signed by the two states in April 1922—it was actually signed individually by Russia and each of the then Socialist Soviet Republics 'allied with the RSFSR' (Georgia, Ukraine, Belorussia, Azerbaijan, Armenia, and the Republic of the Far East). A later secret annex to the Rapollo Treaty permitted the training of German armed forces on Soviet territory. The Treaty ended the diplomatic isolation to which both countries had been subject after the Bolshevik Revolution and the First World War. Lenin was prepared to make an agreement with the Weimar Republic despite the Berlin government's intimidation of the communist party, including the murders of Rosa Luxemburg and Karl Liebknecht.

Here an appreciation is required of the external structural factors that impacted on the communist leadership's foreign and security policy stance. The Russian Revolution coincided with a shift in the global balance of power, in particular the rise of the United States as a major transatlantic power, with interests no longer confined to the western hemisphere (on the rise of the US as a global power see Zakaria, 1998). It was also a period in which imperialism was being challenged by indigenous forces in the Third World, forces based principally on nationalism as noted in the previous chapter, but also, as noted in Chapter 4, in some cases on radical leftist ideologies. This would further cause a dilemma for the Soviet leadership's foreign and security policies. Given the ideological justification for revolution in Russia, the Bolsheviks were morally obliged to support socialist revolution elsewhere, thereby operating according to the principles of internationalist working class solidarity. However, faced with the external factor of being opposed by stronger powers the new leaders were also obliged to act according to the logic of the balance of power. Hence, ideals would often clash with the realities of the international system. During the first decades, given the power realities pertaining after world war, revolution, civil war and then the turmoil of rapid modernization through Stalin's revolution from above, the USSR was not in a position materially, even had it wished to on principle, to challenge the international status quo and the global balance of power through military means. Had it tried to do so, as Lenin predicted, in all likelihood it would have meant the speedy end of the new revolutionary regime. The origins of what one can term the Soviet "national security state" can be identified from these early post-revolutionary years.

The term "national security state" is most often associated with the USA, linked to developments in the security realm following the National Security Act (NSA) of 1947. The NSA established the National Security Council, the Central Intelligence Agency, and increased the powers of the Pentagon at the expense of the US State Department (see Jablonsky, 2002–2003; Stuart, 2012). The term has also been associated with the role of the military in the Third World, especially in parts of Latin America in the second half of the twentieth century (see Mores, 2011). A national security state is one in which overriding attention is paid to military security, with a key role played by the military industrial complex in the political and economic realms of decision-making. By the early 1980s the cost of defending the Soviet empire would take 40 percent of the total Soviet budget, and between 15 and 20 percent of GDP (Brooks and Wohlforth, 2000/2001). This was at least four times the level that the USA spent on defence as a proportion of GDP.

In a national security state there is a strong emphasis on perceived enemies of the state and a tendency towards secrecy and a lack of transparency when it comes to military expenditure. I argue here that the concept is a useful one to apply to the Soviet Union in the security realm. It was a well-founded fear of both external and internal threats to the regime that created a militarized and centralized system of tight controls in the USSR. This highly centralized system was to develop to excess under Stalin. The structure of the international system, the balance of power, and the security dilemma faced by the new Soviet regime pushed revolutionary ideology to a subordinate place when it came to issues of survival and national (state) interests.

The Significance of the Great Patriotic War

Justifying the Five Year Plan in his report to the Central Committee of the CPSU in January 1933, Stalin said it was necessary to 'create in the country all the necessary technical and economic prerequisites for increasing to the upmost the defensive capacity of the country, to enable it to organize determined resistance to any and every attempt at military intervention from the outside' (Stalin, 1943, p. 410). The logic for the rapid build-up of Soviet industry and agriculture was geared to military requirements and the perceived need to counter the threat of capitalist aggression, thus solidifying the national security state. Iron and steel provide the bedrock for military might, as well as the necessary engine for growth—hence the motivating factor was in large part not modernization for its own sake, but for the greater good of Soviet security. Stalin used the threat of foreign invasion to justify rapid industrialization, and it is common to quote from his speech on the tasks of economic executives that he made in February 1931: 'We have fallen fifty to one hundred years behind the developed countries. We must make up the distance in ten years. Either we will or they will crush us' (Stalin, 1955). It is important to bear in mind also the ideological justification: it was claimed that western neo-imperialism was inherently aggressive, and as long as capitalism continued to exist then war was seen not just as a possibility but an inevitability. Hence it was absolutely necessary also from a Marxist-Leninist standpoint to develop industry for defensive purposes.

Stalin had taken lessons from earlier epochs in Russia's history that had demonstrated how backwardness in military capabilities threatened national security. The Crimean War (1854–1855) and the Russo-Japan War (1904–1905) highlighted the dangers of being technologically behind in industrial and hence military might. Going back to the time of Peter the Great, Russia's leaders have been concerned with maintaining a modern infrastructure for the upkeep of the military, and also to enable Russia to play an equal role in international diplomacy. Ever since the Battle of Poltava in 1709, when Peter's army defeated those of Sweden's Charles XII, Russia has considered itself to be a great power. During the Soviet period Poltava retained its patriotic appeal, although this lost its resonance after 1991—for Poltava is situated in what has become (at the time of writing still) a foreign country (Ukraine) and was linked to the incorporation of the Baltic states, that are also no longer part of Russia (Hughes, 1998, p. 38) The battle at Poltava marked the demise of the Swedish Empire, and the rise of the Russian Empire.

One component of Stalin's "socialism in one country" was to maintain state control over industry, commerce, and trade, thereby being able to manipulate foreign economic relations in a way that would not leave the USSR vulnerable to outside pressures. Like Peter the Great two centuries before him, Stalin was intent on building the industrial might necessary to construct a strong military to ensure the security of the state. Stalin considered the capitalist world as hostile, untrustworthy, and intent on undermining the communist system in any way possible using any means at its disposal. Although President Herbert Hoover, unlike Woodrow Wilson, did not consider a military solution viable or US military intervention necessary to crush Bolshevism, he was a confirmed ideological opponent of the Soviet Union. Hoover pursued a kind of forerunner of Kennan's policy of a long-term 'patient containment', for any direct intervention he feared would serve to provide the Bolsheviks with a mobilizing dynamic for Russian nationalism that could then be used to legitimate themselves and gain wider support. Like Kennan after him, Hoover predicted that Bolshevism would collapse due to its own internal contradictions, especially in the face of economic recovery in the rest of Europe. This comes out in a remarkable book by one US president (Hoover) about another (Roosevelt) (Hoover, 1962). Hence, for Stalin, autarky was a policy designed to ensure security in the face of capitalist encirclement.

If the turmoil of the first decades of the Soviet regime had helped to establish the Soviet national security state, then subsequent developments only served to reinforce it. On June 21, 1941 over three million German troops in 145 divisions, with some 5,000 tanks, supported by 3,000 aircraft, advanced across the USSR's western border. A further 705,000 men from among Hitler's allies (Romania, Hungary, and Finland) were also involved in the attack (Gray, 2007, p. 131). The Nazi invasion of the Soviet Union was the largest military invasion in the history of warfare. In the first year of the war the Red Army lost on average some 15,000 men each day, or over 100,000 each week. In one city in one year (Leningrad, 1941–1942) the Soviet Union lost more lives (one million) than the combined total for the other western allies for the entire course of the war. One-third of Leningrad's population perished during the siege (see Reid, 2011; Salisbury, 2003). And yet more Soviet lives were lost in one battle, that for Stalingrad, the greatest battle in world history, with almost one million soldiers killed. Over seven million troops on both sides took part. The battle lasted for six months, from September 1941 through to April 1942. In the greatest tank battle of all time, also in the USSR at Kursk, the Germans lost twice as many men in one week than the total number of soldiers the Americans later would lose during the two decades of the Vietnam War.

It was shown in the previous chapter how Stalin invoked Russian national identity and sought to instil a sense of Soviet patriotism in defence of the "Motherland," during the course of what came to be called the Great Patriotic War. The collective suffering in the war and then the relief and pride in coming out eventual victors helped to legitimate the Soviet Communist system internally and inspired people from across the world. The war against Germany also highlighted the internal security problem posed by the national question in the USSR, as it provided nationalist groups with opportunities to seek their freedom from Russian control. It was noted in the previous chapter that Stalin had forcibly deported whole ethnic groups from the Caucasus to Central Asia. At the Battle of Stalingrad it has been estimated that 50,000 of the troops in German uniforms fighting against the Soviets in the 6th Army (Wehrmacht) were Soviet citizens (Beevor, 1999). Beevor leads one to believe that a large number of Soviet defectors volunteered to fight with the Germans, whereas many in fact would have been forced to serve the Wehrmacht, in support roles to the German front line troops. The numbers are also contested. Further west, when German troops first invaded the USSR Ukrainian nationalists initially saw them as saviours. On June 30, 1941 the Organization of Ukrainian Nationalists under the leadership of Stepan Bandera proclaimed an independent Ukrainian state in Lvov. This, however, was short-lived, with the Soviet secret police massacring thousands (Taubman, 2003, p. 193). The Nazis too responded brutally to any manifestation of Ukrainian nationalism.

Stalin's diplomacy during the war years, as even one of his fiercest western academic critics acknowledged, was 'entirely a matter of realpolitik' (Conquest, 2001, p. 150). Another western historian however, argues that the "traditionalist" focus on international power politics 'misinterprets Stalin's ambitions [for] Marxist-Leninist teachings informed everything in his life, from his politics to his military strategy and personal values' (Gellately, 2013, p. 9). But Stalin was far more than an ideologue. As with Lenin, so too in foreign policy matters Stalin acted rationally in pursuit of Soviet state interests, once more involving (for the third time in just twenty years) an agreement with Germany, this time under the Nazis, for purely reasons of state. Stalin had initially stood alone in countering the rise of Nazism in Germany, and the threat this posed to Soviet security led him to seek alliances against Hitler with the UK and France. In the end, out of perceived necessity to preserve Soviet security a non-aggression pact was made between the Third Reich and the USSR in what has been described as the "diplomatic sensation of the century" (Service, 2007, p. 214).

Stalin was criticized for the pact with Germany, yet he had not been the first to sign an agreement with Hitler's Germany. Britain and France had already signed an agreement in Munich on 30 September 1938, which allowed Hitler to annex parts of Czechoslovakian territory bordering Germany (the Sudetenland). The British Prime Minister Neville Chamberlain hailed the Munich Agreement and the Anglo-German Declaration (a non-aggression declaration, also signed at Munich), for ensuring 'peace for our time'. However, at Munich the British and French basically gave Hitler a green light to turn his attention eastwards, to take on the USSR. Stalin, reacting to this appeasement of Hitler sought to prevent such an outcome—or at least delay it—by forming his own agreement with Hitler. Recognizing the dangers that Hitler's expansionist ambitions held for Soviet security, and having had his overtures to the western democracies rebuffed, and then seeing the British and French sign an agreement with Hitler, Stalin had no choice but to turn to Berlin himself. As a Soviet historian, also critical of Stalin, put it: 'From the point of view of state interest the Soviet Union had no other acceptable choice' than to conclude the non-aggression pact with Germany (Volkogonov, 2000, p. 356). Referring to wartime cooperation with the USSR Churchill famously implied that he would make a pact with the devil if necessary to defeat Germany. Well, that is what Stalin was effectively doing with his pact with Hitler. Both Lenin and Stalin were forced to compromise their ideological principles and cooperate with a German regime that was aggressively repressing local communists.

There is no consensus about Stalin's role as war leader, although most studies agree at some level he performed well. This was despite the fact that during the purges in 1937 and 1938 he had decimated the Soviet military high command. As a result of these purges all district commanders were removed, along with

90 percent of district chiefs of staff and their deputies, and 80 percent of divisional commanders and 90 percent of staff officers (Volkogonov, 2000, p. 368). One recent study argues that Stalin's personal role in the war was critical in gaining defeat over Germany. Whereas Churchill and Roosevelt were replaceable as war leaders, Stalin's leadership was indispensable (Roberts, 2008, p. 314). In his memoirs the leading Soviet general in the war paints a picture of Stalin as an outstanding organizer, with both tactical and strategic abilities that were unimpeded by ideological considerations (Zhukov, 1974). Stalin was Supreme Commander of the Soviet Armed Forces, head of the State Defence Council, Commissar for Defence, the head of government as well as being head of the party. However, it was through his military command that he conducted the war, not through the ideological apparatus of the party organization. Zhukov's memoirs paint a portrait of Stalin as an effective war leader able to assimilate advice from his military commanders and then to issue speedy and direct instructions that would be immediately implemented down the chain of command (Zhukov, 1974).

It is worth reminding ourselves what Europe looked like immediately after the war, although from this distance and vantage point it is difficult to imagine just how devastating it was. Europe had been ravaged by war. Thousands of cities had been all but obliterated. In the USSR alone there were 1,760 towns and cities destroyed. 84 percent of the buildings in Budapest were damaged. In the UK 202,000 houses had been destroyed. Millions more had been damaged. In Germany about one fifth of all dwellings were destroyed. In Berlin, and in Hanover, and in Hamburg, the figure was over 50 percent. In Duisburg it was 66 percent. In Cologne 70 percent. Up to 20 million Germans were homeless. Stalingrad was mostly rubble. Across much of Europe there was either none or only sporadic services of water, gas, or electricity. Transportation had been nearly crippled. Large parts of Europe had no functioning institutions, no clear borders, no schools, no hospitals, universities, libraries, functioning governments, post offices, or banks (money for the most part was worthless). There was no law and order, and rape, pillage, starvation, fear and helplessness was the order of the day. A little like Somalia in the first decade of the twenty-first century, perhaps. Civil wars raged in Greece, Yugoslavia, and Poland. Peoples in the Baltic republics and Ukraine were still fighting the Russians.

The total death toll is debatable, but around 35 to 40 million lost their lives as a direct consequence of the fighting, 27 million in the USSR alone. Poland lost 6 million, one in every six of the population. The Jews suffered the biggest genocide in history with 5,750,000 being killed. Only 1.6 million European Jews survived. It was Russian troops who liberated Auschwitz in January 1945. As Russian troops marched towards Berlin, the capital of Hitler's Reich, advanced guards had erected placards by the side of the road on which was written 'Tremble with fear, fascist Germany, the day of reckoning has come'. Ahead of the Russians, Germans were on the run, civilians taking what they could carry, as they raced westwards to avoid Soviet revenge and retribution. Between January–March 1945, around 9 million Germans were on the move. In Berlin alone 50,000 refugees were arriving each day (the figures are taken from Lowe, 2013, pp. 4–33). This was the largest panic migration in history, as the German people were fearful of retribution for the horrors that had been inflicted on Russians in the Soviet Union.

Unsurprisingly the Second World War had a profound effect on the Soviet people, and especially on the Slavs and then particularly the Russians—for much of the war on the eastern front was fought on Russian territory. Gorbachev's father had been a communist during the war, and the war became one of the motivating influences leading the young Gorbachev to seek membership of the CPSU, for he believed, as he put it in his retirement, that Soviet Communism was responsible for 'the great victory over fascism [and hence] proof that the country's cause was the right one'. The year after the war, aged just sixteen, Zdenek Mlynar was motivated by the Soviet defeat of Nazism to join the Czechoslovakian Communist Party. Mlynar went on to study Law in Moscow in the 1950s where Gorbachev was one of his fellow students. He felt that committing himself to the communist party was necessary to make the world safe and more just through socialist development (Gorbachev and Mlynar, p. 14, 15). For many at this time the CPSU was seen as an organization that reflected glory on the Soviet state and as a positive force in the wider cause of socialism. Mlynar would later become one of the leaders of the Prague Spring in 1968.

One should not forget that similar devastation had impacted Asia. At the end of the war in the Pacific some 9 million Japanese were homeless, Nagasaki and Hiroshima had been laid waste by the first use of the Atom bomb, and almost every single Japanese city had been subject to relentless US aerial bombardment. 4 million Indonesians died during the war; 80 percent of Manila's buildings were turned into rubble; and although estimates always will vary, possibly as many as 20 million Chinese people died as a result of the Second World War. British and American casualties in the war were in comparison relatively small. Given the death and destruction experienced in the Soviet Union it is not surprising that Stalin's post-war priority was to rebuild the Soviet state, whilst also ensuring that there would be no further threats to national security. The Gulag in the USSR too has to be factored in to any understanding of Soviet political culture. Some 1.6 million people of the 18 million who passed through camps never came out alive. Many were executed, others were worked or starved to death. The vast majority of those subject to the Gulag nevertheless survived, many having been "re-educated" for integration back into the wider Soviet "community of peoples." The Gulag, as one scholar put it, was not a genocidal institution (Barnes, 2011, p. 2). Many of the Gulag survivors feared not only for their own safety against a restoration of the purges and terror, they also feared contact with foreigners and the threat emanating from the western capitalist powers. Fears about one's own individual liberty and about threats to the Soviet state permeated Soviet society. War touched everyone in the USSR, and so did the Gulag, either directly, or through the fate of family members or friends.

The Onset of the Cold War

Very quickly wartime cooperation between the Soviet Union and the western powers led to mutual suspicions and mistrust. Immediately after the war Stalin set about establishing a security buffer zone whilst ensuring also that the regimes in that part of Europe liberated and controlled by the USSR would remain compliant to Moscow's security wishes. Stalin pursued a clear political goal that was designed to turn the Soviet Union into a respected great power on a level with the West (see Gorlizki and Khlevniuk, 2004). His priority was to ensure that the USSR would be safe, and confident in its own future. In the hierarchy of strategic interests Europe was always critical for the USSR, much more so, in existential terms, than Europe had been for the United

States. In the same year that Russians fought Napoleon in 1812 at Borodino on the outskirts of Moscow, the Americans were engaged in hostilities with the British, but French troops were far more of a threat to Russia than the British ever were to the United States. It was therefore natural after 1945 that the USSR was reluctant to compromise on what were conceived to be key post-war security questions, such as the one over Poland. The issue of Stalin imposing a Soviet-type system on Eastern Europe was much more about securing Soviet state interests than it was about spreading communism. Imposing communist systems on Eastern Europe was to protect Soviet state interests. Stalin expressed concern at the Potsdam meeting that if freely elected governments were permitted in the states of Eastern Europe then 'they would be anti-Soviet, and that we cannot allow' (Leffler, 1986, p. 102). Stalin was not willing to risk the security of an already ravaged Soviet state for the sake of democracy after the loss of nearly thirty million Soviet citizens.

What would come to be called the Brezhnev Doctrine (see Chapter 3) can be seen as a Soviet version of the Monroe Doctrine. The truth is that Roosevelt and Churchill both accepted that Stalin would be unwilling to risk having unfriendly regimes on the eastern borders of the USSR, especially as the western capitalist powers would likely then be their allies. It is remarkable that Gaddis should claim that it was Stalin's 'insistence on equating security with territory' that was responsible for the breakdown of wartime cooperation (Gaddis, 1997, p. 15). Territory is absolutely essential in any state's consideration of its national security—the Monroe Doctrine attests to this in the case of the US—and how could territorial considerations be anything else but central in Moscow after invasion, years of bloody warfare and mass loss of life? (on the link between territory, geopolitics, and war see Mackinder, 1904; and Rosecrance, 2013). Gaddis's acknowledgement of the importance of territory in Stalin's determination of the USSR's security in 1945 also undermines his own central argument that Stalin was guided by a romantic commitment to ideology and his own personal security when formulating foreign security policies. Gaddis's one-sided narrative in which he is clearly seeking to apportion blame to Stalin for the onset of the Cold War, also emphasizes Soviet spying activities, as if the US were itself entirely innocent of such behaviour. For example, Gaddis refers to Soviet penetration of the Anglo-American atomic bomb project and to the bugging of Roosevelt and Churchill's accommodation at the Tehran Conference in November 1943 (Gaddis, 1995, p. 21). Yet no reference is made to the US bugging not only of the communist delegations, but nearly all delegations at the San Francisco Conference. Stalin's approval for the gathering of intelligence on the US Atomic bomb project was simply the rational behaviour that any leader under the circumstances would have sanctioned, irrespective of his ideology or disposition to romanticism.

Poland was the main issue as the war against Germany was coming to an end. Russia had been invaded three times by western powers through Polish territory, and Stalin was adamant this would not be permitted again. During the negotiations with Churchill and Roosevelt at Yalta in February 1945, Stalin made it clear that apart from the priority of defeating Germany, in strategic terms, what he called the 'Polish corridor' 'outweighed all the other problems discussed at the conference' (Plokhy, 2010, p. 176). There was some irony here, in that the UK ostensibly went to war to save Poland in 1939 from German Nazism, and yet ended up accepting its incorporation into the Soviet communist bloc after the war was over.

In the end all had to succumb to the logic of the balance of power. The *Washington Post*, reporting on the Yalta conference, has Stalin rising from his seat when discussing the future of Poland, asking loudly of Churchill and Roosevelt: 'Do you want me to tell the Russian people that I am less Russian than Lord Curzon? Do you want me to tell the Russian people that I am less Russian than Clemenceau? Do you want me to accept less than they proposed for Russia?' Stalin was insisting that the new boundary between the USSR and Poland be based on the Curzon Line that had been proposed by the British Foreign Minister Lord Curzon and agreed to by French Prime Minister Clemenceau, after the First World War. Stalin concluded his tirade by asking rhetorically 'Did your army liberate Poland, Mr. Churchill? Did your army liberate Poland Mr. President?' (cited in Plokhy, 2010, p. 177). In response to Roosevelt and Churchill's insistence on a democratic government in Poland Stalin remarked 'I must say that the Warsaw government has a democratic base equal at least to that of de Gaulle' (Plokhy, p. 177). Stalin felt betrayed by the West on the question of Poland, having been assured (or so he thought) during the war that the USSR's national interests would be respected on its conclusion. Stalin wrote a letter to President

Truman in April 1945 in which he stated bluntly that Moscow had a right to have a 'friendly government' in Warsaw because Poland borders the USSR. Stalin stated: 'Poland is to the security of the Soviet Union what Belgium and Greece are to the security of Great Britain'. He went on to write: 'I am ready to ... do all in my power to reach an agreed settlement. But you are asking too much. To put it plainly, you want me to renounce the interests of security of the Soviet Union; but I cannot proceed against the interests of my country' (Stalin's Correspondence, 1965, p. 220). Stalin made it abundantly clear in his letter to the US president that following the blood shed by Soviet troops on the 'fields of Poland' for the 'liberation' of that country, that he could not agree to a government in Warsaw that would be hostile to the USSR.

It can reasonably be argued that the USSR and the USA stumbled into the Cold War, with no single country, individual, or event as the catalyst for its onset. Gaddis's assertion that the opening of the Soviet and East European archives means that we now know the answer to the origins of the Cold War is an astounding claim to make from a leading historian. One-time member of the post-revisionist school, Gaddis now argues that Stalin's personal behaviour was responsible for the onset of the Cold War, asserting that '*as long as Stalin was running the Soviet Union a cold war was inevitable*' (Gaddis, 1998, p. 292; stress in original). Stalin's behaviour is open to interpretation, but the archives are actually of relatively little assistance in determining a specific cause of the Cold War. Gaddis claims now that each of the key initiatives taken or supported by the USA after 1945, including rehabilitation of economic assistance to (West) Germany, later including rearmament and membership of NATO; and the establishment of the European Coal and Steel Community were a 'response to what Stalin had done' (Gaddis, 1998, p. 125). Gaddis paints a picture of Stalin as being totally inflexible, blinded by ideological blinkers. These blinkers made Stalin distrust the US and the 'whole capitalist world', thereby making it impossible for the US to have a constructive relationship with the USSR. This is simply not credible. Many of the documents demonstrate in fact that Stalin actually hoped that the wartime alliance with the USA and the UK would continue into the post-war period. Stalin's regime was also far less repressive in 1945 than it had been in 1935.

Stalin was inclined to realist considerations, and even at the height of his purges and repressive domestic policies he did not engage in military adventures overseas. He did not even try and take advantage of the new wave of decolonization that took place after the war, by seeking to spread Soviet influence into the Third World. A case can be made that Stalin was wrong, that he misperceived American and British intentions after the war against Hitler, but he surely can be forgiven for suspecting their motives given the previous history of relations. It was not simply Stalin's commitment to Marx that led to the Cold War, but also his concern about Soviet state security. If a Cold War was inevitable as long as Stalin was in power it was much more likely to do with Truman's own perceptions and biases concerning Stalin than the Soviet leader's actual intentions or policies (see Larson, 1985). Stalin had demonstrated his willingness to retreat from previous positions when faced with diplomatic pressures. This was the case in relation to the Turkish Straits, when after the war the USA made it clear that Stalin's wish for Soviet bases there was unacceptable. Stalin withdrew his claims (despite the USA making similar claims in Iceland). Having first refused to recall Soviet troops from Northern Iran as originally agreed immediately after the war, following diplomatic pressure in the new United Nations organization Stalin acquiesced and Soviet troops were withdrawn. Stalin refrained from giving any material support to the communists during the Greek civil war, and did not provide support for communists in Italy or France. In any overall assessment of the prevailing balance of power the USSR was relatively weak in 1945 compared to the United States, and Stalin was afraid that the West would take advantage of this fact.

Stalin did not have any trust in the West going forward, and he predicted that Germany and Japan would rise once more to become great powers. War would always remain a possibility, and it was incumbent on the USSR therefore to ensure its own defence (Stalin, 1972, pp. 34, 37). Meanwhile, the US administration had asked their resident expert on Russia in the American embassy in Moscow to provide them with an evaluation of Soviet objectives and behaviour. The result was George Kennan's famous "long telegram," later published in revised form as the 'Sources of Soviet Conduct' in *Foreign Affairs* (Kennan, 1947). At this time the US had not developed a grand strategy relating to its own role in the world, and Kennan's analysis of the USSR provided the basis for what became the grand strategy of "containment." This was a policy articulated publicly by President Truman, who on 12

March 1947 urged the US Congress to commit aid to Greece and Turkey to prevent the development of Soviet-style communism. The basic strategy that was developed to counter the expansion of Soviet Communism was thereafter labelled the Truman Doctrine. In the Spring of 1947 the US Secretary of State George Marshall launched the US recovery project to help rebuild war torn Europe, thereby providing US economic as well as political and security support to contain the USSR.

Kennan considered that due to Soviet Marxist-Leninist ideology there could never be a 'community of aims' between the Soviet Union and the capitalist powers. This sounds a little odd coming just after the USSR shared a community of aims with the USA and other capitalist powers in opposition to Nazi Germany. As shown above, previously both Stalin and Lenin had demonstrated their willingness to sign agreements with Berlin for non-ideological reasons. Some twenty years after Kennan's long telegram, Arthur Schlesinger argued that Leninism had created a structure of thought and behaviour that made postwar collaboration between Russia and America 'inherently impossible' (Schlesinger, 1967). Kennan's basic argument that relations could only improve after the USSR had implemented domestic reforms and jettisoned Marxist ideology is also perhaps an odd claim to make by a self-proclaimed 'Realist'.

Given that Germany within just twenty years had been responsible for two bloody wars, no one wished to see it rise from the ashes of defeat to once more threaten international security. Neither the US nor the USSR, neither the British nor the French, were prepared to countenance immediately after the war had ended in 1945 any possibility of a renewed and resurgent Germany. Despite the fact that much of the country was in ruins, Germany remained a potential future power in the centre of Europe. It was a matter of controlling Germany's industrial potential so that it could not be used to forge a military machine that Germany could again employ to threaten international security. The division of the country was then in a sense the natural outcome of the balance of power, not the direct result of ideological differences. Famously a French diplomat once said that he was so much in love with Germany that he was pleased there were two of them! Khrushchev told British officials in early 1956 that it was a good thing for everybody that Germany was divided. Reflecting in his old age on the question of East Germany Khrushchev stated 'We had a strategic, economic, and political … stake in its independence'. He went on to state that permitting the establishment of a separate German capitalist state allied with the West 'would have meant for us to retreat to the borders of Poland' (Khrushchev, 1974, p. 358). Andrei Gromyko (Soviet foreign minister between 1957 and 1985) informed one of his advisers in 1977 that 'we don't need a united Germany at all, not even a socialist one. The united socialist China is enough for us' (quoted in Trachtenburg, 2012, p. 173). The USA and the USSR feared a Germany united in the other camp. In part then the origins of the Cold War relate to Germany and traditional conceptions of the balance of power. The defeat of Germany had left a power vacuum in the heart of Europe. The issue was how best to incorporate a defeated Germany into a new post-war international order in a manner to ensure that it would not again cause a threat. The vacuum was filled by the United States and the Union of Soviet Socialist Republics; and Germany remained divided as the best solution to ensure security.

Cold War Crises

After 1945 a number of crises could have led to a major military confrontation between the Cold War protagonists. In June 1948 Stalin enforced a blockade of West Berlin. The old German capital of Berlin was situated well inside East German territory yet it had been divided into four zones, occupied by each of the USSR, the USA, the UK, and France. This truly was an anomaly of the Cold War, and having western powers occupying parts of the East German capital in the middle of the Eastern half of Germany was always a thorn in the side of the communist bloc—or, as Khrushchev would put it the western allied presence in Berlin was a 'bone in the Soviet throat' (cited in Smith, p 28). In the summer of 1947 the western allies had announced their intention to establish a federal German state in the western zones of occupation and proceeded to issue a new currency. Stalin's objectives in instituting a blockade was to force the western allies to return to the Council of Foreign Minsters (CFM) meeting with the Soviet Union to discuss the question of German unification (as a neutral state). Stalin argued that if the West insisted on establishing two separate independent states then the western powers should forgo any rights in Berlin.

Although termed a "blockade," Stalin did not cut off supplies to West Berlin from the Soviet occupied zone and nor was air access denied. All land, rail, and water links were cut to West Berlin from Western Europe. There were rumblings in some quarters in Washington about sending US troops to force the border open, but cooler heads prevailed. In an election year it would have been difficult for the USA to justify war to save the capital of Germany having so very recently fought a war against the Germans. Instead, the US military governor in Germany, General Lucius Clay, ordered a massive airlift to supply West Berliners with food and fuel. An average of 4,500 tons of food were flown in each day. A plane landed every 90 seconds at the two main airports in West Berlin, and the airlift lasted for 324 days, until Stalin called off the blockade in May 1949, when an agreement was reached to reconvene the CFM in Paris at the end of that month. There is surely an irony here too: the same western air forces that had so recently been dropping bombs on the German capital, turning it into rubble, were now flying sorties over the same city, only this time dropping supplies to keep the population alive.

The meeting of the CFM led nowhere, and the western powers formerly established the Federal Republic of Germany (FRG) with a parliament and capital in Bonn, in September 1949. Hence the three western zones became one separate and new (West) German state. The following month Stalin responded by establishing the German Democratic Republic (GDR). Stalin's objective in the blockade was to prevent the establishment of a separate West German state. In this he failed. The crisis over Berlin was to have the psychological impact of finally turning former allies in war against Hitler's Third Reich into feared foes. This mutual fear quickly took on military organizational shape in the form of the North Atlantic Treaty Organization (NATO), tying the western states together, and the Warsaw Treaty Organization (WTO) linking the communist bloc states (see Tables 7.1 and 7.2). NATO was established during the Berlin airlift, in April 1949. It was an alliance that committed the USA to the defence of Western Europe, something that British Foreign Minister, Ernest Bevin, had long been advocating. It was only when the FRG became a member of NATO on 9 May 1955, after having been officially declared a fully sovereign state the previous week, that Khrushchev established the WTO, further demonstrating the key significance of Germany in Soviet perceptions of national and international security.

Table 7.1 Membership of NATO (1949–present)

	(Joining after Cold War)
Belgium	Czech Republic (March 1999)
Canada	Hungary (March 1999)
Denmark	Poland (March 1999)
France	Bulgaria (March 2004)
Iceland	Estonia (March 2004)
Italy	Latvia (March 2004)
Luxembourg	Lithuania (March 2004)
Netherlands	Romania (March 2004)
Norway	Slovakia (March 2004)
Portugal	Slovenia (March 2004)
United Kingdom	Albania (April 2009)
United States	Croatia (April 2009)
Greece (February 1952)	
Turkey (February 1952)	
Federal Republic of Germany (May 1955)	
Spain (May 1982)	

Membership Action plans for Bosnia and Herzegovina, Macedonia, and Montenegro.

Table 7.2 Membership of the Warsaw Treaty Organization (1955–1991)

Albania (withdrew 1968)
Bulgaria
Czechoslovakia
German Democratic Republic
Hungary
Poland
Romania
USSR

Having implied that Stalin was reluctant to engage in risky or adventurist foreign policies in the aftermath of war, and that he eventually backed down over Berlin, it is nevertheless the case that he gave the green light for Kim Il Sung's invasion of South Korea in June 1950. However, this came about following repeated requests from Kim for approval and assistance that had earlier been turned down, and only after Stalin felt reassured that the United States did not consider Korea to be critical to American security. Dean Acheson, the US Secretary of State had publicly excluded South Korea from the "defensive perimeter" in the Pacific that the USA identified as critical to American interests. This led Stalin, understandably, to believe that the US would not intervene. Mao's victory over the Nationalists in China, and the successful testing of the Soviet Atom bomb in 1949, indicated a positive shift in the global balance of power in Moscow's favour, giving added impetus to Stalin to take a more forthright stance.

The Korean War is termed the "Fatherland Liberation War" in North Korea and what came to be the North Korean communist party's ideology of self-reliance, *juche*, is essentially one based on racial purity, nationalism, and homogeneity, fusing also a Stalinist-like personality cult with neo-Confucian values (Soh, 1999; Cha, 2013, p. 74). Stalin's support for Kim was reluctant and it came with conditions attached, as Korea was at the time not considered vital to Soviet national security, even though North Korea shared a border with the USSR. Stalin had no wish to become directly involved in the war, but hoped to make up something for the perceived loss over Berlin. However, the war would have a dramatic impact on the development of the Cold War, giving credence to those who had argued that the Soviet Union was intent on spreading communist systems wherever there was a perceived opportunity to do so, by military means if viable.

Even before the USA took the issue to the United Nations, American troops were being prepared for deployment from their bases in Japan. In the end the United States and China fought on opposing sides in the Korean War, but the war's most significant outcome was to globalize and militarize the Cold War conflict between the two superpowers. Now the USA committed itself to the defence of Taiwan; signed a peace treaty with Japan, which became a base for the US military in the Asia Pacific; and Indochina was now considered in Washington to be "essential to the security of the free world" (Harper, 2011, p. 106). The Korean War also solidified the military bloc system in Europe, stimulated the rearmament of the FRG, and led to a massive increase in the US defence budget. The Korean War gave the arguments central to NSC 68 a massive boost, and it globalized the US policy of containment. The invasion of North Korea took place in the same year that the US National Security Council issued its Policy Paper 68. Although the contents of NSC 68 were soon to leak out, it was to remain officially classified until the 1970s. A policy paper prepared for President Truman, it set the strategic course of US foreign and security policy for the Cold War against the USSR. It was the North Korean invasion of South Korea that globalized and militarized the Cold War. In other words, it was a policy emanating from Pyongyang and Beijing that would have such a major impact on the wider US-Soviet bipolar confrontation. Its impact in Europe was to turn NATO from a prospective to a proper military alliance, and led to a major commitment from the US to station troops in Western Europe. Again, the Third World in Asia came to play a major part in Soviet Communism's existential struggle with western capitalism.

As a result of the electoral cycle a new US president came to power in 1953, whilst coincidently, but due to the natural ageing process, leadership succession was occurring too in Moscow. The American wartime hero Dwight Eisenhower was elected to the White House in January, whilst Stalin's death in March eventually led to the emergence of Nikita Khrushchev as Soviet leader. The tightening of the blocs in Europe as a result of the Korean War led to the Sovietization of the GDR, with this in turn sparking tensions across the country immediately following Stalin's death. Thousands of workers went on strike in opposition to new work quotas. Simultaneously large numbers of East Germans were voting with their feet and leaving for the West. On 17 June, demonstrations turned violent with offices associated with the communist authorities being attacked and set on fire in the GDR's largest cities, including the capital East Berlin. The uprising was put down by Soviet tanks and the East German *Volkspolizei*.

Khrushchev was faced with another uprising in October 1956, when a student revolt in Hungary turned into a major national movement calling for radical reform and a replacement of the communists in power. There was also a demand for Hungary to leave the WTO. Soviet tanks put down the uprising. Khrushchev stated in justification to his Politburo comrades that 'If we leave Hungary, this will encourage the Americans, the English, and the French—the imperialists. They will interpret it as our weakness and take the offensive' (Harper, 2011, p. 21). This was to use almost identical language to that of Lyndon Johnston and the authors of NSC 68 in relation to the need to show American resolve to stop dominoes falling one by one to Soviet Communism. President Johnson argued that if the USA would run from the fight in Vietnam then no countries would ever again have the same confidence in US protection. Johnson considered Vietnam vital to US interests, fearing that if the USA lost Vietnam, then this would be followed by the loss of all of Southeast Asia (Schandler, 1977, p. 9). The world of bipolarity had become a tight zero-sum game.

Despite the interventions in Germany and Hungary to hold the Soviet Communist block together, Khrushchev engaged in liberal reforms in the domestic realm, including his denunciation of Stalin at the 20th Party Congress. He also allowed many of the deported peoples to return to their homelands in the Caucasus, removed some restrictions on the arts and literature, and undertook limited economic reforms. However, now Khrushchev was convinced that the Soviet Union would eventually catch up with the West in economic terms. He had been hankering after an official invitation to visit Washington to invest prestige on the USSR as a major world player. When it eventually came he 'relished the notion that it had been the might of the Soviet economy ... and the entire socialist camp that had prompted Eisenhower to seek better relations' (Kempe, 2011, p. 30). As his plane, the new TU-114, the world's tallest aircraft at the time, was descending over Washington to Andrews Air Force Base in September 1959 Khrushchev said: 'We'd come a long way from the time when the United States wouldn't even grant us diplomatic recognition' (Kempe, 2011, p. 30). Khrushchev was carrying a gift that he presented to Eisenhower at the White House: it was a model of the *Lunik* space capsule that had very recently landed on the moon (Carlson, 2009). The USSR had two years previously launched the first satellite to orbit the earth. Khrushchev was full of pride for what was generally perceived at the time to have been a remarkable technological breakthrough in space exploration. It would lead to fears in the USA about a "missile gap" thereby stimulating further the nuclear arms race. In China, Mao condemned Khrushchev's visit to the USA as representing 'communist betrayal' (Kempe, p. 33). By the time John F. Kennedy entered the White House Khrushchev had seemingly successively penetrated parts of the Third World, having gained some influence in the Middle East, beginning with supplies of military equipment to Egypt.

In Berlin (the bone in the throat for Khrushchev) things had reached choking point by the summer of 1961. Free movement between the two halves of the city, connected by road, water, rail and underground trains, was a bane for the East Germans. West Berliners crossed the border to do cheap shopping; East Berliners worked in the West or simply disappeared (defected) to the West across open borders. Khrushchev also maintained that unrestricted movement was used as a free pass by western intelligence services. By July 1961 some 30,000 East Germans were fleeing to West Berlin each month—most of these were young skilled workers who could not be easily replaced. Since 1949 some three million people had left East Germany to live in the West. New border restrictions were considered essential to stem the tide. On 13 August 1961 East German soldiers began constructing the Berlin wall.

On the same day that the Warsaw Pact issued its Declaration on 13 August justifying construction of the wall, the Mayor of West Berlin, Willy Brandt, referred to the 'inhuman measures' taken by the 'oppressors' of East Berlin and described the so-called new border controls as the construction of an outer wall of a 'concentration camp' drawn right across Berlin. The East Germans referred not to a "wall" but to the "anti-fascist protective barrier." Kennedy was quoted as telling his advisers that although not a perfect solution to the German Question, 'a wall is a hell of a lot better than a war' (quoted in Dallek, 2003, p. 426). Khrushchev said that without the wall the USSR would have had to send workers to East Germany to take up the jobs left behind by fleeing East Germans, and that 'we didn't want our [i.e., Soviet] workers to clean their [i.e., German] toilets' (Khrushchev, 1990, p. 169). Khrushchev told GDR leader Walter Ulbricht 'Imagine how a Soviet worker would feel. He won the war and now he has to clean your toilets. It will not only be humiliating—it will produce an explosive reaction in our people' (Khrushchev, 1990, p. 169). The wall did deal with the immediate issue at hand, and it did help to resolve a crisis that seemed to be heading for a major confrontation. However, it was surely another nail in the coffin that was being built for the Soviet communist experiment.

The following year the world came close to nuclear Armageddon during the Cuban missile crisis, in October 1962. Khrushchev claimed that 'Our only goal in placing the missiles in Cuba was to prevent any encroachment on Cuban sovereignty and to ensure the capability of the Cuban people to be the masters of their own country' and this could not be done through 'diplomatic notes and TASS [press] statements' (Khrushchev, 1990, pp. 170, 171). Khrushchev stressed that the missiles were designed as a deterrent against what was otherwise seen as an inevitable US attack on Cuba. It was evident due to a number of factors that the US objective was indeed to overthrow the regime in Cuba. There had been a failed attempt to do so at the Bay of Pigs in April 1961. Since then statements from US policy makers, US military exercises blatantly practising invasion of a small Caribbean island, and the evident visceral hatred the Kennedy brothers (president and attorney general) had for the Castro brothers in Havana, made it clear what US objectives were. The Soviet leader considered the only way to deter a US attack would be the placement of "defensive" missiles on the island. Khrushchev thought that it would also be appropriate for Americans to experience what it was like to have enemy missiles aimed at them from nearby bases (there were US missiles in Turkey targeted at the USSR).

Most analyses of the missile crisis have Kennedy as the hero who, through his great leadership and willingness to negotiate a compromise brought the world back from the brink. However, it was Kennedy's own brinkmanship that could well have brought about the world's first war between nuclear powers. Kennedy actually threatened the world with nuclear devastation not due to any real strategic threat to the USA, nor to ensure any vital US interests, but rather to secure his own political position in Washington. Thankfully for the rest of the human race Khrushchev agreed to remove the missiles from Cuba. The crisis did have the positive result of making both sides reflect upon the futility of war in the nuclear age. The psychological impact led immediately to the establishment of the "hot line" (a telephone link to be used in crises and emergencies) and ultimately to arms control agreements and the establishment of nuclear deterrence, or mutually assured destruction (MAD) as the basis of strategic policies on both sides of the iron curtain.

From Détente to Retrenchment

Khrushchev was removed from power in a bloodless coup in 1964. There was an unwritten agreement by his successors that there should be no more turbulence, uncertainty, inconsistency, or attempts at radical reform. Brezhnev's leadership was marked by the rise and fall of détente with the United States. As with his predecessors in the Kremlin, Brezhnev too would be faced with discontent and uprisings in Eastern Europe, which once more would result in military intervention to ensure Soviet control and maintenance of the buffer zone. The Soviet-led WTO intervention in Czechoslovakia in August 1968 put the rest of the bloc on notice that no radical deviation from the communist path would be tolerated by Moscow. The main fear was that if Moscow was to loosen its grip on one bloc country then the other dominoes could fall, and eventually contagion could spread into the USSR itself: into Moldova, Ukraine, Belarus, and the Baltic republics. The fear was that this would not only undermine the security buffer zone that Stalin had established after 1945, but it would also infect non-Russians with the virus of nationalism, hence undermining the security and stability of the Soviet state. Although the official justification for the intervention was made in ideological terms, it was always clear that reasons of national security were critical. However, it did also clearly demonstrate just how dependent the CPSU was on following Marxist-Leninist doctrine, for bloc cohesiveness could not withstand any radical reform of the system.

Despite the intervention in Czechoslovakia, Brezhnev continued with his policy of forging a more cooperative relationship with the United States and the West. The main motivations for decreasing tensions with the West were the following:

• Gain official recognition of the USSR as a superpower and to accept its control over Eastern Europe
• Gain official recognition of the territorial status quo in Europe
• Manage the arms race
• Prevent a superpower conflict in the Third World
• Gain access to western technologies
• Counter the power of China

These were all linked to Soviet security interests, particularly: ensuring maintenance of the Soviet sphere of influence in Eastern Europe; institutionalizing strategic nuclear parity; preventing client states from dragging the superpowers into a direct showdown in the Third World; increasing trade with the western powers to assist the USSR in the development of the scientific revolution, considered necessary for the survival of the national security state; and finally and perhaps most importantly to counter the growing power and threat of China. Managing the arms race through arms control would also free up funds for investment in other areas of the economy. Détente did not mean an end to the Cold War. As a leading Soviet official put it, détente was necessary to ensure that the Cold War competition was managed in such a way that it did not end on a heap of radioactive rubble (Arbatov, 1977). Although the Soviet economy was still growing, by the late 1970s the rate of growth was slowing. Furthermore, as Brooks and Wohlforth note, measuring and comparing growth rates between the USSR and western capitalist states was always an inexact science (Brooks and Wohlforth, 2000–2001, p. 16). Growth rates are calculated by productive output, and yet much of what the Soviet Union produced in its farms and factories was all but useless. It's all very well for a country to manufacture large quantities of consumer goods, but if they are not worth consuming domestically let alone selling internationally then it did not say much for growth compared, say to the Asian Tigers in the 1970s and 1980s. The system that Stalin constructed in the 1930s to rapidly modernize the economy was effective in creating the iron and steel required for basic infrastructure development and building a modern military at that time, but by the 1960s it was already proving to be inadequate to keep productive pace with the market economies of the West. Half-hearted attempts at reform had led nowhere—and then reforms that had been tried in the wider communist bloc ended up threatening the system and requiring military intervention before things got out of control. Hence, détente with the West (what Brezhnev called a 'peace programme') was a foreign policy orientation designed in large part to save the Soviet domestic political economy. It was the fear that domestic reform could undermine the CPSU's control—a fear that turned out to be justified by subsequent events under Gorbachev—that was an important motive for détente.

Under a tottering conservative leadership that had lost any revolutionary zeal, the 1970s nevertheless saw the USSR engage more actively in overseas military ventures, either by assisting allies or through direct intervention. In the end it was Soviet policy in the Third World that led the USA in the 1970s to take a harder line towards Moscow, engage more actively itself in the Third World, and move away from détente. It has been stated that détente was "buried in the sands of the Ogaden" (following the

Soviet-assisted intervention of Cuban troops in the conflict in the Horn of Africa). However, the most significant event leading to the deterioration in US-Soviet relations was the Soviet invasion of Afghanistan in December 1979. The rise of indigenous communist groups in Kabul created a dilemma for the USSR. There were two main communist factions and in the mid-1970s the KGB was urging the Khalk communist grouping not to forcibly take power from the regime of Mohammed Daoud in Kabul. In the end, Nur Muhammed Taraki and the Khalk leadership removed Daoud in a military coup, in April 1978, without having any prior consultations with Moscow. The Afghan government had been requesting the Soviet Union to intervene since March 1979. Ultimately members of the Politburo, led by Defence Minster Marshall Dmitry Ustinov, persuaded Brezhnev that Afghanistan now provided Moscow with an opportunity that should not be missed to counter US power in the region. During a Politburo meeting in Moscow Ustinov chimed in: 'Why shouldn't we be entitled to act in the proximity of our borders as the US are doing in their Latin American backyard?' (cited in Grachev, 2008, p. 23). The USSR shared a border of 2,348 kilometres with Afghanistan. If Central America (e.g., Nicaragua and El Salvador) was viewed by the US in strategic terms as its backyard, then Afghanistan was perceived in the Kremlin as the strategic backyard of the USSR on its own southern periphery. The context was one also of radicalizing Islamic forces in the region, with neighbouring Iran (which shares 2,180 kilometres of border with Afghanistan) having undergone an Islamic Revolution. The war would last over nine years and kill or injure 55,000 Soviet citizens. It would put the last nail in the coffin of détente. It also impeded any improvement of relations with China and Pakistan. The war would prove to be unwinnable for the USSR.

From 1917 through to the mid-1980s Soviet foreign relations were determined by considerations of state security. The stress on national security was a natural outgrowth of early and then ongoing experiences of warfare and the fears this instilled about internal and external enemies of state. These fears then resulted in the creation of a national security state and the development of a military industrial complex within a one-party communist system. Marxism-Leninism was always an essential component of Soviet identity and purpose, but the ideology in the realm of international security did not always determine Soviet international behaviour. Interventions in the Eastern bloc and in Afghanistan had national security goals, although spreading communism (in the Third World) or maintaining it (in Eastern Europe) were also significant considerations. These ideological considerations were also closely tied up with the very survival of the communist system in Moscow, and Russia's control over its internal empire. By the time Gorbachev succeeded to power Soviet Communism was in crisis, and hence the USSR threatened with extinction. It is true that in 1917 the Bolsheviks were radical uncompromising revolutionaries wedded to Marxist ideology. But the further away one gets from 1917, the more bureaucratic and ossified the Soviet system became.

Gorbachev and Retrenchment and the End of the Cold War

On coming to power in 1985 Gorbachev represented a new more energetic and less fearful generation. When he joined the Politburo Gorbachev was shocked to discover that military expenditure was rising twice as fast as Soviet GNP, although he was frustrated that even at the highest levels statistics concerning the military were top secret 'inaccessible even to members of the Politburo' (Gorbachev, 1996, p. 136). The Soviet national security state was so lacking in transparency in this field that even the dominant leader in a totalitarian country was unaware of how much the military industrial complex was costing. The new Soviet leader discovered that 'In virtually all branches of the national economy, military expenditure sapped the vital juices' (Gorbachev, 1995, p. 136). Gorbachev still did not know how much money was, as he put it, being 'poured into this bottomless pit' (quoted in Grachev, 2008, p. 7). There was a consensus in the Soviet military high command too that military expenditure in the 1980s was much too high, and that the USSR could not continue to bear such a burden (Odom, 2000, p. 225). It was simply no longer tenable for the Soviet leadership to continue this profligate spending on arms, especially if it wished to stimulate the domestic economy and satisfy the rising expectation of an increasingly less cowed population. It is wrong to credit Gorbachev alone for initiating the reforms of the 1980s, for there was support within all levels of the CPSU apparatus for something to be done to reverse the economic decline and the social crisis inflicting the USSR at that time. It was recognized that spending on arms needed to be cut, and it was this that initially explained Gorbachev's priority on improving relations not only with the USA and Western Europe, but also with China. The USSR and China shared the longest border of any two states in the international system, and in 1969 came very close to all-out war during bloody clashes along parts of the border.

It is important also to note that the USSR in the 1980s was 'the first industrialized country to register peacetime declines in life expectancy and infant mortality' (Brooks and Wolhfortth, 2000/01, p. 18). The downward shift among key economic performance indicators began in the mid 1970s—the Soviet economic slowdown was not a temporary blip, but seemingly permanent and irreversible without a radical and fundamental restructuring of the system. The problem then was systemic, not a simple policy or cyclical problem. The Soviet system could no longer bear the burden of the national security state. Gorbachev noted in a speech he gave the year before he gained power that if the USSR was to continue into the next century as a great power an acceleration of the economy was essential (Gorbachev, 1987, p. 86). In the foreign and security realms a "New Political Thinking" (NPT) was improvised in dealing with the West. Gorbachev stated that 'The roots of the new thinking lay in the understanding that there would be no winners in a nuclear war and that in any such event both "camps" would be blown to kingdom come' (Gorbachev and Mlynar, 2002, p. 139). Gorbachev recalled in his memoirs that for him the most difficult of the 'international Gordian knots' to untie in relations with the West was 'undoubtedly the military rivalry between the superpowers' (Gorbachev, 1988, p. 403). In his speech to the House of Commons in December 1984 Gorbachev stated that the 'the nuclear age inevitably dictates a new political thinking' (Gorbachev, 1988, p. 427). Central to NPT was an attempt to break out of the arms race to help domestic economic reform (see Shearman, 1993).

A number of measures were taken, including a unilateral moratorium of nuclear testing; the unilateral withdraw of half a million Soviet troops from Eastern Europe; the withdrawal of troops from Afghanistan; and an end to the Brezhnev Doctrine. However, none of this worked in the end because of the very nature of the Soviet national security state. The Soviet economic system required more than an injection of savings from cuts in arms expenditure; and the political system could not accommo-date radical change due in large part to the fact of the USSR being an empire; all empires it seems come to an end when the colonial powers are unable or unwilling to commit the resources necessary to hold them together. In relation to the nuclear arms issues the logic of mutual assured destruction compelled both sides to coexist and to manage their relations in such a way that the ideological and power struggle did not result in out-and-out warfare. Perhaps the nuclear bomb would have been more deserving of the Noble Peace Prize than Gorbachev. Although we can never be certain, a strong case can be made that it was the nuclear stand-off that was responsible for keeping the Cold War from turning into a hot one.

Conclusion

There are those who argue that the demise of the Cold War can best be explained with reference to the revolution in military affairs that had begun in the 1970s, leading to a situation in which the USSR could no longer compete with the United States Certainly the nature of the Soviet political economy prevented the USSR from being able to match the United States in the development of precision-guided missiles and other new military features arising from the micro-electronic revolution and new information technologies. Increased defence expenditure in the United States had begun under Carter in 1979, but it was Reagan who deliberately sought to win the Cold War through a high-tech arms race. However: 'The main impact of Reagan's policies was to propel the Soviets to adopt ever-more offensive military doctrines, which rendered the bilateral balance of power in Europe increasingly unstable' (DeVore, 2010, p. 242). It was despite Reagan's policies, not because of them, that Gorbachev instigated decisions that led to a defensive Soviet military posture, thereby undermining the arms race. The Soviet communist system was in crisis, and it was this that was responsible for the radical new thinking and policies in the security realm under Gorbachev. In the final analysis, it was Soviet national security that was the key determinant of foreign policies throughout the entire history of the USSR, and not Soviet Communism. Although in theory the October Revolution was designed to transcend the nation and the idea of security pertaining only to the nation state, in the end it was the logic of anarchy in the interstate system that determined Soviet international behaviour.

Initially Gorbachev sought to win the war in Afghanistan by a surge in Soviet troops, but soon came to realize it was unwinnable and withdrew the army in 1989. Gorbachev sought to maintain the stability of the communist bloc by making it more viable through economic and political reform, but the reforms would lead to crisis and collapse and a renunciation of the Brezhnev Doctrine. Gorbachev sought to save the socialist enterprise in the USSR and hold the Union together through reforms, but this would eventually spark dissolution of the country and an end to communism. In the end it was Soviet Communism's funeral dirge, and not that of capitalism. But Soviet Communism endured for some 74 years. Founded during the First World War of the previous century, Soviet Communism was strengthened during and immediately after the Second World War. War, as it were, made the Soviet state; but then the state made war: it made war on its own people, on the peoples of Eastern Europe, and finally on Afghanistan. The Soviet communist state was always fearful of internal and external enemies (and rightfully so). It was ultimately this fear that prevented any serious attempts to reform the system, until it was manifestly too late to save it. The Soviet national security state would wither away from age and disease largely due to a sense of insecurity that was always well founded. The remarkable thing is that it lasted as long as it did. Gorbachev had no real option but to retrench. And retrenchment marked the final denouement of the long Cold War drama that so dominated international security during the second half of the twentieth century. In the end, although Marxist theory predicted that the state (in general) would wither away, it was only the Soviet state that did so.

Conclusions

There is no single explanation of any important event, let alone of a long historical period such as that covered in this book. There will always be differences of view and emphasis, and history is a controversial matter, and interpretations of history are often used as tools in political contestation. What I have sought to do in this book is to provide an assessment of Soviet Communism and an examination of the rise of fall of the USSR and its impact on world politics, by focusing on the roles of ideology, power, and the state, and where these all interplay with and have been determined to an extent by the forces of nationalism, whilst trying to avoid any political biases. The previous chapters have shown how events coming out of the Revolution of October 1917 and the rise of Soviet Communism went on to shape the international politics of the twentieth century, whilst leaving a legacy that well into the twenty-first century was still being played out in Ukraine. Without the challenge of Soviet Communism there would have been no Cold War, that tense, dangerous ideological and balance of power contestation that brought the world so close to nuclear war in October 1962. In this final chapter I will highlight the main findings from the study and suggest any lessons that might be drawn, whilst also returning to the question of how academics failed to foresee the collapse of Soviet Communism and the subsequent radical impact this had on the international system. In rethinking the international politics of the twentieth century it is necessary to highlight the power of ideological challenges to the international order, as well as the more traditional notions of the balance of power defined in material terms. This book has shown how the Soviet communist state was central to both.

So What Was the USSR?

As this book highlights, the birth of the Union of Soviet Socialist Republics created a challenge to the international status quo from the left. Yet it was from the right that the main challenges to the international order came between the two world wars of the twentieth century: from Italian Fascism, and its variants in Spain and Japan, and from German Nazism. As Hobsbawm notes, during this period the left was not responsible for the over-throw of a single government, and 'all anti-democratic regime changes, by coup, conquest, or by other means, were moves to the right' (Hobsbawm, 2007, p. 609). Hence, nationalism was really the main direct challenge to the international order during this period, and not communism. However, these far right regimes, in Germany under Hitler, in Spain under Franco, and in Italy under Mussolini, can only be understood as reactions to the forces of communism on the left. Hence it was Soviet Communism arising from the Bolshevik Revolution in 1917 that provided the impetus for the rise of the nationalist far right. But, as this book has also shown, Marxism-Leninism was itself, although an ideology based upon class relations, forced to make compromises with national-ism, and indeed was employed in the Third World as an ideology of national liberation. In the end, too, Soviet Communism's own demise came through the power of the national idea. In regard to the balance of power, Soviet Russia became the second pole in a bipolar confrontation that would come to be defined as a Cold War. But this materialized not through any initial intention by the Bolsheviks to expand Soviet influence to the West by military force, but rather through a perceived need to construct a national security state to counter what was seen as a threat from the main capitalist powers to the survival of the Russian Revolution. By the middle of the twentieth century the USSR posed both an ideological challenge and a military security threat to the West, as it emerged from the war against Germany as a major power with increased geopolitical influence. The earlier chapters to this book trace how first ideational and then material factors led to the perception of a Soviet threat among leaders in western states.

If we fast-forward to the end of the century, the Union of Soviet Socialist Republics was dismantled, without a shot being fired, in December 1991. The dismantling of the USSR was a major transforming event not just for the former fifteen republics of the union, but again, as with 1917, for world politics. Radical transformative political events in Russia at both the opening and the closing of the previous century were instrumental in having systemic and psychological impacts in world politics. The end of the Soviet system in 1991 was analogous to other major transformations in world politics such as the decline of the Roman or Ottoman empires, both of which occurred over hundreds of years. The decline and demise of the USSR occurred in historical comparison, however, in the blink of an eye.

The USSR renewed its diplomatic relations with Israel, broken since the six-day war in 1967, when Alexander Bovin, the new Soviet ambassador was presenting his credentials in Tel Aviv on December 25, 1991—just as the country he represented ceased to be a legal entity later that same day (Bovin, 2003). Soviet diplomats throughout the world went to bed that Christmas night representing the USSR and woke up the next morning representing the Russian Federation, or in the case of non-Russian diplomats, representing other parts of the former Union. Yuri Vorontsev went to work one day in New York as Soviet delegate to the UN and finished the day representing Russia. The diplomatic staff in Soviet embassies across the world contained representatives of many different nationalities from across the USSR, and these officials suddenly found themselves representing new fledgling states, but having temporarily to share office space with diplomats from what was now a foreign country as they shuffled chairs and swapped offices. Although in terms of material power the USSR by this time had not kept pace with its potential foes, and its economy was in a "pre-crisis" situation, the world was still essentially bipolar in military terms. It turned out that the real crisis was not in relation to Soviet decline in the military balance of power, although this was also important, but in relation to the unravelling of the Soviet belief system, and the related challenges to the communist regime coming from the nations that comprised the Soviet "outer empire," and from those nations within the USSR itself.

Reflecting more than twenty years later on contemporary international relations and Russia's role in world politics it has been useful to examine what Soviet Communism actually was and why the Soviet system collapsed. This has been a useful exercise for a number of reasons. First, the collapse of Soviet Communism had major unanticipated consequences on the international political system. An understanding of the Soviet communist past helps us to contextualize and better understand some contemporary issues in global politics, for many of these have their origins in the Soviet era (for example, the rise in ethnic conflicts, the re-emergence of the far right, and the increasing manifestations of radical fundamentalist ideologies linked to religion, the Russian annexation of Crimea and the crisis in Ukraine, and the issue of ethnic Russians in other parts of the former USSR). Second, Russia was the central component of the Soviet Union, hence understanding the Soviet era is important for appreciating both the historical background and the political, social, and cultural legacies that continue to impact on Russian thinking and behaviour today. Although this book ends with the dismantlement of the USSR and the collapse of Soviet Communism, anyone wishing to understand contemporary Russia under Vladimir Putin would need to appreciate the rise and fall of Soviet Communism as covered in this book. Third, it is instructive to reflect upon the failure of International Relations (IR) and Soviet Studies to get the Soviet Union and Soviet Communism right: for it is a remarkable fact the field of Soviet Studies and the discipline of International Relations failed to foresee the collapse of the USSR and the end of the Cold War. There was a general consensus that Soviet Communism still had a long life yet—just as it was about to expire—and that there was no end in sight to the Cold War. International Relations as a discipline failed to predict or even, for the most part allow for the possibility of, the end of the Cold War that would result from the demise of the Soviet communist system. Given these facts it is remarkable that most scholars and policy makers in the West were also taken by surprise when Russia failed to successfully consolidate into a liberal democracy, and then under President Vladimir Putin's leadership would become more anti-western and assertive in its foreign policy, leading to what some observers referred to as a new Cold War (Lucas, 2008). This conception was given added currency with first the Russian war with Georgia in 2008, and then the annexation of Crimea in 2014.

USSR as an Ideological Empire State

The book's main message is that we should recognize what the Union of Soviet Socialist Republics essentially was: *an empire*.

This directs us to the most important finding of this study, for in all chapters the fact of empire is central: central to the development of both the ideology and the practice of Bolshevism; to the development of the Soviet national security state; for explaining the difficulties Soviet Communism had both at home and in the wider world of international relations; and the failure of an ideology based on class relations to supplant the stronger sense of national identity in the context of empire. Hence the failure of Soviet Communism can in large part be seen as linked to the fact of empire. This should always have been a self evident, basic, and essential fact: that the USSR was the Russian Empire in a new Soviet guise. It is worth noting that the Russians had experienced the collapse of empire on three previous occasions before the dismantlement of the USSR in 1991: the Kievan Empire (850–1240), the Muscovite Empire (1400–1605), and the Romanov Empire (1613–1917). Hence the most recent reconstituted Russian Empire was in the guise of the Soviet Union from the 1920s. Yet this was something that was actually rarely if ever considered or even acknowledged in either the fields of Soviet Studies or IR. However, the fact of empire, as previous chapters have shown, was always evident to the original Bolshevik revolutionaries, for they were operating in direct ideological opposition to what they clearly recognized as an empire at the beginning of the twentieth century (Lenin, 1963). The Bolsheviks may have been opposed to both empire and nationalism, but they had no option but to deal with those facts: for they inherited a Russian Empire with a large number of separate nationalities.

Russia had *officially* been an empire (*Rossiskaya Imperiya*), since 1721, and for centuries Russia had continually been expanding across vast tracts of territory in Eurasia. This included Ukraine, occupying the largest landmass in Europe of any single country apart from Russia itself. In previous centuries Kiev, the Ukrainian capital, was even considered to be the original heartland of "Mother Russia." On official maps of the Tsarist Russian Empire Ukraine appeared as "Little Russia" (*Malorossiia*). Putin recalled this fact in April 2014, when he noted that Ukraine was only accorded official administrative status in the Soviet era, in 1920 (Putin, 2014). The golden age of Ukrainian national identity was not then under the Russian Tsars, but under the Soviet Communist Commissars. Lenin, whose statues were being torn down during the Maidan events in Ukraine in 2014, was responsible for the policy of indigenisation (*korenizatsia*) that allowed for the flowering of Ukrainian language and culture in the 1920s. During the communist era Soviet leader Nikita Khrushchev transferred Crimea from the jurisdiction of the Russian Republic to that of the Ukrainian Soviet Socialist Republic in 1956, at a time when no one could envisage Ukraine splitting off from Russia and the wider Union. The last Soviet leader's wife, Raisa Gorbacheva, was of Ukrainian origin. Chernenko, Gorbachev's predecessor was from a Ukrainian family. Brezhnev was born in Ukraine, and Khrushchev was born near the border of Russia and Ukraine and served as Party First Secretary in Kiev. Many other leading figures in the former USSR had family connections in Ukraine. So too do some Russian officials at the time of writing. The problems pitting the EU and Russia for influence in a fractured Ukraine in 2014 can only be understood within this historical framework.

Ukraine is pivotal to Russia for a number of reasons, but an extremely important factor relates to sentiment, to history, to the politics of identity. Certainly, as events in early 2014 revealed, eastern and southern parts of Ukraine, and particularly Crimea, are thought to be integral parts of the Russian nation. A Levada poll taken during the events that removed Viktor Yanukovich from power in February 2014 found that nearly half of Russians saw the events as a violent coup conducted with western support (Interfax, 27 February, 2014). As George Mirsky put it Ukraine is 'pivotal to the great Russian state—whether yesterday's Soviet Union or today's federation' (Mirsky, 2014). It is pivotal for reasons relating to the Russian conception of where Ukraine fits within the idea of the Russian nation, and also due to geopolitics and Moscow's political and strategic relationship toward the West. This was not the first time that Ukrainians had been torn about which way their country should look, whether to the East or to the West. In 1926 Oleksander Shumskyi, the Commissar for education in Kiev clashed openly with Lazar Kaganovich, the First Secretary of the Communist Party in Ukraine, at a meeting of the Ukrainian Politburo, when he accused ethnic Russians of dominating local affairs. Shumskyi was associated with a group of Ukrainian communists that was pushing for a 'pro-European orientation for Ukraine' (Smith, 2013, p. 89). Shumskyi was strongly identified with the policy of indigenization in Ukraine. Events in Ukraine since the collapse of the Soviet Union demonstrate that the consequences emanating from the end of the

Soviet Russian Empire are still playing out. The same is true in the North Caucasus.

I noted how the Russian Empire should be distinguished from other European empires. It has been said that whereas England and France had empires, Russia was an empire. For example, the British and French empires expanded in non-contiguous areas, creating colonies in distant lands administered separately from the central institutions of the (nation-) state, whereas Russia's empire expanded across neighbouring lands thereby incorporating ever more peoples into a larger (empire-) state. Hence, when the British and French empires collapsed, as difficult as it was for many to accept this in London and Paris, there were no resulting crises in the British and French states themselves. Of course the French and British left behind bloody conflicts in their former colonies in Africa, Asia, and the Middle East, with many unresolved to this day (e.g., Palestine, Iraq, and Syria). The experience of post-colonial conflicts based upon ethnic, religious and tribal differences adds further evidence in support of arguments developed in this book about the USSR, Russia, and the post-Soviet space. In contrast to the end of other empires, given the different nature of the Soviet/Russian empire-state, there would be major systemic ramifications when it was eventually dismantled in 1991. During the Russian Empire it was never clear where Russia proper ended and the rest of Empire began. There were no fixed territorial boundaries on the map delineating the settlements of other nations. All school children in the UK up until 1948 could easily identify India and other colonies on a map of the world, marked in pink (or sometimes red) clearly as India, a colony separate from (even if considered by some integral to) the home country. Russia itself in contrast only began to appear as a separate geographical entity on maps in the Soviet period, as the Russian Socialist Federative Soviet Republic.

In addition to being the latest incarnation of the Russian Empire the USSR was also an ideological and a revolutionary state. Whereas the Tsarist Russian Empire was a conservative counter-revolutionary state (forming the Holy Alliance with Prussia and Austria in 1815 to preserve the existing dynastic order in Europe after the Napoleonic Wars) the USSR was a revisionist, revolutionary state. Lenin's objective in taking power in 1917 was to foment socialist revolution in the more developed capitalist states in the West. When it became clear after the Russian Civil War that this was no longer a feasible prospect in the near term, following Lenin's death in 1923, a leadership struggle broke out in which different contenders offered alternative visions for establishing a socialist society, each articulating programmes with reference to Marxist ideology. It was shown how Leon Trotsky pushed for 'permanent revolution', considering that socialism could not survive in Russia if revolution did not also take place in the advanced capitalist countries. Nikolai Bukharin supported a continuation of the New Economic Policy (NEP) started by Lenin in 1921: pursuing a mixed economy with the state holding the commanding heights of industry until such time as a stage of development would be reached that would be conducive for further developing socialism. Stalin's conception was for "socialism in one country" which involved rapid and enforced industrialization and collectivization and the institutionalization of state planning. Stalin won out in this struggle for power, using purges and terror against his opponents (termed "enemies of the people") and the USSR was labelled in the West a "totalitarian state."

The USSR was then what we would call today a fundamentalist state, in that its basic policy directions were determined by a rigid set of ideological precepts, and the objective of foreign policy, in theory if not always in practice, was to remake the world in its own Soviet image. From the Russian Revolution of 1917 through to the collapse of the USSR in 1991, during the period Hobsbawm (1994) called the 'age of extremes', Soviet Russian identity had been tied up with the conception of their country as the central component of international communism, or what came to be officially termed after 1945 the world socialist movement, or the world socialist system. Stalin may have devised the conception of socialism in a single country as a mobilizing force to modernize and industrialize the USSR in the face of capitalist encirclement, yet throughout the entire Soviet period, from 1917 through to the New Political Thinking under Gorbachev, the USSR was an ideological state whose leaders saw it as their duty to support communism internationally, in what one might term a form of "communist imperialism." Official Marxist-Leninist doctrine gave legitimation to Soviet control over the East European communist states after 1945, and also gave legitimation to the CPSU leadership, providing it with its title to rule across the USSR.

As previous chapters have demonstrated, ideology was at times adapted to meet changing domestic and international circumstances. For example the conception of "peaceful coexistence" implied a less imperial or revolutionary momentum in Soviet foreign policy in the 1950s under Khrushchev, yet this was, as with Brezhnev's "peace programme" in the 1970s, a recognition of the existential dangers of nuclear weapons. Nevertheless, Marxist-Leninist ideology was still a powerful force. Peaceful coexistence and the peace programme were in effect different methods for conducting what was still seen as a global class conflict between two socio-economic systems. With the advent of weapons of mass destruction, however, it was deemed necessary to try and ensure that this global conflict with international capitalism did not lead to a *nuclear* end of history—hence adaptations to the ideology.

Yet Ideology served several functions—cognitive, socializing, and revolutionary. Marxism-Leninism provided a worldview, created a system of beliefs, and prescribed an operational code for action. The extent to which ideology determined Soviet behaviour is disputed, but it is clear that it did play an important role, particularly, but not only, in the domestic realm. This has been borne out by archives that have been made available since the collapse of the system (for example, see Courtois, 2001). It is clear also that each successive Soviet leader was not only obliged to articulate policies in line with the writings of Marx and Lenin, but that they each genuinely believed in the non-capitalist path of development. Stalin, for example, was far from being simply a dictatorial tyrant, for his tyranny was based upon a genuine (no matter how distorted it may have been) Marxist understanding of the world, hence his terrorist state policies were conducted with the objective, as he saw it, of building communism. Gorbachev too, even after the August coup attempt to remove him from power, right to the every end, was a committed Leninist. In terms of the national question, by the 1970s the official ideology had melded this with Marxism-Leninism into the formulation of a "meta-ethnic" Soviet community held together by socialist characteristics. Yury Bromley was the leading Soviet academician working on ethnicity, and this is his formulation (see Bromley, 1975). It would have been impossible to explain some of the Soviet Union's foreign policies towards the Third World during this same period without an appreciation of the ideological dimension. One irony that would become evident with the fall of the USSR was that whilst the Soviet communist party leadership felt obligated to support revolutions of national liberation in the Third World as a step towards socialist orientation, its own national minorities were restive and would eventually undertake their own revolutions of national liberation as a step towards independence and capitalist development.

As noted earlier the concept of the nation may originally have been a social construction, or an imagined community, but the national community is far from being an imaginary one—for most peoples across the world it is very real, and the power of the national idea is perhaps the single most potent one when it comes to political mobilization of the masses. One factor that inhibited a more complete understanding of this issue was that for the vast majority of Soviet Area Studies specialists, Russia was the main focus. There was a very strong Russo-centric tendency in Soviet Area Studies, and whilst this is understandable given that Russia was the dominant force in the USSR, it would have serious impediments, for we could not know enough about the Soviet Union as a whole. It is interesting to recall that specialists on nationalism tended to ignore the USSR in their studies, whilst Soviet Area Studies specialists tended to either dismiss the national question entirely, or argue that it was not an important issue and was unlikely to destabilize the system. The development of the Soviet multinational state has been equated to that of the USA, contrasting these to the European experiences (Rutland, 1984). It has been suggested that both Russia and the USA over the centuries had engaged in a process of integrating peoples from different national communities into a larger national collective (Soviet and American).

However, notwithstanding the expansion of the USA into what was once Mexican territory, the US experience is fundamentally different from the Soviet/Russian experience. Like Australia, the US is an immigrant society comprised of peoples who voluntarily left their original homelands to settle there (not forgetting the penal colonies in Australia's earlier development). In contrast, Russia incorporated national communities by force into an expanded empire-state. Rutland refers also to Scots, Irish, Welsh, and English, who have separate identities but nonetheless share identity as members of the wider United Kingdom as their most important reference point. But the USSR was radically different from the US, UK, or Australian experiences of national integration. In addition to misreading and underplaying the forces of nationalism in the USSR itself, most academics also failed to grasp the inherent problems the Soviet Union had in managing its outer empire in Eastern Europe, for it was always going to be difficult to impose a Soviet-type communist system on countries with such vastly different experiences, cultures, languages, and religions (such as Bulgarians, Hungarians, Germans and Poles). What held these together was not common bonds of identity and ideology, but the Soviet national security state's military might. Also, whilst Stalin's crimes against his own people were recognized in the West, for the most part the focus was on his terror campaign against the old Bolshevik revolutionaries and high communist officials, rather than the far larger numbers of ethnic minorities that suffered the consequences of high Stalinism as documented in previous chapters.

Ideological Contradictions and New History under Gorbachev

Stalin's attempt to create socialism in one country and a new post-nationalist international community of peoples was riddled with inherent contradictions from the outset. First there was the contradiction of trying to manufacture a common history and culture out of such a diverse and complex mix of uncommon pasts—as, for example, those of Ukraine on the one hand and Uzbekistan on the other. For a number of clear reasons it would be extremely difficult to form a union between such different groups. It would be similar to an attempt to make a new community and union between Sweden and Tadzhikistan. It would be much easier to imagine a union between Sweden and Norway, although even here previous historical attempts at Union between these two Scandinavian countries would not inspire optimism. Sweden and Norway were in fact a union from 1814 until the dissolution of the union in 1905. The Soviet communist leadership imagined a new Soviet nation but this, as it turned out, did prove to be imaginary.

A second contradiction was in the construction of political and cultural institutions through which national identities were fostered and guaranteed, whilst seeking at the same time to construct a post-national Soviet identity. Each of the major nationalities had their own constitutions and national organizations (including party, state, and cultural bodies) that reinforced their own sense of nationhood rather than encouraging identity as a Soviet meta-ethnic community. Rather what emerged was a federal entity made up of separate nations, and whilst attempting to create a new loyal citizenry, by enabling the flowering of national cultures, the ultimate Soviet project of integration was undermined.

A third contradiction in Soviet nationalities policy was the fact that, although privileging the Russians politically, and linking the Soviet state with a dominant Russian culture, the Russians were in fact the only national group without an identity that was distinct from the wider Soviet one. Other titular nationalities had two identities, two languages, two cultures, two histories, and two sets of institutions. Russians on the other hand had to share theirs: their history, their language, and their culture. Whereas other languages were allowed to flourish, the Russian language was meshed with Sovietization. Soviet Communism did not offer a realistic alternative to the national idea and failed to create a sense of community that would be solid, deep, and long lasting.

These contradictions were ultimately played out to their logical conclusion when Gorbachev began to institute reforms after 1985. Glasnost provided for freedom of expression. Perestroika allowed for the development of civil society and for groups to operate free from state controls, and ultimately for partial democratization and political contestation. It quickly became clear that the Soviet system was far from enjoying legitimacy as the peoples of the USSR rallied around their national flags in what became a struggle for independence from the Union. Nation in the end trumped class. Although it was Yeltsin who was instrumental in bringing the system down when he used the newly created Russian political institutions as a base for his power struggle against Gorbachev, it was already by that time (December 1991) clearly in its death throes, as some republics had made unilateral declarations of independence. This included Ukraine, whose new parliament had passed a Declaration of State Sovereignty in July, which was ratified in a referendum on 1 December. Although Yeltsin during his struggle for power with Gorbachev had wanted to save the Union in a different form, he recognized that without Ukraine this would be impossible. Yeltsin would in later years express regret at having 'lost Ukraine', and the 'guilt' he felt about this would give him sleepless nights in his retirement (Khineyko, 2007).

It was noted how Brezhnev's "stability of cadres" had stifled creativity and led to a period of economic stagnation. *Glasnost* under Gorbachev can be viewed as an information policy, a policy designed to help save Soviet Communism from complete stagnation. *Glasnost* means openness, and Gorbachev hoped that by allowing more freedoms in the media, and in academic research, and more transparency in public policy-making, his objective of accelerating economic growth would be better realized. One aspect of this new openness was to allow for a more comprehensive evaluation of Stalinism than that provided by Khrushchev in his speech to the 20th Party Congress some thirty years earlier. Khrushchev could only go so far in his denunciation of Stalinism in 1956, as he himself had carried out some of the policies linked to the terror and the purges twenty years earlier. Khrushchev denounced Stalin the individual, but not the system he had helped Stalin to build. Of the six defining features of totalitarianism Khrushchev is widely admired for removing one of them: the use of terror. He may not have been able to go so far as to criticize the fundamentals of the political economy, but totalitarianism without the terror was a major improvement over the pure Stalinist system.

Gorbachev did not have any concerns that a reassessment of the 1930s could rebound on him personally, for he was only a young undergraduate student when Stalin died in 1953, hence he could afford to go beyond a critique of the cult of personality. Unlike Khrushchev, Gorbachev, through a more open environment, would let others do the talking for him. This was done through the pages of academic reports and serious journalism, as well as the more popular media. However, unravelling the strict controls that the Party/state had over the means of communication would quickly open up the floodgates for a radical reassessment of the entire Soviet period. Removing strict censorship enabled other points of view and interpretations of history to be articulated, separate from the official Leninist one handed down from above. Removing this second element of the totalitarian system—the party's control over all means of communication— had unanticipated consequences. People were no longer afraid of the knock on the door in the middle of the night, and now they had an opportunity to engage in a debate through the various media available (pre-internet) on the burning issues of the day. Yet the burning issue of the day was history: basically it began as a continuation of the debate that Khrushchev had opened up but then quickly shut down in 1956, about Stalin's role in Soviet history.

Glasnost was initially designed by Gorbachev to forge a coalition to buttress his position against the conservative forces in the higher echelons of the national security state, especially among the security organs and military high command, and within the Central Committee of the CPSU. The hope was, by opening up a space for free expression it would be possible to enlist support for *perestroika* among the creative intelligentsia and the more reformist-minded members of the party apparatus. Stalin had destroyed the original Bolshevik intelligentsia in the purges; Khrushchev was essentially anti-intellectual; and in Brezhnev's corporatist deal with the leading institutions of the national security state there was no room for creativity, and no role for the liberal intelligentsia that had emerged in the post-Stalin era. The Soviet people were also hungry for information about and analyses of the Stalinist past. The command economy was defined by being non-capitalist, non-market based—that is to say, what was produced was based on central planning and what the party leadership considered to be appropriate from a political standpoint, rather than being based on the desires and demands of the consumer. Glasnost provided this first manifestation of the market, in the realm of ideas, and it produced an unstoppable hunger for history. This resulted in saturation coverage of the crimes and evils of the Stalinist system, reflecting a desire among Soviet citizens for the "truth" to be told about their country's past. But this went beyond Stalin, logically going back to a discussion about the very foundations of the Soviet state under Lenin and the Bolsheviks to discover what gave rise to Stalinism. A sort of "history wars" was being conducted in the media in which a new liberal (anti-Leninist) interpretation of the Soviet era was becoming dominant.

Glasnost helped to undermine the legitimacy of the CPSU's title to rule. It revealed openly what many already knew anyway: that the Soviet Communist system was rotten to its core. *Glasnost* provided oxygen, not for *perestroika,* as Gorbachev initially had hoped, but for opposition to the CPSU and the Soviet national security state. Increasing openness led to the development of civil society, to the blossoming of organizations independent of the state. It also led to the articulation of nationalist sentiment and calls for national liberation. Rather than remaining supporters of *perestroika,* national elites and the indigenous intelligentsia in the republics wrapped themselves in their national flags—they all did, liberals as well as conservatives and the old communists. On the national question, as Jeremy Smith put it, Gorbachev was 'hopelessly utopian', as he considered the nations of the USSR to be one single family, the Soviet people (Smith, p. 257). Gorbachev did not foresee the consequences of his information policy because he did not appreciate sufficiently the power of the national idea.

The first groups to take advantage of Gorbachev's licence to form independent associations were environmental movements. Yet part of the motivation for these too was nationalist in origin, for areas suffering the terrible environmental consequences of highly polluting industries were often found in the non-Russian republics. In these republics it was considered a deliberate ploy on the part of the Soviet leadership in Moscow to situate polluting industries far away from Russia. Opposition in the Baltic republics to the construction of a hydro-electric dam, a phosphate plant, and nuclear power plant; opposition to pollution in Lake Sevan in Armenia; a movement to reverse the gradual disappearance of the Aral Sea in Central Asia—all these issues increased nationalist tendencies and led to groups pushing for independence from the USSR (see Smith, 2013). Accidents, such as the nuclear disaster at Chernobyl in 1986 and the Armenian earthquake in 1988, also helped to mobilize anti-regime and pro-nationalist movements, for many Ukrainians and Armenians considered that the reaction to these events demonstrated that Russians who dominated the political system in Moscow cared little for their plight.

There are those who argue that a smaller voluntary union could have been preserved if Gorbachev had instituted direct elections for an all-Union presidency, and then put himself forward for election under universal suffrage. Archie Brown has suggested that being elected in free and open elections would have provided legitimacy to Gorbachev, who could then have used the office of Soviet president to preserve a smaller Union (it is accepted that the Baltic states would still most likely have broken away) (Brown, 2009, p. 51). Stephen Cohen (2004) has similarly argued that the Soviet system was on the path of being successfully reformed, and that the Union could have been saved. What prevented this from happening according to Cohen was the attempted coup against Gorbachev in August 1991. The date of the coup was significant, for it was to be the next day that the new Union Treaty was to be signed, providing those Soviet republics that signed it with "sovereignty" in a new Union of Soviet Sovereign Republics. Gorbachev himself states that one of his biggest mistakes was not dealing with the national question, stating that 'What we needed was decentralization of the USSR, rather than its disintegration' (Gorbachev, 2009, p. 299). Gorbachev also acknowledged later that he should have put himself forward for democratic elections as USSR president for, as he writes: 'legitimacy of the president's authority could have allowed us to make more determined actions against the destroyers of the USSR' (Gorbachev, 2009, p. 300)

Brown, Cohen, Gorbachev and others also refer to the referendum of April 1991 asking Soviet citizens if they wished to endorse a new reformed Union of Sovereign Soviet Republics as evidence that the Union could have been saved if it was not for the coup. The evidence they give is the seemingly strong endorse-ment that the referendum received from the majority of those that voted. Four things should be noted: First, six republics refused to take part: Estonia, Latvia, Lithuania, Moldova, Armenia, and Georgia. Second, the official results are surely suspect when in some of the Central Asian republics turnout was recorded to be almost 100% with over 90% in favour of the proposed Treaty. In the Turkmen SSR, for example, the turnout was 97.66% and 98.26% voted in favour. This is simply not credible. Third, many of those voting in favour would have seen it as the first step in gaining complete national independence. Fourth, it was already surely too late and there could be no turning back the momentum for disintegration as the USSR and the communist party had lost legitimacy. Leninism that held the USSR together had suffered a terminal crisis and nationalism had been mobilized to fill the ideological void.

It would have been most unlikely that a multi-national entity such as the USSR could have been preserved in any form other than a centralized authoritarian empire, and those who now make claims that the Union could have been saved underestimate the power of the national idea and the failure that comes in the end to all great empires. The idea that the USSR could have become a functioning plural democracy is naïve at best. The history of empires simply does not support such an argument. The Soviet empire was held together by military might, not by a common belief system. Leninist ideology as it developed in the USSR can be seen as a sort of secular religion. The leader of the secular church (the General Secretary of the CPSU) chaired the councils that dealt with matters of faith (the Politburo and Secretariat of the CPSU) and oversaw appointments to other offices responsible for ensuring adherence to the teachings of the church (the Central Committee and Republican Party Secretaries). The important distinction to be made between a secular religion such as Leninism and otherworldly religions is that Leninism was a "scientific" class-based theory that could be tested empirically through observation and the scientific method, whereas otherworldly religions are based on pure faith. The fact that the teachings of Leninism could not be empirically verified, but on the contrary were seen to be false (given the dynamic nature of western capitalism for example, and the absence of freedoms under Soviet socialism) led to a cognitive dissonance in which everyday reality did not fit with the Leninist doctrine. It became necessary therefore to move away from the strictures of the church's teachings if one wanted to make better sense of the world. There could be no salvation in an afterlife, as the religion of Leninism believed in no such idea, for it offered the good life on earth. The failure in ideology then became a systemic problem for the regime.

IR, the Balance of Power and the USSR as a National Security State

Whilst ideology was an important component explaining Soviet perceptions and behaviour, and providing a large part of the reason for the final collapse, geopolitics and the balance of power were also significant factors. It should be noted that it was not only sympathizers on the left that supported the USSR in the West, for so too, for a while at least, did western governments; but they did so from pure calculations of material interests and national security. Churchill might have hated communism, but he nevertheless cooperated with Stalin in 1941 against Hitler's Germany. This was not out of any preference for communism over Nazism, but out of a consideration of the balance of power. No matter what Stalin had been doing to his own people, as long as he was fighting Germans there would be no criticism. The British, for example, kept quiet about the massacre of more than 20,000 Polish military officers in the Katyn Forest. It was clear to Churchill and Roosevelt by the Spring of 1943 that Stalin had been responsible for these killings three years earlier, but it was decided that the blame should nevertheless be officially apportioned to the Germans to buttress the coalition with Stalin and to denigrate Hitler's regime. The British War Department issued a directive stating that 'It is our job to help ensure that history will record the Katyn Forest incident as a futile attempt by Germany to postpone defeat by political methods' (Mearsheimer, 2011, p. 79). State security interests tend to override values in the formulation of policy especially in times of international crises and conflicts. The same was true of the Soviet state. It was noted how the structure of the international system and the dire situation that Soviet Russia faced after the Revolution led Lenin to a series of compromises as he sought to construct the necessary instruments of the state that could guarantee its security. This included the establishment of the NKVD (later KGB) to ensure security within the state, and the build-up of the armed forces to ensure security from outside threats. Stalin took this further, to construct under the guise of socialism in one country the national security state. This book has demonstrated how the development of Soviet material power and the USSR's control over Eastern Europe after 1945 very quickly resulted in changing threat perceptions and the construction in the West of a Cold War mentality and the strategic priority of "containing" the USSR and Soviet Communism. This Cold War competition became global, and it was in the Third World where it would become most intense.

It is useful here to reflect further, briefly, upon how the western discipline of IR dealt with the USSR. One of the many myths that had developed in the undergraduate teaching of IR by the middle of the second half of the twentieth century was that IR as a separate discipline began with the establishment of the Woodrow Wilson Chair at the University of Wales, Aberystwyth in 1919 (see Schmidt, 2002). Yet there was still no internal integrity or canonical authority or standardized discourse or accepted curriculum making for a coherent IR discipline before 1945. Therefore, as with Soviet Studies, so too with IR, it was the rise of Soviet power and the political vacuum in Europe following Germany's defeat in war that stimulated the development of a real community of scholars working in a more disciplined field. The IR community that emerged sought to describe and explain the most important issues in international politics, and then to prescribe the most appropriate strategy and policies to deal with them. This focus, as the world became bipolar meant addressing how to contain what was seen as America's main global competitor, the USSR, and much of the IR focus was on security and grand strategies linked to this perceived Soviet threat.

Realism was the dominant approach in IR for much of the Cold War period, and by definition this did not allow for a serious consideration of the internal dynamics of the main protagonists' domestic systems (see Morgenthau, 1948; Waltz, 1979; Vasquez, 1983). Realists, especially adherents of what became the dominant brand of Waltz's structural realism, not only downplayed ideology, ideas, and culture: they also largely discounted the actual decision-making processes (Waltz, 1979). Hence, there was assumed to be a logical (if not moral) equivalence between the two superpowers, with states personified as unified rational actors behaving according to the logic of anarchy and the security dilemma in pursuit of the national (state) interest. The very foundation of American IR and the early stranglehold of Realism in the post-Second World War period can be traced to the actions of a number of influential institutions and individuals in the early 1950s. As with Soviet Studies, a number of key individuals and institutions helped to finance and influence IR's development. The Rockefeller and Carnegie Foundations, Yale, Chicago, and Columbia Universities, and others helped to finance and forge what became an influential foreign-policy establishment and separate IR discipline on the East Coast of the United States in the mid-1950s. Key individuals in this development included Hans Morgenthau, William T. R. Fox, Arnold Wolfers, Walter Lippmann, and Paul Nitze (names familiar to any student of IR). A young graduate student by the name of Kenneth Waltz was also a participant, as a rapporteur, in the founding conference in 1954 when IR theory was, it has been suggested, "invented" (see Guilhot, 2011; Palmar, 2011). However one sees the making of IR, it is argued that a field (or discipline) was constructed that was, as Ole Waever has put, 'self-organizing around Realism' (Waever, 2011, p. 122). Its construction was also very closely linked to the Cold War and the desire of US foundations and influential individuals to define what was in the American national interest, and particularly to help devise US foreign and security policies towards the USSR. Hence, one can perhaps rather say that IR owes its founding to the threat posed, in western perceptions, by the Soviet state, principally the threat of hard, Soviet military power. It might be more appropriate to say then that IR as a discipline and the dominance of Realism self-organized around the Soviet threat.

Then the so-called great debates in IR did not enhance understanding of the nature of Soviet Communism and the USSR—rather it was portrayed as just another Great Power, for example in interdependency theory, Soviet Russia remained still a normal state actor in what was essentially the traditional realist mode. And IR tended to use the terms Soviet and Russia interchangeably, indicating the tendency to see the USSR and Russia as the same single entity, without recognising the Soviet Union's complex social make up. Yet these were not so much debates—insofar as they were really debates at all—about theory, but rather about method. And in none of those that involved the USSR was nationalism or ideology a salient factor. Much was made of the so-called "levels of analysis" problem in international relations, and out of this developed a separate field of comparative foreign policy (CFP). Yet, even though the emphasis of CFP clearly was on the domestic level of analysis, little work was done on communist states, and then in those few cases where the USSR was used as a comparative case study it was the scientific methodology that determined the analysis, and little account was taken of the role of culture, ideas, or the politics of identity (for example, Jonson, 1984). The main debate in the discipline of IR in the Cold War period was about polarity: whether or not a bipolar or a multipolar system was more conducive to international order and stability, and which particular power configuration would most likely lead to war, and which one was most conducive to keeping the peace. But no account was made about the actual nature of the poles. It did not matter who the poles were. Linked to this were debates about the meaning, feasibility, and strategies of nuclear deterrence. IR counted Soviet missiles and tanks and army personnel, but did not account for the politics of identity or the actual nature of the Soviet (multi-) national security state. As noted in Chapter 7, over-determining hard material power and misunderstanding the nature of Soviet Communism made it impossible for IR and policy makers in the West to develop effective strategies to counter the real threat that existed.

Thus, like the Soviet Area Studies specialists so too the IR community failed to account for the important role ideology played in Soviet decision-making, or the saliency of the politics of identity and the role of nationalism. The Soviet Union was never really a superpower in any other sense than in the realm of military power and then nuclear power especially. For the most part IR specialists seriously exaggerated other facets of Soviet power. It has become passé to talk about soft power as if this is really something new, rather than something leaders have appreciated for as long as the state system has existed: the important role of diplomacy, culture, and other non-material power assets in state-to-state relations. It is therefore even more surprising that soft power considerations were largely ignored during the Cold War, although structural realism by definition could not account for it. On almost any measure the USSR was no competitor against the USA, due mainly to the two factors of ideology and nationalist sentiments. If America could in any way have been called an empire in the Cold War then it was an empire by invitation: American military bases in Western Europe were there not by imposition but by invitation. American democracy and popular culture was clearly of magnetic attraction across most of the world during the Cold War, but especially during its final years after the US had withdrawn from Vietnam. In contrast, Eastern Europe was involuntarily held in the Soviet embrace, with tanks ensuring compliance. And tanks had to be used to put down uprisings in Hungary in 1956 and again in Czechoslovakia in 1968. It was the national idea that mobilized Poles under the banner of Solidarity, in coalition with the (Polish) Pope, to break away from the Soviet bloc, inspiring other nations throughout Eastern Europe to do the same in a wave of anti-communist (and hence also anti-Soviet) revolutions of national liberation. These events further demonstrate the power of the national idea and the crisis in Marxist-Leninist ideology.

The Soviet national security state constructed by Stalin's forced and rapid modernization campaign helped the USSR to survive against its external (and internal) opponents, and without its construction the Soviet Union could not have defeated Nazi Germany. Also Soviet military might for a while was effective in maintaining control over Eastern European "fraternal" communist party states. But in the end the nature of the national security state became a burden on the Soviet economy. As a model of rapid modernization Stalinism might have been effective in creating the industrial infrastructure for a national security state, but without radical reforms it proved inept and a hindrance to building an economy that was competitive in an increasingly globalized market place. And the national security state could not prevent Soviet Communism from losing its legitimacy, for the reasons discussed above. An old Soviet joke defined Soviet Communism as the longest and hardest road to capitalism.

Impact and Legacies

The experience of Soviet Communism was not all awful, notwithstanding the terrible suffering it brought to many, especially in the USSR itself. Soviet Communism did lift people out of poverty, produced high levels of literacy, provided a decent education, good health care, guaranteed employment for all, with decreasing infant mortality rates and increased life expectancy (at least until the late-Soviet period) and other important basic features in what is termed the "physical quality of life index." The Soviet Union was instrumental in defeating Hitler's Nazi expansionist regime. Whatever faults he had Stalin personally played a critical role in bringing about the defeat of Germany. Again, whilst not ignoring the selfish motives of and the tensions created by Soviet aid to national liberation movements in the Third World, the USSR did assist many former colonial powers to gain their independence and their dignity, and enabled them to survive against internal and external foes. The Soviet model of development provided inspiration for peoples in the poorer countries of the world.

Opinion polls in Russia since the end of Soviet Communism, have consistently reported that a majority of citizens considered the Soviet experience on the whole to have been a positive one. In 2007, more than two-thirds of respondents considered the period between 1922 and 1953 (i.e., the Stalin era) to have been a golden age, when people were kinder, less selfish, and more sympathetic and the country was kept in order. People had a sense of pride in the Soviet past, and Stalinist repression was viewed as having been necessary to modernize Russia. Despite the fact that over 90 percent of Russians are aware of his many victims, Stalin as *vozhd*, as great leader, was perceived by the majority as having continued the legacy of the greater history of the Russian Empire (see Khapaeva, 2012, p. 109). Khapaeva notes that Russians not only condone rather than condemn the Soviet past, but they see it as 'an epic of glorious national history' (pp. 118–119). It is an interesting fact that those who actually lived under really existing socialism now have a rosy view of it in retrospect, whereas those in the West who had once admired it from afar are now very critical. Having noted this, it must be said that no political group or leader with any prospect of gaining power in Russia (or, for that matter anywhere else in the former communist bloc) advocates the restoration of the Soviet Communist economic model, and this includes the CPRF.

Nevertheless it is important to recognize that many Russian citizens do look back with nostalgia at life in the USSR. It should also be born in mind that the Communist Party of the Russian Federation (CPRF) has continued to be a major force in electoral politics right through the post-Soviet era, a party that plays on its Soviet heritage as the successor to the CPSU (the leader of the party Gennady Zyuganov used to deal with questions of ideology in the CPSU apparatus). In the first elections to the parliament since the violent conflict between Yeltsin and the Duma two years previously, in December 1995 the CPRF won the majority of seats in both (what was then) the party list and the constituency sections of the ballot in parliamentary elections (see Table C.1).

By this time the CPRF had actually taken on many features of a far right party rather than being a standard Leninist party (see Cox and Shearman, 2000). During the late-Soviet period Zyuganov joined forces with a group of ultra-nationalists and elements of the Orthodox Church and the military industrial complex to try and prevent the disintegration of the USSR. Zyuganov was also instrumental in forging an alliance of communists with various nationalist organizations that attracted the label the "red-brown alliance." As with the communists in Russia at the beginning of the century, due to changing circumstances so too at the end of the century it was necessary for the communists to combine elements of nationalism into their ideology. Leading up to the presidential election of 1996, when Yeltsin was seeking re-election (under the banner of an anti-communist democrat), it seemed to be almost certain, according to polls, that Zyuganov, representing a form of neo-Soviet Russian nationalism (with the national-patriotic bloc), was set to win. Yeltsin's popularity was in single figures. Yet Yeltsin would eventually prevail in the second round (see Table C.2).

Some commentators claim the election was fixed, but either way Yeltsin could not have won if it were not for the critical help,

Table C.1 Election to the Duma on 17 December 1995
(Turnout: 64.73%)

Party/bloc	Leader	Party list seats	PList percent	Single M seats	Tot seats
CPRF	Zyuganov	99	22.3	58	157
LDPR	Zhirinovsky	50	11.2	1	51
Our Home is R	Chernomyrdin	45	10.3	10	55
Yaboloko	Yavlinsky	30	6.9	15	45
Agrarian Party	Lapshin	0	3.8	20	20
Russia's Choice	Gaidar	0	3.9	9	9
Congress of RC	Lebed	0	4.4	5	5
Women of R	Fedulova	0	4.6	3	3
PRUC	Shakrai	0	0.4	1	1
Beer Lovers party	Tsinov	0	0.6	0	0
Independents		0	.0	95	95

Table C.2 Russian presidential election (1996)

Candidate	Votes	Percentage of voters	
1st Round: 16 June 1996			
B. Yeltsin	26,665,495	35.28%	
G. Zyuganov (CPRF)	24,211,686	32.03	
A. Lebedev (CRC)	10,974,736	14.52	
G. Yavlinksy (Yab)	5,550,752	7.34	
V. Zhirinovsky (LDPR)	4,311,479	5.70	
S. Fedorov (PWSR)	699,158	0.92	
M. Gorbachev	386,069	0.51	Turnout: 69.7%
M. Shakkum (RSPP)	277,068	0.37	
Y. Vlasov (PP)	151,282	0.20	
V. Bryntsalov (RSP)	123,065	0.16	
Against all	1,163,921	1.54	
2nd Round: 3 July 1996			
B. Yeltsin	40,208,384	53.8%	
G. Zyuganov (CPRF)	30,113,306	40.3	Turnout: 68.*%

both financial and practical, of the oligarchs. The election was deliberately portrayed as a choice between the "democratic" Yeltsin offering a new and better future, or a return to the Soviet Communist past under Zyuganov. Despite the power of money and the media (controlled then by the oligarchs) and the constant denigration on television, the CPRF candidate still came a very close second in the first round of voting. Taking into consideration the fact that other candidates (Lebedev and Zhirinovsky) also represented a form of the far right it is clear that Russian nationalism had become a major force in electoral politics. Gorbachev's miserable vote (see Table C.2) reflected the fact that most people associated him, negatively, with allowing the USSR to collapse and causing Russia to suffer the inequities of economic dislocation, and having to go cap in hand begging to the West for help.

Again, despite the dominance of United Russia (UR), the tight control of the Putinist state over the media, and the greater sums available to UR, it is remarkable that still in 2012 Zyuganov as head of the CPRF managed to garner over 12 million votes (17% of total votes cast), and in the elections to the Duma in December 2011 the CPRF gained 19 percent of the total vote. There is still then a very significant support base for the communists in Russia. Although in terms of demographics CPRF membership tends to be higher among the older generations, the party does have a better-organized structure than many other parties that seem to come and go as tools for individuals in pursuit of power. In the event of a major economic crisis, however, it is possible that the CPRF could gain a higher vote still, perhaps in alliance with other "patriots." Western-oriented liberal parties have consistently fared poorly in elections to both the Duma and the presidency.

Brezhnev ruled for 18 years, Khrushchev for 11 years, and Stalin for 31 years. A problem in the Soviet system was the absence of an institutionalized method for leadership succession, hence when the incumbent leader died or was forced out of office a potential crisis of succession ensued. In post-Soviet Russia, with the development of a multi-party system and regular competitive elections for the parliament and presidency it was assumed that there would now be regular changes in leadership, which would then stimulate initiatives in public policy and hold leaders accountable to the wider population. However, following the anarchy, turmoil, and uncertainty of the 1990s, with the advent of Putinism, despite regular elections taking place, the Russian political system reverted back to some of the essential elements of the old Soviet system (see White, 2011 and Sakwa, 2008). Although far from being totalitarian, the political system as it developed under Putin, has come to take on some Soviet-type features. There is no functioning competitive party system, as the party of power has no effective opposition and is more a tool of the incumbent leadership, hence UR operates in Russia much like the CPSU did in the Soviet system. The Russian parliament, the Duma, is more of a rubber stamp for decisions made at the top by Putin. Putin has also established a cult of personality around himself. State controls over much of the media and the almost total control over television is also a feature of the contemporary Russian system. Putin and a handful of very wealthy oligarchs control and own much of the Russian economy. And oppositionists, as in Soviet days, risk imprisonment if they challenge the Putin regime.

Another feature of contemporary Russia that resembles the Stalin era is accusing opponents of the regime of acting in the interests of foreign powers ("enemies of the people" under Soviet Communism). For example, an NGO that receives funds from outside Russia's borders is obligated by law to register as a foreign agent (*inostrannyi agent*), reminiscent of a Cold War discourse. This links in also to the increasingly anti-US rhetoric that became dominant under Putin. Putin has on a number of occasions also directly intervened in policy discussion relating to the teaching of Russian and Soviet history, criticizing those who have taken what he considered to be too critical a view of the Stalin period, and in particular Stalin's role in the Second World War.

The Russian Orthodox Church has also taken on a much more significant political role, with the church leaders often seen in public with the political elite, including Putin. The Church published a calendar in 2014 dedicated to a celebration of Stalin, with each of the 12 months of the year showing an image of the former Soviet leader, from when he was a young boy through to him as elder statesman.

A youth movement, *Nashi* (Ours, in English) with some resemblance to the Komsomol was established and was widely considered to be an organization specifically designed to support Putin personally and as an activist organisation to directly challenge any other groups that might oppose the regime. Putin has also embraced Russian nationalism and the term "Russia for the

Russians" has returned into vogue, a term that goes back to the time of the pogroms under the Tsars. Putin himself, before the Soviet Union collapsed, had a career in the KGB, and he brought into government a large number of people who had previously served in the military/security apparatus (the so-called *siloviki*). By 2008, by the end of Putin's second presidential term, 42 percent (at least) of leadership positions in Russia were held by individuals that could be clearly identified as *siloviki* (there were thought to be more who had not declared their earlier roles in the security apparatus) (see Kryshtanovskaya and White, 2009, p. 301). Putin's goal of creating a Eurasian Union was seen by many as an attempt to reconstitute the USSR. Whilst it is the case that Putin revived the old Soviet national anthem—the same music, with different words, although composed by the same individual—he did not envisage reconstituting the Soviet Union through the Eurasian Union. Rather, Putin conceived the Eurasian Union as enhancing Russian interests and helping to reinforce its status as a great power. However, given Ukraine's trajectory towards the European Union rather than the Eurasian Union since the toppling of President Victor Yanukovich in February 2014 there is little prospect of this original goal being fulfilled. As with Yeltsin's earlier attempt to salvage a Union by incorporating some former Soviet states, so too with Putin without Ukraine any Eurasian Union lacks the international clout that he was hoping for—there is very little prospect of yet another renewal and creating a fifth version of the Russian empire, although there are potential conflicts still over Russian speakers in some former Soviet Republics.

What is remarkable is the force in the first quarter of the twenty-first century not of internationalism and the left, but of nationalism and the extreme right, and this is the case across large parts of Europe, not just in Russia. China continues to be ruled by the communist party, but as it has developed the mode of the capitalist market it has had to revise its ideology. And instead of rigid adherence to Marxism-Leninism the party has adapted its ideology with an increasing stress on nationalism. One of the lessons that we can glean from a reassessment of how Soviet Communism was misinterpreted in the previous century is the dangers of focussing on "high" politics and hard power and underplaying the forces from below, linked to the power of the politics of identity, and especially those of the ethnic nation or tribe. Specialists on the Arab world failed to foresee the radical events that took place from Tunisia through Egypt, Libya and Syria and other parts of the Middle East, due to their focus on elites and ignorance of mass sentiments (see Gause, 2011). Similarly, although there are terrorists that act internationally, seeing terrorism in global terms is conceptually and strategically wrong. Terrorism has local roots, hence the solutions cannot be found in a "global war on terror." Samuel Huntington perhaps had the correct focus in his thesis on a clash of civilizations (on cultural differences) but he too was operating at the wrong level of analysis. Since the collapse of the USSR and the end of the Cold War the world has been afflicted by numerous violent conflicts in which cultural differences, if not determining, play an important part—but these are not between civilizations, but within them (for example in Iraq, Syria, Afghanistan, and Ukraine).

Another legacy is the continued Cold War mind set on both sides of the former iron curtain, and a tendency for the West, the USA particularly, to continually suspect Russian motives even when Russia is simply asserting its own rational, national interests. This is not the place to give any detailed assessment of Russia's development since the collapse of communism and the USSR in 1991, but it should be noted that the manner in which Russia has been excluded from any meaningful participation in western institutional structures, despite attempts by both Yeltsin and Putin (in his earlier terms as President especially) to effectively integrate with the West, has led to increasing resentment in the Russian Federation. NATO was established to counter the Soviet threat. That threat disappeared in 1991, yet NATO did not die what many considered should have been a natural death but has expanded to incorporate both former communist bloc states in Eastern Europe and former republics of the Soviet Union (see Table 7.1). Conflicts over Georgia in 2008 and Ukraine in 2014 must be seen in light of Russian concerns about western intentions, perceived from Moscow as designed to weaken the Russian Federation and undermine what are considered to be its vital security interests. There seems to be a flawed logic in American strategic thinking when it comes to assessing Russian policy, perhaps a psychological legacy of the long Cold War and the inter-systemic competition of the previous century.

Although Russia under Putin is not an American-type liberal democracy, it does not offer a realistic model for other countries to follow. It does not pose an ideological challenge. In terms of the relative balance of military power, although remaining a world nuclear power, Russia no longer has armed forces realistically capable of challenging US interests (even it wanted to). However, what Russia does have is a very strong national identity and a sense of being wronged by the West since the Soviet collapse. This could easily be mobilized into an anti-western, anti-US stance in the event of international crises where it is perceived that Russia's interests are being challenged. There is great danger here. Hyper patriotism/nationalism is potentially far more threatening to international order and stability than communism ever was (we should consider here that the Cold War ideological conflict ended without war between the major powers). Putin's popularity during the crisis over Crimea reached astronomical proportions, based on a potent mix of Russian nationalism and antipathy to the West for what was perceived (however accurately) as meddling in the internal affairs of a state (Ukraine) with a large Russian population. One lasting legacy of the Soviet era, remarkable for still being resonant a quarter of a century after the Berlin Wall fell, is a continuing trend of mutual suspicions between the two main Cold War adversaries. In the event of a West-Russia crisis it would be very difficult, should it be mobilized, to rein in Russian hyper-nationalism and then to be able to step back from the brink. It should be recognized that Soviet Communism and the specific threat that it posed to the world is long gone, and that the Russian Federation today has normal state interests.

One final conclusion is to stress that Communism was (and still is) an emancipatory ideology that has at its core equality for all. The inequalities that gave rise to communism at the beginning of the twentieth century continue to exist. That Soviet Communism as practice was eventually used as a tool of repression by a totalitarian regime does not alter that fact. Hence, although Soviet Communism was defeated as practice, communism was not defeated as an idea, and the fact that nationalism helped to distort it and then dig the grave for it does not mean that communism cannot be resurrected, or that a new internationalism around radical ideas of justice and equality within a non-capitalist framework cannot be envisaged in the future. This book has not been an obituary of communism so much as one of the Soviet Leninist Empire-State.

Bibliography

Acton, E. 'The Three Traditions and Revisionism', in Alistair Kocho-Williams (ed.) *The Twentieth Century Russian Reader* (London: Routledge, 2011).

Ali, T. 'Introduction', in Tariq Ali (ed.), *The Stalinist Legacy: Its Impact on 20th Century World* Politics (Harmondsworth, Middlesex, 1984, 9–29).

Amis, M. *Koba The Dread: Laughter and the Twenty Million* (London: Jonathan Cape, 2002).

Anderson, B. *Imagined Communities* (London: Verso, 1983).

Anderson, P. 'Sino-Americana', *London Review of Books,* February 9, 2012, 20–22.

Andrew, C. and Gordievsky, O. *Comrade Kryuchkov's Instructions* (Stanford: Stanford University Press, 1993).

Andrew, C. and Mitrokhin, V. *The Mitrokhin Archive II: The KGB and the World* (London: Allen Lane, 2005).

Ang Cheng Guan, 'The Origins of the Cold War in Southeast Asia: The Case of Vietnam', in Malcolm H. Murfett, (ed.) *Cold War Southeast Asia* (Singapore: Marshall Cavendish, 2012).

Applebaum A. *Iron Curtain: The Crushing of Eastern Europe 1945–1956* (New York: Doubleday, 2012).

Applebaum, A. *Gulag: A History* (New York: Anchor Books, 2004).

Arbatov, G. *Cold War or Détente: A Soviet View,* (London: Zed Books, 1977).

Arendt, H. *Origins of Totalitarianism* (New York: World Publishing Company, 1951).

Arnason, J.P. *The Future that Failed: Origins and Destinies of the Soviet Model* (London: Routledge, 1993).

Aron, R. *The Opium of the Intellectuals* (New Brunswick: Transaction Publishers, 2005) Berlin 2004

Ascher, A. *The Revolution of 1905: Russia in Disarray* (Stanford: Stanford University Press, 1988).

Bacon, E. *The Gulag at War: Stalin's Forced Labour System in Light of the Archives* (London: Macmillan, 1994).

Barner-Barry C., and Hody, C. 'Soviet Marxism-Leninism as Mythology', *Political Psychology*, vol. 15, no. 4, 1994, 609–630.

Barnes, J. *The Porcupine* (London: Jonathan Cape, 1992).

Barnes, S. *Death and Redemption: The Gulag and the Shaping of Soviet Society* (Princeton: Princeton University Press, 2011).

Barnett, V. 'Understanding Stalinism—The "Orwellian Discrepancy" and the "Rational Choice Dictator"', *Europe-Asia Studies*, 58, 3, May 2006, 457–466.

Becker, M. 'Mariategui, the Comintern, and the Indigenous Question in Latin America', *Science in Society*, 70/4, 2006, 450–479.

Becker, M. 'Mariategui and Latin American Marxist Theory, *Latin American Series*, 20, (Athens: Ohio University Monographs in International Studies, 1993).

Beschloss, M. R. and Talbott, S. *At the Highest Levels: The Inside Story of the End of the Cold War* (London: Little Brown, 1993).

Beevor, A. *Stalingrad: The Fateful Siege, 1942–1943* (London, Penguin, 1999).

Beyme, K. 'The Concept of Totalitarianism: A Reassessment After the End of the Cold War' in Achim Siegel (ed.), *The Totalitarian Paradigm After the End of Communism. Towards a Theoretical* Reassessment (Amsterdam: Radopi, 1998, 39–54).

Bloom, W. *Personal Identity, National Identity and International Relations* (Cambridge: Cambridge University Press, 1990).

Bolshaya Sovietskaya entsiklopediia edited by Alexander Prokhorov, A. (Moscow: Progress, 1969).

Bovin, A. *XX vek kak zhizn': vospominaniia* (Moscow: Zakharov, 2003).

Bowker, M. (ed.) *Russia After The Cold War* (Harlow: Longman, 2000).

Bowker, M. and Shearman, P. 'The Soviet Union and the Left in Britain' in Alex Pravda and Peter Duncan (eds) *Soviet British Relations Since the 1970s* (Cambridge: Cambridge University Press, 1990, 147–167).

Bradley, M. P. 'Decolonization, the Global South, and the Cold War, 1919–1962'. In Melvyn P. Leffler and Odd Arne Westad (eds) *The Cambridge History of the Cold War*, Vol. 1., (Cambridge: Cambridge University Press, 2011, 464–485).

Braithwaite, R. *Across the Moscow River: The World Turned Upside Down* (New Haven: Yale University Press, 2002).

Brandenberger, D. *National Bolshevism: Stalinist Mass Culture and the Formation of Modern Russian National Identity* (Cambridge, Mass: Harvard University Press, 2002).

Breslauer, G. *Khrushchev and Brezhnev as Leaders: Building Authority in Soviet Politics* (Boston: Allen and Unwin, 1982).

Bromley, Y. *Sovremennye etnicheskie protessy v SSSR* (Moscow, 1975).

Brooks, J. '*Thank You Comrade Stalin': Soviet Public Culture From Revolution to Cold War* (Princeton, New Jersey: Princeton University Press, 2000).

Brooks S. and Wohlforth, W. 'Power, Globalization, and the End of the Cold War: Reevaluating a Landmark Case for Ideas', *International Security*, 25/3, Winter, 2000/01, 5–53.

Brown, A. 'Gorbachev at Eighty: Evaluating his Achievements' available at www.opendemocracy.net/od-russia/archie-brown-gorbachev-at-eighty-evaluating-his-achievements, accessed 25 February, 2011.

Brown, A. 'Perestroika and the Five Transformations', in *Breakthrough to Freedom. Perestroika: A Critical Analysis* (Moscow: R. Valent, 2009).

Brown, A. *The Rise and Fall of Communism* (London: Bodley Head, 2009).

Brown, A. 'The Soviet Union: Reform of the System or Systemic Transformation', *Slavic Review*, 63/3, Autumn, 2004, 489–504.

Brown, A. *Soviet Politics and Political Science* (London: Macmillan, 1974).

Brutents, K.N. *National Liberation Movements Today* (Moscow: Progress, 1977).

Brutents, K.N. *Sovremennie natsional'no-osvoboditel'nie revolyutsii* (Moscow, 1976).

Brzezinski, Z. *Strategic Vision: American and the Crisis of Global Power* (New York: Basic Books, 2012).

Buchanan, P. 'Putin vs. the Neo-Comintern', available at http://antiwar.com/pat/?articleid=8176 accessed July 5, 2011.

Buczkowski, P. and Klawiter, A. (eds) *Theories of Ideology, and Ideology of Theories* (Amsterdam: Rodopi, 1986).

Bukharin, N. *The ABC of Communism* (Ann Arbor: University of Michigan Press, 1966).

Bush, G. and Scowcroft, B. *A World Transformed* (New York: Vintage, 1998).

Cadbury, D. *Space Race: The Epic Battle Between America and the Soviet Union for Dominion of Space* (New York: HarperCollins, 2006).

Carlson, P. *K Blows Top: A Cold War Comic Interlude, Starring Nikita Khrushchev, America's Most Unlikely Tourist* (New York: Public Affairs, 2009).

Carr, E.H. *Twilight of the Comintern* (New York: Pantheon, 1982).

Carr, E.H. *What is History?* (London: Penguin, 1961).

Carrere d'Encause, H. *L'Empire eclate* (Paris: Flammarion, 1978).

Carrillo, S. *Eurocommunism and the State* (Westport, Ct: Lawrence Hill, 1978).

Castro, F. *My Life* (London: Penguin, 2008).

Cha, V. *The Impossible State: North Korea, Past and Future* (London: Vintage, 2013).

Chang, J. and Halliday, J. *Mao; The Unknown Story* (London: Jonathan Cape, 2005).

Chavez, TV address available at www.marxist.com/chavez-transistional-programme. htlm. accessed February 1, 2010).

Chernyshevsky, *What Is To Be Done?* (Ithaca: Cornell University Press, 1989).

Churchill, W. Quoted in the *International Herald Tribune*, May 10, 2011, 2.

Clark, M. *Meeting Soviet Man* (Sydney: Angus and Roberston, 1960).

Cohen, S. 'Was the Soviet System Reformable?' *Slavic Review*, 63/3, 2004, 459–488.

Cohen, S. *Bukharin and the Bolshevik Revolution: A Political Biography* (Oxford: Oxford University Press, 1980).

Connor, W. *Ethnonationalism: The Quest for Understanding* (Princeton: Princeton University Press, 1994).

Conquest, R. *Reflections on a Ravaged Century* (New York: W.W. Norton, 2001).

Conquest, R. *The Great Terror* (London: Macmillan, 1968).

Constitution (Fundamental Law) of the Union of Soviet Socialist Republics (Moscow: Novosti, 1977).

Coughlin, C. *Saddam: The Secret LIfe* (London, Macmillan, 2002).

Courtois, S. 'Introduction: The Crimes of Communism', in Stephen Courtois, Nicolas Werth, Jean-Louis Panne *et al.* (eds) *The Black Book of Communism: Crimes, Terror, Repression* (Cambridge, Mas: Harvard University Press, 1999, pp. 1–32).

Cox, M. and Shearman, P. 'After the Fall: Nationalist Extremism in Post-Communist Russia', in Paul Hainsworth (ed.) *The Politics of the Extreme Right: From the Margins to the Mainstream* (London: Pinter, 2000, pp. 224–246).

Cox, M. (ed.) *Rethinking the Soviet Collapse: Sovietology, the Death of Communism and the New Russia* (London: Pinter, 1998).

Dallek, R. *John Kennedy: The Unfinished Life* (London: Penguin, 2003).

Dallin, A. and Firsov, F. *Dimitrov and Stalin 1934–1943: Letters from the Soviet Archives* (New Haven: Yale University Press, 2000).

Daniels, R.V. *The Rise and Fall of Communism in Russia* (New Haven: Yale University Press, 2007).

Dreznev, D., www.foreingpolicy.com/posts/200/09/24/must_stop_consuming_ideological_ analogies accessed 19 September, 2014.

Davis, J. W. and William C. Wohlforth, 'German Unification', in Hermann R. K. and Richard Ned Lebow (eds) *Ending the cold War: Interpretations, Causation, and the Study of International Relations* (New York: Palgrave Macmillan, 2004, pp. 131–160).

Dawisha, K. 'The Question of Questions: Was the Soviet Union Worth Saving?', *Slavic Review*, 63/3, 2004, 513–526.

De Mesquita, B.B. and Smith, A. *The Dictator's Handbook: Why Bad Behavior Is Almost Always Good* (New York: Public Affairs, 2011).

Deutcher, I. *The Prophet Armed: Trotsky 1879–1921* (London: Verso, 2003).

Deutcher, I. 'Socialism in One Country' in Ali (ed.), 1984, 95–111.

DeVore, M. 'A Dangerous Utopia: The Military Revolution From The Cold War to The War on Terror', in George Lawson, Chris Armbuster and Michael Cox (eds) *The Global 1989: Continuity and Change in World Politics* (Cambridge: Cambridge University Press, 2010, pp. 219–242).

Dikotter, F. *Mao's Great Famine* (London: Bloomsbury, 2011).

Djilas, M. *The New Class: An Analysis of the Communist Systems* (San Diego: Harvest/HBT, 1957).

Dostoevsky, F. *Notes from Underground* (London: Penguin, 1984).

Dowler, W. *Russia in 1913* (DeKalb, IL: Northern Illinois University Press, 2010).

Drakulic, S. *How We Survived Communism and Even Laughed* (New York: Harper Collins, 1992).

Eatwell, R. and Wright, A. *Contemporary Political Ideologies* (London: Continuum, 1999).

Empire Census (Russian Census of January 1897) available at http://demoscope.ru and www.eastview.com/research-collections accessed July 9, 2013.

Engerman, D. *Know Your Enemy: The Rise and Fall of America's Experts* (Oxford: Oxford University Press, 2009).

English, R. D. *Russia and the Idea of the West: Gorbachev, Intellectuals and the End of the Cold War* (New York: Columbia University Press, 2000).

Enloe, C. *Bananas, Beaches, and Bases: Making Feminist Sense of International Relations* (Berkeley: University of California Press, 1989 and 2014 (revised and updated).

Fainsod, M. *Smolensk Under Soviet Rule* (London: Macmillan, 1958).

Fainsod, M. *How Russia is Ruled* (Cambridge, Mass: Harvard University Press, 1953).

Ferguson, N. available at www.commonwealth/maazine.org/blog/?p=469), accessed February 10, 2012.

Figes, O. *The Whisperers: Private Life in Stalin's Russia* (London: Penguin, 2008).

Figes, O. *Natasha's Dance: A Cultural History of Russia* (New York: Metropolitan Books, 2002).

Figes, O. *Revolutionary Russia* (London: Penguin, 2014).

Figes, O. *A People's Tragedy: A History of the Russian* Revolution (New York: Viking, 1996).

Fischer, L. *The Soviets in World Affairs* (Princeton: Princeton University Press, 1951).

Fitzpatrick, S. *The Russian Revolution* (Oxford: Oxford University Press, 2008).

Friedrich, C. and Brzezinski, Z. *Totalitarian Dictatorship and Democracy* (Cambridge: Cambridge University Press, 1956).

Fukuyama, F. 'The Modernizing Imperative: The USSR as an Ordinary Country', *The National Interest*, no. 31, Spring 1993, pp. 10–18.

Fukuyama, F. *The End of History and the Last Man* (New York: Free Press, 1992).

Fukuyama, F. 'The Nature of the Problem: A Systematic Soviet Strategy for the Third World?' in Dennis L. Barker (ed.) *The Red Orchestra*, (Stanford: Calif. Hoover Institute Press, 1986).

Furet, F. and Nolte, E. *Fascism and Communism* (Lincoln: University of Nebraska Press, 2001).

Fursenko, A. and Naftali, T. *Khrushchev's Cold War: The Inside Story of an American Adversary* (New York: W.W. Norton, 2006).

Holsti, K.J. 'Scholarship in an Age of Anxiety: The Study of International Politics During the Cold War', *Review of International Studies*, 24, 1998, 17–46.

Gaddis, J.L. *The Cold War* (London: Allen Lane, 2005).

Gaddis, J.L. *The Landscape of History: How Historians Map the Past* (Oxford: Oxford University Press, 2002).

Gaddis, J.L. *We Now Know: Rethinking Cold War History* (Oxford: Oxford University Press, 1997).

Gause, F.G. 'Why Middle Eastern Studies Failed to See the Arab Spring', *Foreign Affairs*, 90/4, July-August, 2011, 81–90.

Gettately, R. *Stalin's Curse: Battling for Communism in War and Cold War* (New York: Alfred. A. Knopf, 2013).

Getty, J. and Naumov, O. *The Road to Terror* (New Haven, Yale University Press, 2010).

Gellately, R. *Stalin's Curse: Battling for Communism in War and Cold War* (New York, Alfred Knopf, 2013).

Gellately, R. *Lenin, Stalin, and Hitler: The Age of Social Catastrophe* (New York: Alfred A. Knopf, 2007).

Gellner, E. *Encounters with Nationalism* (Oxford: Blackwell, 1994).

Glaser, D. and Walker, D.M. *Twentieth Century Marxism: A Global Introduction* (London: Routledge, 2007).

Goldman, W.A. *Terror and Democracy in the Age of Stalin: The Social Dynamics of Repression* (Cambridge: Cambridge University Press, 2007).

Gooding, J. *Socialism in Russia: Lenin and His Legacy* (Basingstoke: Palgrave, 2002).

Goncharov, I. *Oblomov* (London: Penguin, 1976).

Gorbachev, M. 'Historical Significance of Perestroika', in *Breakthrough to Freedom. Perestroika: A Critical Analysis* (Moscow: R. Valant, 2009).

Gorbachev, M. 'Foreword' in Valery Tishkov *Chechnya: Life in a War-Torn Society* (Oakland: University of California Press, 2004).

Gorbachev M. and Milnar Z *Conversations with Gorbachev* (New York: Columbia University Press, 2002).

Gorbachev, M. *Memoirs* (London: Transworld Publishers, 1995).

Gorbachev, M. *Memoirs* (New York, Doubleday, 1993).

Gorbachev, M. 'On Socialist Democracy', Report and Concluding Speech at the Plenary Meeting of the CPSU Central Committee 27–28 January 1987, in Gorbachev, *Writings, Speeches and Reports* (London: Atlantic Highlands, 1987, 113–16).

Gorbachev, M. *Izbrannye rechi i stat'i* (Moscow: Izdatel'stvo politicheskoi literatury, 1987).

Gorlizki, Y and Khlevniuk, O. *Cold Peace: Stalin and the Soviet Ruling Circle, 1945–1953* (Oxford: Oxford University Press, 2004).

Grachev, A. *Gorbachev's Gamble: Soviet Foreign Policy and the End of the Cold War* (Cambridge: Polity, 2008).

Gray, C. *War, Peace and International Relations: An Introduction to Strategic Studies* (London: Routledge, 2007).

Gray, J. *Black Mass: Apocalyptic Religion and the Death of Utopia* (London: Allen Lane, 2008).

Gromyko, A. *Memoirs* (London: Arrow Books, 1989).

Grushin, O. *The Dream Life of Sukhanov*, (London: Viking, 2006).

Guilhot, N. (ed.) *The Invention of International Relations Theory: Realism, the Rockefeller Foundation, and the 1954 Conference on Theory* (New York, Columbia University Press, 2011).

Gvosdev, N. K. (ed.) *The Strange Death of Soviet Communism: A Postcript* (New Brunswick, Transaction Books, 2008).

Hahn, G. M. *Russia's Islamic Threat* (New Haven: Yale University Press, 2007).

Halliday, F. *Revolution and World Politics: The Rise and Fall of the Sixth Great Power* (London: Palgrave, 1999).

Halliday, F. 'Third World Socialism: 1989 and After' in George Lawson, Chris Armbruster and Michael Cox (eds) *The Global 1989: Continuity and Change in World Politics* (Cambridge: Cambridge University Press, 2010, 112–134).

Halliday, F. *The Making of the Second Cold War* (London: Verso, 1983).

Harper, J. *The Cold War* (Oxford: Oxford University Press, 2011).

Harrison, M. 'Stalin and Our Times', in Geoffrey Robertson (ed.) *Stalin: His Times and Our Times*, (Dublin: Irish Association for Russian and East European Studies, 2005, 67–84).

Harvey, R. *Comrades: The Rise and Fall of World Communism*, (London: John Murray, 2003).

Haslam, J. *Russia's Cold War* (New Haven: Yale University Press, 2011).

Haynes, M. *Nikolai Bukharin and the Transition from Capitalism to Socialism* (Beckenham Kent: Croom Helm, 1985).

Heer, J. 'Trotsky's Ghost Wandering in the White House', *The National Post*, June 7, 2003.

Herman, R.G. 'Identity, Norms, and National Security: The Soviet Foreign Policy Revolution and the End of the Cold War', in Kazenstein (1996).

Herrmann R.K. and Lebow, N. (eds) *Ending the Cold War: Interpretations, Causation, and the Study of International Relations* (New York: Palgrave, 2004).

Heywood, A. *Political Ideologies: An Introduction* (Houndmills, Basingstoke: Palgrave Macmillan, 4th edition, 2007).

Hill, C. *Lenin and the Russian Revolution* (London: English Universities Press, 1972).

Hill, R.J. and Frank, P. *The Soviet Communist Party* (Boston: Allen and Unwin, 3rd edition, 1986).

Hitchens, C. *The Nation* July 10, 1991.

Hitchens. C. *The Missionary Position: Mother Teresa in Theory and Practice* (London: Verso, 1995).

Hitchens, C. *No One Left to Lie: The Triangulations of William Jefferson Clinton*, (London: Verso, 1999).

Hitchens, C. *The Trial of Henry Kissinger* (London: Verso, 2001).

Hitchens, C. *Hitch 22: A Memoir* (New York: Twelve, 2010).

Hitchens, S. 'Let's Not Get Too Liberal', *Guardian*, September 21, 2001.

Hobsbawm, E. *Revolutionaries* (London: Abacus, 2007).

Hobsbawm, E. *Age of Extremes: The Short Twentieth Century 1914–1991* (London: Michael Joseph, 1994).

Hochschild, A. *The Unquiet Ghost: Russians Remember Stalin* (New York: Mariner, 2003).

Hollander, P. *The End of Commitment: Intellectuals, Revolutionaries, and Political Moralilty* (Chicago: Ivan R. Dee, 2006).

Holmes, L. *Communism: A Very Short Introduction* (Oxford: Oxford University Press, 2009).

Holmes, L. *The End of Communist Power: Anti-Corruption Campaigns and Legitimation Crisis* (New York: Oxford University Press, 1993).

Holsti, K. 'Scholarship in an Era of Anxiety', *Review of International Studies*, 24, 1998, 17–46.

Hoover, H. *The Ordeals of Woodrow Wilson* (Washington, D.C: Woodrow Wilson, Center Press, 1962).

Hopf, T. *Reconstructing the Cold War: The Early Years, 1945–1958* (Oxford: Oxford University Press, 2012).

Hough, J. *The Soviet Union and Social Science Theory* (Cambridge, Mass: Harvard University Press, 1977).

Hough, J. *The Soviet Prefects* (Cambridge, Mass: Harvard University Press, 1969).

Hough. J. and Fainsod, M. *How the Soviet Union is Governed* (Cambridge, Mass: Harvard University Press, 1979).

Hughes, L. *Russia in the Age of Peter the Great* (New Haven: Yale University Press, 1998).

Huntington, S. *Who Are We: The Challenge to America's National Identity* (New York: Simon & Schuster, 2004).

Huntington, S. *The Clash of Civilizations and the Remaking of World Order* (New York: Simon and Schuster, 1996).

Huntington, S. *The Third Wave: Democratization in the Late Twentieth Century* (Normal: Oklahoma University Press, 1993).

Igmen, A. *Speaking Soviet With an Accent: Culture and Power in Kyrgyzstan* (Pittsburgh, PA: University of Pittsburgh Press, 2012).

Ignatieff, M. 'Interview with Eric Hobsbawm', *Times Literary Supplement*, October 28 1994.

Inkeles A. and Bauer, R. *The Soviet Citizen: Daily Life in a Totalitarian Society* (New York: Atheneum, 1968; originally published by Harvard University Press in 1959).

Interfax, February 27, 2014.

Interfax, December 11, 2006. Available at www.interfax_religion.com/?act=news.& div=2359 accessed July 17, 2013

International Herald Tribune, November 24, 2011.

Jablonsky, D. 'The State of the National Security State', *Parameters*, Winter, 2002–2003, 4–20.

Jian, C. *Mao's China and the Cold War* (Chapel Hill: University of North Carolina Press, 2001).

Johnson, C. 'Abolish the CIA', *The London Review of Books*, vol. 26, no. 20, October 21, 2004, pp. 25–28.

Johnson, C. (ed.) *Change in Communist Systems* (Stanford: Stanford University Press, 1970).

Jones, B. *The Russia Complex: The British Labour Party and the Soviet Union* (Manchester: Manchester University Press, 1977).

Jones, D. and Smith, M. 'Is There a Sovietology of South East Asia Studies?' *International Affairs*, 77/4, 2001.

Jonson, C. *Superpowers: Comparing American and Soviet Foreign Policy* (London: Francis Pinter, 1984).

Judt, T. *Postwar: A History of Europe Since 1945* (London: Pimlico, 2007).

Kalinovsky, A. 'Decision-Making and the Soviet-War in Afghanistan From Intervention to Withdrawal', *Journal of Cold War Studies*, 11/4, Fall 2009, 46–73.

Kanet, R. 'The Superpower Quest for Empire: The Cold War and Soviet Support for "Wars of National Liberation"', *Cold War History*, 6/3, 2006, 331–352.

Katzenstein, P.J. (ed.) *The Culture of National Security: Norms and Identity in World Politics* (New York: Columbia University Press, 1996).

Kautsky, J.H. *Marxism and Leninism: Different Ideologies* (New Brunswick: Transaction Publishers, 2002).

Kautsky, K. *Marxism and Bolshevism: Democracy and Dictatorship* available at www.marxists.org/archive/kautsky/1934/bolshevism/ch01.htm, accessed April 17, 2014.

Kempe, F. *Berlin 1961,* (New York: Berkley Books, 2011).

Kennan, G. ("X") 'The Sources of Soviet Conduct', *Foreign Affairs*, 25/4, 1947, pp. 566-82.

Khapaeva, D. 'Russia Fractures in the Fabric of Culture', in Peter Furtado (ed.), *Histories of Nations: How Their Identities Were Forged* (London: Thames and Hudson, 2012, 108–119).

Kheng, C.B. 'The Communist Insurgency in Malaysia, 1948–1989: Was it Due to the Cold War?', in Malcolm Murfett (ed.) *Cold War Southeast Asia* (Singapore: Marshall Cavendish, 2012).

Khineyko, I. 'Boris Yeltsin and Ukraine' April 24, 2007, available at ukraineanalysis. wordpress.com/2007/04/24/boris-yeltsin-and-ukraine accessed May 6, 2014.

Khrushchev, N. *Khrushchev Remembers: The Glasnost Tapes* (Boston: Little Brown, 1990).

Khrushchev, N. *Khrushchev Remembers: Volume 2, The Last Testament,* edited by Strobe Talbott, (Boston: Little Brown, 1974).

Khrushchev, N. *Khrushchev Remembers,* edited by Strobe Talbott, (London: Book Club Associates, 1971).

Kiernan, B. *The Pol Pot Regime: Race, Power, and Genocide Under the Khmer Rouge 1975–1979* (New Haven: Yale University Press, 2008).

Kim, G. 'Sovietskii Soyuz i natsional'no-osvoboditel'noe dvizhenie', *Mirovaia ekonomokia i mezhdunarodnye otnoshenia,* 9, 1982, 19–33.

King, D. *Red Star Over Russia: A Visual History of the Soviet Union From 1917 to The Death of Stalin* (London: Tate Publishing, 2008).

Kissinger, H. 'Conversations on Diplomacy', www.state.gov/secretary/20092013 clinton/rm/2011/04/161435.htm, accessed May 12, 2014.

Kissinger, H. *Years of Upheaval* (Boston: Little Brown, 1982).

Knei-Paz, B. *The Social and Political Thought of Leon Trotsky* (Oxford: Clarendon Press, 1979).

Knight, N. 'Applying Marxism to Asian Conditions' in Glaser and Walker, 2007. 141–153.

Konchalovsky, A. 'Gorbachev: The Wrong Man for Andropov's Reforms', *Open Democracy* available at www.opendemocracy.net/od-russia/andrei-konchalovsky/ orbachev-wrong-man-for-andropov's-reforms, accessed March 30, 2011.

Kosukhin, *Afrikantskaia revolyutsionnaia demokratiia: ideologiia i politika* (Moscow: 1980).

Koval, B.I., Semenov, S.I., and Shul'govski A.F. *Revolyutsionnye prtotessy v Latinskoi Amerike,* (Moscow, 1974).

Kozlov, V.A., Fitzpatrick S., and Mirovenko S. V. (eds) *Sedition: Everyday Resistance in the Soviet Union Under Khrushchev and Brezhnev* (New Haven: Yale University Press, 2011).

Kryshtanovskaya, O. and White, S. 'The Sovietization of Russian Politics', *Post-Soviet Affairs*, 25/4, 283–289.

Landau, K. 'The League against Imperialism', *The Militant*, 3/1, 1930, 5; atvailable at www.marxists.org/history/etol/writers/landau/1930/02/lai.htm accessed on April 13, 2013.

Lane, C. 'Legitimacy and Power in the Soviet Union Through Socialist Ritual', *British Journal of Political Science*, 14/2, 1984, 207–217.

Lane, C. *The Rites of Rulers: Ritual in Industrial Society: The Soviet Case* (Cambridge: Cambridge University Press, 1981).

Lane, D. and Ross, C. *The Transition from Communism to Capitalism: Ruling Elites from Gorbachev to Yeltsin* (London: Macmillan, 1998).

Lane, D. *The Roots of Russian Communism* (London: Martin Robertson, 1968).

Larson, D. *Origins of Containment: A Psychological Explanation* (Princeton: Princeton University Press, 1985).

Larys, M. and Mares, M. 'Right-Wing Extremist Violence in the Russian Federation', *Europe-Asia Studies,* 63/1, 2011, 129–54.

Lawrence, M. 'The Rise and Fall of Non-Alignment' in Robert J. McMahon (ed.) *The Cold War in the Third World* (Oxford: Oxford University Press, 2013, pp. 139–55).

Lebow, R.N. and Risse-Kappen, T. (eds) *International Relations Theory and the End of the Cold War* (New York: Columbia University Press, 1995).

Leder, M. *My Life in Stalinist Russia* (Bloomington: Indiana University Press, 2001).

Lee, K. *From Third World to First: The Singapore Story, 1965–2000* (New York, HarperCollins).

Lee, S. *Lenin and Revolutionary Russia* (London, Taylor and Francis, 2003).

Leffler, M. and Westad, O. (eds) *The Cambridge History of the Cold War* (Cambridge: Cambridge University Press, 2010).

Leffler, M. *The Specter of Communism: The United States and the Origins of the Cold War, 1917–1953* (New York: Hill and Wang, 1994).

Leffler, M. 'Adherence to Agreements: Yalta and the Experience of the Early Cold War', *International Security*, 11/1, Summer 1986, 88–123.

Leitenberg, M. 'Deaths in Wars and Conflicts in the 20th Century', Cornell Peace Studies Program, Occasional Paper, No. 9, 3rd edition, 2006.

Lenin, V. *The Tasks of the Proletariat in the Present Revolution (a.k.a. The April Theses)*, Published April 7, 1917, *Pravda*, no. 26. Available at www.marxists.org/archive/lenin/works/1917/apr/04.htm accessed February 3, 2013.

Lenin, V. *The Proletarian Revolution and the Renegade Kautsky*, 1918. Available at www.marxists.org/archive/lenin/works/1918/prrk/index.htm (accessed February 2, 2013).

Lenin, V. 'Term of Admission into the Communist International', available at www.maraxists.org/archive/lenin/works/1920/jul/x01htm, accessed February 17, 2014.

Lenin, V. 'Better Fewer, but Better', written March 2, 1923 (Moscow: Progress, 1979, 287–294).

Lenin, V. *The State and Revolution* (Moscow, Progress, 1977).

Lenin, V. *On the Great October Socialist Revolution: Articles and Speeches* (Moscow: Progress, 1976).

Lenin, V. *What is to be Done?* (Peking, Foreign Languages Publishing House, 1973).

Lenin, V. 'Left Wing Communism: An Infantile Disorder' in Lenin *Against Revisionism* (Moscow: Progress, 1976 (Original April 27, 1920).

Lenin, V. *The Development of Capitalism in Russia* (Moscow: Collected Works, Vol. 3, 1970).

Lenin, V. *Imperialism, The Highest Stage of Capitalism* (Moscow: Progress, 1963).

Lenin, V. *The Right of Nations to Self-Determination* (Moscow: Progress, 1947).

Lenin, V. *Selected Works* (Moscow: Corporative Publishing Society, 1935, VIII, 297).

Lermentov, M. *Hero of Our Time* (London: Penguin, 1977).

Levine, S. 'Commentary', *Journal of Cold War Studies*, 12/1, 2010, 128–133.

Li, Mingjiang, *Mao's China and the Sino-Soviet Split: Ideological Dilemma* (London: Routledge, 2012).

Ligachev, Y, *Inside Gorbachev's Kremlin* (Boulder, Westview, 1996).

Light, M. (ed.) *Troubled Friendships: Moscow's Third World Ventures* (London: British Academic Press/Royal Institute of International Affairs, 1993).

Light, M. *The Soviet Theory of International Relations* (London, Wheatsheaf Books, 1988).

Lih, L.T. *Lenin*, (London: Reaktion Books, 2011).

Lih, T. *Lenin Rediscovered* (Leiden, Brill, 2006).

Longworth, P. *Russia's Empires* (London, John Murray, 2006).

Lowe, K. *Savage Continent: Europe in the Aftermath of World War II,* (London: Penguin, 2013).

Lucas, E. *The New Cold War* (London: Bloomsbury, 2008).

Luthi, L.M. *The Sino-Soviet Split: Cold War in the Communist World* (New Jersey: Princeton University Press, 2008).

Machiavelli, N. *The Prince*. Quentin Skinner (ed.) (Cambridge, Cambridge University Press, 1988).

Mackinder, H. 'The Geographical Pivot of History', *The Geographical Journal*, 23/4, April 1904, 421–37.

Macintyre, B. *A Spy Among Friends: Kim Philby and the Great Betrayal*, (London: Bloomsbury, 2014).

Macintyre, S. and Clark A. *The History Wars* (Carlton, Victoria: Melbourne University Press, 2003).

Malia, M. *The Soviet Tragedy: A History of Socialism in Russia, 1917–1991* (New York: The Free Press, 1994).

Mandel, E. 'A Critique of Eurocommunism', *Marxist Perspectives*, 2/4, Winter, 1979–1980, 114–142.

Mandela, N. *Long Walk to Freedom* (New York: Back Bay Books, 1995).

Mandelbaum, M. *The Ideas that Conquered the World: Peace, Democracy, and Markets in the Twenty-First Century* (New York: Public Affairs, 2002).

Marsh, C. *Religion and the State in Russia and China: Suppression, Survival, Revival* (New York: Continuum International, 2011).

Marx, K. *18th Brumaire of Louis Bonaparte* (Moscow: Progress, 1937).

Marx, K. *A Contribution to the Critique of Political Economy* original 1859; on-line version: www.marx.org1993(Preface,1993, accessed November 2, 2012.

Marx, K. and Engels, F. *The Communist Manifesto* (London: Penguin, 2002).

Matthews, M. *Poverty in the Soviet Union* (Cambridge: Cambridge University Press, 1986).

Matthews, M. *Privilege in the Soviet Union* (London: Unwin Hyman, 1978).

Matthews O. and Nemstova A. 'Fascist Russia?' *Newsweek*, August 15, 2011, 20–23.

Matthews, O. *Stalin's Children: Three Generations of Love and War* (London: Bloomsbury, 2009).

McArgo, D. 'Rethinking Southeast Asian Politics', Working Paper 4, Leeds University, 2008.

McDaniel, T. *Autocracy, Modernization, and Revolution in Russia and Iran* (Princeton: Princeton University Press, 1991).

Mearsheimer, J. *Why Leaders Lie: The Truth about Lying in International Politics* (Oxford: Oxford University Press, 2011).

Mearsheimer, J. *The Tragedy of Great Power Politics* (New York: W.W. Norton, 2001).

Medvedev, R. (*Christian Science Monitor*, Sep 15, 2009).

Medvedev, R. *Sotsializm v Rossii?* (Moscow: Kraft, 2006).

Medvedev, R. *Let History Judge: The Origins and Consequences of Stalinism* (New York: Alfred Knopf, 1971).

Memorial: '"Ot Pol'skoi komissii Obshchestva "Memorial"' available at www.memo.ru/history/POLAcy/INTROD.htm, accessed on January 26, 2010.

Menashe, L, 'Eurocommunism and the USSR: End of the Bolshevik Tradition in the West?' in Carl Boggs and David Plotke (eds) *The Politics of Eurocommunism: Socialism in Transition* (London: Macmillan, 1980, pp. 291–334).

Merridale, C. *Night of Stone: Death and Memory in Russia* (London: Granta, 2000).

Mesquita, B. and Smith, A. *The Dictator's Handbook: Why Bad Behavior is Almost Always Good Politics* (New York: Public Affairs, 2011).

Meyer, A.G. 'Theories of Convergence', in Chalmers Johnson (ed.) *Change in Communist Systems* (Stanford: Stanford University Press, 1970, 313–314).

Milne, T. *Kim Philby: The Unknown Story of the KGB Master Spy* (London: Biteback Publishing, 2014).

Mirsky, G. 'Russia is Right to be Upset over Events in Ukraine', *Financial Times*, February 26, 2014.

Molyneux, J. www.johnmolyneuxblogspot.com accessed May 10, 2008.

Montefiore, S.S. *Stalin: The Court of the Red Tsar*, (London: Phoenix, 2004).

Mores, D. 'The National Security State', in Thomas H. Holloway (ed.) *A Companion to Latin American History*, (Chichester: Blackwell Publishing, 2011, pp. 386–405)

Morgan, T. *Reds: McCarthyism in Twentieth-Century America* (New York: Random House, 2004).

Morgenthau, H.J. *Politics among Nations* (New York: Knopf, 1948).

Morrison, J. *Boris Yeltsin: From Bolshevik to Democrat* (London: Penguin, 1992).

Mount, F. 'When Our World Turned Upside Down', *The New York Review of Books*, LX/11, June 20-July 10, 2013, 35–38.

Munk, R. 'Marxism in Latin America/Latin American Marxism' in Glaser and Walker 2007, 154–173.

Naimark, N. M. *Stalin's Genocides* (Princeton, N.J: Princeton University Press, 2010).

Nauchnii kommunizm. Slovar' edited by Rumyantseva, A.M. (Moscow: Politizdat, 1980).

O'Clery, C *Moscow: December 25, 1991* (New York: Public Affairs, 2011).

O'Connor, K. *Intellectual and Apparatchiks: Russian Nationalism and the Gorbachev Revolution* (Plymouth: Lexington Books, 2008).

Odom, W. *Collapse of the Soviet Military* (New Haven: Yale University Press, 2000).

Offord, D. 'Dostoevsky and the Intelligentsia', in W. J. Leatherbarrow (ed.) *The Cambridge Companion to Dostoevsky*, (Cambridge: Cambridge University press, 2002, pp. 111–130).

O'Malley, K. 'The League Against Imperialism: British, Irish, and Indian Connections', *Communist History Network Newsletter*, 14, Spring 2003; available at: www. workersrepublic.org/Ireland/leftnationalism/leagueagainstimperialism.html accessed May 9, 2009.

Orwell, G. 'What is Fascism', on line www.mtholyoke.edu/acad/intrel/orwell46.htm accessed 20 September, 2014.

Orwell, G. *Homage to Catalonia* (London: Penguin, 1989).

Orwell, G. *Animal Farm* (London: Penguin, 1984).

Orwell G. *1984* (London: Penguin, 1978).

Overy, R. *The Dictators: Hitler's Germany, Stalin's Russia* (London, Allen Lane, 2004).

Parmar, I. 'American Hegemony, The Rockefeller Foundation, and the Rise of Academic International Relations in the United States', in Nicolas Guilhot (ed.), *The Invention of International Relations Theory: Realism, the Rockefeller Foundation, and the 1954 Conference on Theory* (New York, Columbia University Press, 2011, pp. 182–209).

Pavlenko, A. *The World Revolutionary Process* (Moscow, Progress, 1983).

Pavlova, V.I. 'Contemporary Western Historians on Stalin's Role in the 1930s (A Critique of the Revisionist Approach)', *Russian Studies in History,* 40/2, Fall, 2001.

Perrault, G. (ed) *Le Livre Noir du Capitalisme* (Paris: Le Temps des Cerises, 1998).

Philby, K. *My Silent War: the Autobiography of a Spy* (Grove Press, 1968).

Pipes, R. *Communism: A History* (New York: Modern Library Paperback, 2003).

Pipes, R. *The Unknown Lenin: From the Secret Archive* (New York, Yale University Press, 1998).

Pipes, R. *The Three Whys of the Russian Revolution* (London: Pimlico, 1996).

Pipes, R. *The Russian Revolution 1899–1919* (London: Collins Harvill, 1990).

Pipes, R. *The Formation of the Soviet Union: Communism and Nationalism, 1917–1923* (Cambridge, MA: Harvard University Press, 1964).

Plokhy, S.M. *Yalta: The Price of Peace* (London: Penguin, 2010).

Powell, N. *Amis and Son: Two Literary Generations* (London, Macmillan, 2008).

Priestland, D. *The Red Flag: Communism and the Making of the Modern World* (London: Penguin, 2009).

Pushkin, A. *Evgennii Onegin* (London: Penguin, 1985).

Putin, V. 'Direct Line with Vladimir Putin', 17 April, 2014 available at kremlin.ru/transcipts/7034 accessed May 5, 2014.

Putin, V. Interviews compiled on Youtube.com/watch?v=3d_yxJk&feature=youtu.be accessed July 17 2013.

Putin, V. *First Person* (New York: Public Affairs, 2000).

Rappaport, H. *Conspirator: Lenin in Exile* (London: Hutchinson, 2009).

Rashid, A. *Descent into Chaos: The US and the Disaster in Pakistan, Afghanistan, and Central Asia* (London: Penguin, 2008).

Read, A. *The World on Fire: 1919 and the Battle with Bolshevism* (London: Jonathan Cape, 2008).

Reed, J. *Ten Days That Shook the World* (London: Penguin, 1977).

Rees, E.A. 'Leader Cults: Varieties, Preconditions and Functions', in Apor Balazs, Jan C. Behrends, Polly Jones and E.A. Rees (eds) *The Leader Cult in Communist Dictatorships: Stalin and the Eastern Bloc* (Houndmills: Palgrave Macmillan, 2003, 3–26).

Rees, L. *World War Two Behind Closed Doors: Stalin the Nazis and the West* (London: BBC, 2008).

Reid, A. *Leningrad: Tragedy of a City Under Siege, 1941–1944* (London: Bloomsbury, 2011).

Reid-Henry, S. *Fidel and Che* (London: Hodder & Stoughton, 2009).

Rentoul, J. *Tony Blair Prime Minister* (London: Time Warner, 2001).

Rigby, T. H. *Communist Party Membership in the USSR, 1917–1967* (Princeton N.J: Princeton University Press, 1968).

Rigby, T. H. and Feher (eds) *Political Legitimation in Communist States* (Houndmills, Macmillan, 1982).

Risse-Kappen, 'Ideas Do Not Float Freely: Transnational Coalitions, Domestic Structures, and the End of the Cold War', *International Organization,* 48, Spring, 1994, 185–214.

Roberts, G. *Stalin's Wars: From World War to Cold War* (New Haven: Yale University Press, 2008).

Rosecrance, R. *The Resurgence of the West; How a Transatlantic Union Can Prevent War and Restore the United States and Europe* (New Haven: Yale University Press, 2013).

Rostow, W.W. *The Stages of Economic Growth: A Non-Communist Manifesto*, Cambridge: Cambridge University Press, 1960).

Rummel, R.J. *Lethal Politics: Soviet Genocide and Mass Murder since 1917* (New Brunswick: Transaction Publishers, 1990).

Rustow, D. 'Transitions to Democracy: Towards a Dynamic Model', *Comparative Politics,* 2, 1970.

Rutland, P. 'Sovietology: From Stagnation to Perestroika? A Decade of Doctoral Research in Soviet Politics', The Woodrow Wilson Center, Kennan Institute for Advanced Russian Studies Occasional Paper, 241, 1990.

Rutland, P. 'The National Problem and the Soviet State', in Harding, N. (ed.) *The State in Socialist Society* (Albany: State University of New York Press, 1984).

Sakharov, A. *Memoirs* (London: Hutchinson, 1990).

Sakwa, R. (no date) 'Modernization, Democratization and the Soviet Collapse', available at http://mhf.su.en.mode.288 accessed January 22, 2012.

Sakwa, R. *Putin: Russia's Choice* (London: Routledge, 2008).

Sakwa, R. 'Russian Nationalism and Democratic Development', in Mike Bowker (ed.) *Russia after the Cold War* (Harlow: Pearson, 2000, pp. 199–220).

Salisbury, H. E. *The 900 Days: the Siege of Leningrad* (Cambridge, MA: Da Capo, 2003).

Samuel, R. *That Lost World of British Communism*, (London: Verso, 2006).

Schandler, H.R. *Lyndon Johnson and Vietnam: The Unmaking of a President* (Princeton, New Jersey: Princeton University Press, 1977).

Schlesinger, J. 'Origins of the Cold War', *Foreign Affairs*, 46/1, 1967, 22–52.

Schmidt, B. 'On the History and Historiography of International Relations', in W. Carsnaes, T. Risse, and B Simmonds (eds) *Handbook of International Relations* (London: Sage, 2002).

Schweizer, P. *Reagan's War: The Epic Story of His Forty-Year Struggle and Final Triumph Over Communism* (New York: Anchor Books, 2002).

Service, R. *Spies and Commissars: Bolshevik Russia and the West* (London: Macmillan, 2011).

Service, R. *Communism a World History* (London: Macmillan, 2007).

Service, R. *A History of Modern Russia* (London, Penguin, 2009).

Shapiro, L. *Totalitarianism* (London, The Pall Mall Press, 1972).

Shearer, D. 'Social Disorder, Mass Repression and the NKVD During the 1930s', in Barry McLoughlin and Kevin McDermott (eds) *Stalin's Terror: High Politics and Mass Repression in the Soviet Union* (Basingstoke: Palgrave Macmillan, 2003, 85–117).

Shearman, P. 'Nationalism, the State, and the Collapse of Communism', in Sarah Owen Vandersluis (ed.) *The State and Identity Construction in International Relations* (Basingstoke: Macmillan, 2000, 76–106).

Shearman, P. 'Soviet Foreign Policy, 1917–1991', in Peter Shearman (ed), *Russian Foreign Policy Since 1990* (Boulder: Westview Press, 1995, 1–22).

Shearman, P. 'New Political Thinking Reassessed', *Review of International Studies*, 19/2, 1993, pp. 139–158.

Shearman, P. 'The Soviet Union and Cuba: The "Best" of Friends', in Margot Light (ed.) *Troubled Friendships: Moscow's Third World Ventures* (London: British Academic Press/Royal Institute of International Affairs, 1993, 166–190).

Shearman, P. *The Soviet Union and Cuba* (Routledge, 1987).

Shearman, P. 'Soviet Foreign Policy in African and Latin America: A Comparative Case Study', *Millennium*, 15/3, 1986, 339–365.

Shearman, P. 'The Soviet Union and the New Jewel Movement', *International Affairs*, 61/4, 1985, 661–674.

Shearman, P. 'The Demographic Imbalance in the Soviet Union and the National Question', *The Mid-American Journal of Political Science*,1/1, Spring 1984, 42–58.

Shearman, P. 'Language, Sovietization and Ethnic Integration in the USSR', *The Journal of Social Political and Economic Studies*, 8/3, 1983, 227–256.

Shelton, C. *Alger Hiss: Why He Chose Treason* (New York: Threshold Editions, 2012).

Shestakov, A. *Istoriia SSSR: Kratkii kurs* (Moscow: Gosudarstvennoe uchebno-pedagogicheskoe izdatel'stvo Narkomprosa RSFSR, 1939).

Shlapentokh, V. *A Normative Totalitarian Society: How the Soviet Functioned and How it Collapsed* (New York: M.E. Sharpe, 2002).

Siegel, A. (ed.) *The Totalitarian Paradigm After the End of Communism: Towards a Theoretical Reassessment* (Amsterdam: Radopi, 1998).

Silnitsky, F. 'The Nationality Problem', in Frantisek Silnitsky, Larisa Silnitsky, and Karl Reyman (eds) *Communism and Eastern Europe* (Brighton: Harvester, 1975, pp. 33–43).

Simon, R. 'Eurocommunism', in Daryl Glaser and David Walker (eds), *Twentieth Century Marxism: A Global Introducion* (London: Routledge, 2007, 81–94).

Skilling, H.G. and Griffiths, F. *Interest Groups in Soviet Politics*, (Princeton, N.J: Princeton University Press, 1971).

Smith, A. *National Identity* (London: Penguin, 1991).

Smith, D. *Former People: The Last Days of the Russian Aristocracy* (London: Pan Books, 2012).

Smith J. *Red Nations: The Nationalities Experience in and After the USSR* (Cambridge: Cambridge University Press, 2013).

Smith S. 'Mandela: Death of a Politician', *London Review of Books*, January 9, 2014, 17–19.

Smith, S.A. *Red Petrograd: Revolution in the Factories, 1917–1918* (Cambridge: Cambridge University Press, 1983).

Snyder, T. *Bloodlands: Europe between Hitler and Stalin* (London: Vintage, 2011).

Soh, Y. 'Russian Policy Towards the Two Koreas', in Peter Shearman (ed.), *Russian Foreign Policy Since 1990* (Boulder: Westview, 1999, 181–200).

Solzhenitsyn, A. *The Gulag Archipelago* (London: Penguin, 1973).

Stalin, J.V. *Stalin's Correspondence With Roosevelt and Truman, 1941–1945*, published originally in Moscow by the Ministry of Foreign Affairs of the USSR (New York: Capricorn Books, 1945).

Stalin, J.V. 'The Task of Economic Executives', in Stalin, *Problems of Leninism* (Moscow: Foreign Languages Publishing House, 1955, 519–531).

Stalin, J.V. 'On the Draft Constitution of the USSR: Report Delivered at the Extraordinary Eighth Congress of Soviets of the USSR', November, 25, 1936, in Stalin, *Problems of Leninism* (Moscow: Foreign Languages Publishing House, 1955, 561–590).

Stalin, J.V. *Economic problems of Socialism in the USSR* (Peking: Foreign Languages Press, 1972; original in Russian: 1952).

Stalin, J. V. 'The Results of the First Five Year Plan', Report delivered at the Joint Plenum of the Central Control Commission of the CPSU (B), January 7, 1933; in J. Stalin, *Problems of Leninism* (Moscow: Foreign Languages Publishing House, 1943, 401–440).

Stalin, J.V. *Marxism and the National and Colonial Question* (London: Lawrence & Wishar, 1936).

Stalin, J. *Foundations of Leninism* originally published 1924, online: www.marxists.org/reference/archive/stalin/works/1924/foundations-leninism accessed September 20, 2014.

Stone, O. and Kuzniki P. *The Untold History of the United States* (London: Ebury Press, 2013).

Stuart, D. *Creating the National Security State: A History of the Law that Transformed America* (Princeton, N.J: Princeton University Press, 2012).

Sussex, M. (ed.) *Conflict in the Former USSR* (Cambridge: Cambridge University Press, 2012).

Swain, H. (ed) *Big Questions in History* (London: Jonathan Cape, 2005).

Talbot, S. *The Great Experiment*, (New York: Simon & Schuster, 2008).

Taubman, W. *Khrushchev: The Man and His Era*, (New York: Norton, 2003).

Taylor, A. 'Introduction', in John Reed, *Ten Days That Shook the World* (London, Penguin, 1977, pp. vii-xi).

Taylor, R.N. article in the *Guardian*, February 4, 1999.

Tishkov, V. *Chechnya: Life in a War-Torn Society* (Oakland, University of California Press).

Tismaneanu, V. *The Devil in History: Communism, Fascism, and Some Lessons of the Twentieth Century* (Berkeley, CA: University of California Press, 2012).

Tosh, J. *Why History Matters*, (Basingstoke: Palgrave, 2008).

Townshend, 'Right-Wing Marxism', in David Glaser and David M. Walker (eds) *Twentieth Century Marxism*, (London: Routledge, 2007, 46–58).

Trachtenberg, M. *The Cold War and After: History, Theory, and the Logic of International Politics* (Princeton, N.J: Princeton University Press, 2012).

Trenin, D. V. *Getting Russia Right* (Washington D.C: Carnegie Endowment for International Peace, 2007).

Trotsky, L. *The History of the Russian Revolution* on line: www.marxists.org/archive/trotsky/hrr; note the original book was published in 1932, not 1922.

Trotsky, L. *The Basic Writings* (edited by Irving Howe, London: Mercury, 1964).

Trotsky, L. *The Revolution Betrayed* online www.marxists.org/archive/trotsky/1936/revbet/ch05.htm accessed 20 September, 2014.

Truman Library (1942–1948) chronology, available at: www.trumanlibrary.org. Accessed July 17, 2013).

Tsipko, A. *Is Stalinism Really Dead?* (New York: Harper Collins, 1990).

Tucker, R. *Stalinism: Essays in Historical Interpretation* (New Jersey, Transaction).

Urquhart, B. 'A Great Day in History' *New York Review of Books*, 15 January, 2004, 8–10.

Vasquez, J. *The Power of Power Politics* (New Brunswick: Rutgers University Press, 1983).

Vodolazov, G. 'Gorbachev: A Nomenklatura Utopia' *Russian Studies in History*, 42/4, (Spring 2004, 80–87).

Volkogonov, D. *Stalin* (London: Phoenix Press, 2000).

Volkogonov, D. *The Rise and Fall of the Soviet Empire: Political Leaders from Lenin to Gorbachev* (London: Harper Collins, 1999).

Volkogonov, D. *Lenin: Life and Legacy* (London: HarperCollins, 1994).

Volkov. S. *The Magical Chorus: A History of Culture From Tolstoy to Solzhenitsyn* (New York: Vintage, 2008).

Waever, O. 'The Speech Act of Realism: The Move that Made IR', in N. Ghuilhot (ed.), *The Invention of International Relations Theory: Realism, the Rockefeller Foundation and the 1954 Conference on Theory* (New York: Columbia University Press, 2011).

Walt, S. *Revolution and War* (Ithaca: Cornell University Press, 1997).

Waltz, K.N. *Theory of International Politics* (New York: Random House, 1979).

Weber, M. 'Politics as a Vocation', in Gerth, H.H. and Mills, C.W. (eds) *From Max Weber: Essays in Sociology* (Oxford: Oxford University Press, 1958, 77–128).

Webb, S. and Webb B. *The Letters of Sidney and Beatrice Webb, Vol. 3. Pilgramage*, (edited by Norman Mackenzie, Cambridge: Cambridge University Press, 2008).

Webb, S. and Webb, B. *Soviet Communism: A New Civilization?* (London: Longman's Green, 1937).

Weddel, J. *Collision and Collusion* (New York: Palgrave, 2001).

Weinstein, A. *Perjury: The Hiss-Chambers Case* (New York: Knopf, 1978).

Wendt, A. *Social Theory of International Politics* (Cambridge: Cambridge University Press, 1999).

Westad, A. *The Global Cold War: Third World Interventions and the Making of Our Times* (Cambridge: Cambridge University Press, 2007).

Wheen, F. *Das Kapital: A Biography* (London: Atlantic Books, 2006).

Wheen, F. *Karl Marx: A Life*, (New York: Norton, 2005).

White, G.E. *Alger Hiss's Looking Glass War: The Covert Life of a Soviet Spy* (New York: Oxford University Press, 2004).

White, J.D. *Lenin: The Practice and Theory of Revolution*, (Basingstoke: Palgrave, 2001).

White, S. *Understanding Russian Politics* (Cambridge: Cambridge University Press, 2011).

White, S. *Political Culture and Soviet Politics* (Basingstoke: Macmillan, 1979).

Wilson, A. *Our Times: 1953–2008* (London, Arrow Books, 2008).

Wilson, D. *Tito's Yugoslavia*, (Cambridge: Cambridge University Press, 1979).

Wood, T. *Chechnya: The Case for Independence* (London: Verso, 2007).

Worger, P. 'A Mad Crowd: Skinhead Youth and the Rise of Nationalism in Post-Communist Russia', *Communist and Post-Communist Studies*, 45, 2012, 269–279.

Yew, L.K., *From Third World to First: Singapore and the Asian Economic Boom* (New York: HarperCollins, 2011).

Zakaria, F. *From Wealth to Power: The Unusual Origins of America's World Role* (Princeton: Princeton University Press, 1998).

Yakovlev, A. *A Century of Violence in Soviet Russia* (New Haven: Yale University Press, 2002).

Zamyatin. *We* (New York: Penguin, 1993).

Zhukov. G.K. *Vospominaniya i razmyshleniya* (Moscow: Novosti, 1974).

Ziegler, W. *Wilson: The Authorised Life* (London: Harper Collins, 1993).

Zinovieff, S. *Red Princess: A Revolutionary Life* (London: Granta Books, 2007).

Zhdanov, 'Report on the International Situation' report to the First Conference of the Communist Information Bureau, September 1947, in Giulanio Procacci. (ed.) *The Cominform: Minutes of the Three Conferences, 1947/1948/1949* (Milan: Fondazione Giangiacomo Feltinelli, the Russian Centre of Conservation and Study of Records of Modern History, 1949, 217–251 [text in original Russian and in English translation).

Index